Our minds must be considered among the wonders of the natural world. It seems hardly credible that an organised assemblage of molecules can generate vivid feelings and sensations, yet the brain is such an assemblage and it does . . . So, how does our conscious mind arise from our physical brain? *Evolving the Mind* examines this question by following two main themes: how theories of the mind have evolved in science and how the mind itself evolved in Nature.

This book is written in a very accessible way. It is amusing, serious, informative and at times conversational. It starts in history and follows a trail for a physical theory of consciousness inadvertently laid down by twentieth century science.

Graham Cairns-Smith is a Reader in Chemistry at the University of Glasgow and a Fellow of the Royal Society of Edinburgh. Both his undergraduate degree and his PhD were taken at Edinburgh, the latter in the field of organic and solid-state chemistry. He then moved to a lectureship at Glasgow, teaching organic chemistry, molecular biology and the history and nature of science. He is well known throughout the world for his ideas on the nature, origin and evolution of life, themes which have appeared in his string of successful books: *The Life Puzzle* (1971), *Genetic Takeover* (1982), *Seven Clues to the Origin of Life* (1985) and *Clay Minerals and the Origin of Life* (1986). *Seven Clues to the Origin of Life* has so far been translated into eight languages. In addition to his books, Dr Cairns-Smith has given invited lectures worldwide and made numerous contributions to the radio and television programmes.

A.G. CAIRNS-SMITH

Evolving the Mind

on the nature of matter and the origin of consciousness

CAMBRIDGE
UNIVERSITY PRESS

Published by the Press Syndicate of the University of Cambridge
The Pitt Building, Trumpington Street, Cambridge CB2 1RP
40 West 20th Street, New York, NY 10011–4211, USA
10 Stamford Road, Oakleigh, Melbourne 3166, Australia

First published 1996

Printed in Great Britain by Biddles Ltd, Guildford & King's Lynn

A catalogue record for this book is available from the British Library

Library of Congress cataloguing in publication data
Cairns-Smith, A. G. (Alexander Graham)
Evolving the mind : on the nature of matter and the origin of
consciousness / A. G. Cairns-Smith.
p.   cm.
Includes bibliographical references and index.
ISBN 0 521 40220 4
1. Consciousness. 2. Intellect. 3. Mind and body. I. Title.
BF311.C146 1966
153-dc20   94-39376 CIP

ISBN 0 521 40220 4 hardback

Contents

Preface

Two outstanding problems of science are the origin of life and the origin of conscious mind. The origin of life was the obsession of my earlier books where I suggested that molecular biology fails to tell the whole story because 'geochemicals' rather than 'biochemicals' would have been the most critical early players.

I think that on the origin of consciousness molecular biology again falls short, although in a rather different way. Brains are made of standard types of biochemical molecules, essentially the same materials as are found in all living things today. And very much of what goes on in brains can be well understood in terms (ultimately) of the activities of these kinds of molecules. But most of what goes on is unconscious. Consciousness remains a mystery. What today's molecular biology fails to provide is an understanding of the origin of consciousness as a phenomenon, a proper understanding of what consciousness is in physical terms.

The story which I will be telling is based mainly on ideas expressed by many other people. It goes something like this. The root phenomena of consciousness are feelings and sensations, for example feelings of hunger or pain, the sensation of the colour blue, and so on. And I take it that the means to produce all such forms of consciousness evolved: that the ability to make sensations such as pain and hunger was perfected by natural selection because these sensations were useful. (There is nothing very odd about this, you might say, but not everyone agrees.) Now the ultimate means of production of any evolved function lies in material genes, in messages written in DNA molecules, and the only thing that DNA molecules can do is to organise other molecules. Therefore consciousness comes from an organisation of molecules. It is part of the material world, the world of molecular machinery, quite as much as the ability to contract a muscle or convert the energy of sunlight into fuel. They are all evolved functions. They are all on a par.

Of course they don't seem to be. Molecular mechanics may explain how a muscle contracts, but how can it ever explain the sensation of a colour, or the nature and quality of a pang of guilt? Molecular mechanics and conscious experience seem to be worlds apart, as Descartes had insisted they were. But that is not what the theory of evolution says.

William James gave us a general resolution of this dilemma more than a hundred years ago. In a nutshell: *matter* is not what it seems. Or as we should say now there must be more to biological material than is summarised in the models of molecular biology. To make any sense of this we will come to dig a bit deeper: *science* is not what it seems . . .

It would be a scandal if a book like this turned out the way the author had expected; I have duly changed my mind about many things over the several years I have taken in writing it. A number of books on the general subject have appeared in the meantime to inspire or disturb, or sometimes both: few things can be as annoying as finding what one thought was one's own idea expressed rather better by someone else. And then I have had the advantage of numerous discussions with colleagues, often of course with far more knowledge than me on dauntingly various topics which come in. Many of these kind people read and commented on chapter drafts. I would like to thank in particular David Bell, Sarah Cairns-Smith, Emma Cairns-Smith, John Carnduff, Bruce Charlton, Alan Cooper, Hyman Hartman, Neil Isaacs, Ian Marshall, Stephen Mason, Pippa Orr, Karl Overton, Mike Russell, Victor Serebriakoff, Henry Stapp, Brian Webster and George Wyllie. I would have liked to be able to say that you can blame them for any errors or foolishness which you may find, but then I didn't always take the advice offered. Finally my wife Dorothy Anne deserves praise or blame for the whole enterprise: I could not have done it without her interest in the subject, her practical help and her love.

Graham Cairns-Smith

1

Material things

To anyone who has ever had toothache there is no doubt that feelings and sensations are real phenomena. Will they ever become part of science, that science which deals with atoms, molecules and so on? The questions 'Why not?' and 'How on Earth?' follow fast on each other.

Here I start with matter, with how the current common-sense view of the nature of matter evolved. Most of the chapter is straight physics and chemistry, and it may help to provide background – information or reminders – of use later when we come to the molecular machinery within cells and brains. But I must warn you that the main purpose of the chapter is seditious. It is to begin to cast a doubt about the whole story that there *really* is a world out there of atoms and molecules of which we have a good understanding . . .

I suppose I was about eight when my father told me that nobody knew what electricity was. I went into school the next day, I remember, and made this information generally available to my friends. It did not create the kind of sensation I had been banking on, although it caught the attention of one whose father worked at the local power station. His father actually made electricity so obviously he would know what it was. My friend promised to ask and report back. Well, eventually he did and I cannot say I was much impressed with the result. 'Wee sandy stuff' he said, rubbing his thumb and forefinger together to emphasise just how tiny the grains were. He seemed unable to elaborate further.

It was years before I understood what my friend must have been talking about. 'Wee sandy stuff' was a description of electrons: I imagine his father had been trying to explain that, although electricity is some sort of stuff that flows along wires it has a grain to it, it is not infinitely subdivisible, there is a smallest possible quantity of the stuff that flows.

More strictly, the ultimate unit of the electricity-stuff is not an electron but an electric charge, since electricity can be a flow of other charged particles as well. For example, when electricity flows through water it consists not of a movement of (negatively charged) electrons, as it does in a metal, but of larger charged particles, ions, both negative and positive. Electricity gets through bath water like this:

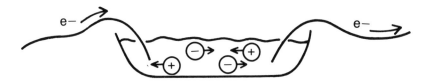

Pure water conducts electricity a little bit because water molecules easily break into oppositely charged ions:

$$H_2O \rightleftarrows H^+ + OH^-.$$

But the reverse arrow indicates that the pieces also re-join, and even more easily, as it happens, so that only a tiny proportion of water molecules are broken up like this at any instant. Very pure water is a poor conductor of electricity, but even tiny amounts of dissolved salts (as in, say, tap water) dramatically increase the ability of water to conduct electricity. This is because salts are entirely made up of ions.

To take some examples: sodium chloride exists in water as singly charged ions, sodium ions, designated Na^+, and chloride ions, Cl^-. Silver nitrate exists as silver ions, Ag^+, and nitrate ions, NO_3^-. There is a difference here in that one of the ions, the nitrate, has several atoms in it. A copper sulphate solution contains doubly positive copper ions and doubly negative sulphate ions – Cu^{2+} and SO_4^{2-} – while a solution of copper chloride has Cu^{2+} and (twice as many) Cl^- ions in it.

All such ions are thousands of times more massive than the negative electrons whose movement constitutes an electric current in a wire. Indeed, these carriers of the current in solutions are hydrated, that is to say surrounded by water molecules more or less firmly attached.

We have already improved on my friend's description of electricity; an electric current *is* a flow of charges, whatever the medium, and positive charges going one way are equivalent to negative charges going the other.

The whole thing depends on the property of a charged particle that it will be repelled by another particle with the same kind of charge and attracted to one with a charge of the opposite sort. *Why* charges should show such mysterious attractions and repulsions across space is another matter. This is usually just taken to be a fundamental property, which is another way of saying that your guess is as good as mine. This somewhat vindicates my father's attitude to electricity. Now there is a theory – quantum electrodynamics it is called – but as you might imagine it has built into it still deeper mysteries. More of that much later. In the meantime let us go further back into history.

'The discovery of electricity'

Electricity, or rather the electricity-stuff charge, is indeed one of the most fundamental aspects of material things (more so in some respects than mass, as we shall see shortly). Yet it is normally hidden. Charges are usually balanced so that they produce no obvious effects. Indeed electricity, anyway its usefulness, is a comparatively recent discovery.

Static electricity   It had been known since antiquity that rubbing various materials together can produce strange repulsions and attractions, as when a pen rubbed on the sleeve can then pick up little pieces of paper, or your hair stands on end after taking off a pullover on a frosty night. But such phenomena do not seem to have been taken very seriously until the eighteenth century.

In 1730 in France, C. F. Du Fay (1698–1739) formulated a two-fluids theory of electrostatic effects, interpreting the rôle of friction as that of separating these fluids, which had a natural tendency to come together again and neutralise each other. Then in 1747 the American statesman and scientist Benjamin Franklin (1706–1790) proposed a one-fluid theory: that of an 'electric fire' that was a constituent of all matter. For him a charged body was one with either an excess (plus) or a deficiency (minus) of the fiery fluid. Again there was seen to be a powerful tendency for such imbalance to put itself right, a tendency that operated across space, creating forces across space. However strange, it was perhaps no stranger than gravity, which was now seen to be manifestly a force that could operate at great distances. Anyway Franklin's theory could fit the facts quite well, although you might have thought that his understanding should have dissuaded him from flying a kite (in more ways than one) into a thunder cloud to check that lightning was a form of electricity. As it turned out he was right and he was lucky.

An analogy with gravity was indeed suggested by Joseph Priestley (1733–1804), the English chemist and social reformer. But it was the

French engineer Charles-Auguste Coulomb (1736–1806) who was to show, in 1785 with the aid of a clever torsion balance, that in one respect at least there was a quantitative similarity. He showed, as Priestley had inferred must be the case, that the force between charges diminished with the square of the distance between them: that is to say, doubling the distance reduces the force to a quarter, and so on.

Electric currents   The next part of the story starts in two of the ancient Universities of northern Italy. Luigi Galvani (1737–1798), professor of anatomy at Bologna, was interested in electrical causes and effects in animals – in electric eels among others – or what was to be dubbed 'galvanism'. In 1786 Galvani was studying the nerves and muscles of a detached frog's leg and he noticed that the muscle twitched when the copper hook from which it was hung was placed on an iron support. Galvani supposed that the nerve or muscle was the source of the effect, that it was due to electricity generated there, perhaps in some way analogous to the shock generator in electric eels.

The professor of natural philosophy (physics) at Pavia, Alessandro Volta (1745–1827) suggested rather that it was the dissimilarity of the metals that had been in contact with the nerve or muscle that was the source of the electricity and that the twitching muscle was simply a detector. He was to show that this sort of electricity was not peculiar to animals, indeed did not require biological material at all.

Volta then put a whole series of paired discs – silver and zinc – between pieces of paper soaked in salty water and found he could magnify the effect indefinitely. He had invented a battery, a 'Voltaic pile', which was a source for the first time of a real, continuous, controllable electric current. It was one of the greatest inventions ever.

The '1800' revolution

Volta published an account of his work in the *Transactions of the Royal Society* in 1800. The scene shifts to England: in the same year Nicolson and Carlyle, using a Voltaic pile, found that water could be decomposed with electricity – 'electrolysed' – into hydrogen and oxygen. Then, at the Royal Institution in London, Humphrey Davy (1778–1829) electrolysed various salt solutions. Using fused salts he isolated for the first time the highly reactive metals sodium and potassium, and went on to discover many other new elements using this technique.

Davy's brilliant and largely self-taught protégé at the Royal Institution, Michael Faraday (1791–1867), was later to clarify these processes, announcing (in 1833) two 'laws of electrolysis'. The first of these was that the mass of a product liberated in electrolysis is proportional to the quantity of electricity that has passed.

To understand this let us come back to the present for a moment. We can think of a piece of metal as consisting of positive ions held together by oppositely charged electrons. The electrons here are neither really wee nor sandy, as I will be discussing later on; but in the meantime an image of metal ions packed like oranges in a box with tiny mobile electrons in spaces between them will do.

Now think of what might happen when the positive silver ions in a silver nitrate solution come in contact with a metal wire that is having extra electrons pumped into it by a power source, as in a typical electrolysis set-up. The silver ions in solution are being pulled towards the negative wire by opposite charge attraction, and when they arrive there they simply join up with excess electrons on the wire *and deposit there as silver metal*, electroplating the wire, and it is an easy matter to find the mass of silver that has been deposited.

Now two such electrolysis cells can be put in series so that exactly the same amount of electricity must flow through each. We might have, say, copper chloride in one cell and silver nitrate in the other. The amount of copper and silver deposited will then each be proportional to the total amount of electricity-stuff that has passed through the cells, in line with Faraday's first law. But the masses of each will not be the same. In fact for every gram of copper metal found to have been deposited in one cell 3.4 g of silver metal will have been deposited in the other. In general – and this was Faraday's second law – the masses of products liberated in electrolysis are always proportional to the 'chemical equivalents' of these products (here, in effect, a measure of the masses of the copper and silver atoms divided by the charge they carry). But this now takes us into new territory. It is time to return to history.

Three strands

The start of the nineteenth century was bringing with it a revolution in our understanding of the nature of matter, one that had been fermenting through the second half of the eighteenth century. The discovery of electrolysis was a strand of this revolution. Even before Faraday's laws were known it was beginning to look as if electrical forces were somehow built into the structure of matter, that water, for example, could be broken into its component elements by electricity because the forces normally holding those elements together in water were, as in all materials perhaps, electrical . . .

The second strand I want to talk about was an idea from further back, a gift from physics to chemistry: that mass was the measure of matter, allowing a third strand to be woven in, the modern atomic theory, dating from 1803.

There was to be another many-stranded revolution, at the turn of the twentieth century, which was to show that material things are in some ways more simple, but in other ways far more complicated and interesting than can be encompassed within the classical notions of atoms, charges, masses, and so on. Right on time for the turn of another century the indications are that we are at the edge of yet another mind-expanding revolution with perhaps, at last, the phenomena of consciousness having a place . . . But again I race ahead. Back to the first revolution, and my second of its three strands.

Mass as the measure of matter?

Neither of the founding fathers of modern science, Galileo (1564–1642) or Descartes (1596–1650), would have said that mass was the critical attribute of matter. For them it was extension, occupancy of space, that was of the essence.

Descartes understood the principle of inertia, later to become Newton's first law of motion, that it is as natural for a body to keep moving in a straight line as it is for it to stay at rest. But Descartes was determined to avoid the idea of action at a distance and sought to explain the motions of the planets, of falling bodies and so on, in terms of minute invisible particles jostling against each other, influencing each other by contact action alone.

Galileo, experimenter and theorist, founded the modern science of dynamics. Yet he had one critical misconception and it had to do with the principle of inertia. Like Descartes he saw that Aristotle (384–322 BC) had been wrong to suppose that a force has to be applied to keep a body moving, and among many other things solved the problem of how it could be that the Earth was rotating daily, with thus every object on it moving at a fantastic speed (we all serenely 'go round the world' once a day). Yet his solution was not quite the same as Newton's was to be. For Galileo circular motion was natural, an Aristotelian idea he had inherited from Copernicus (1473–1543) whose heliocentric view of the solar system Galileo was particularly intent on promulgating. For Newton (1642–1727) the motions of the planets had to be explained through a combination of the inertia idea and the idea of a Universal gravitational force.

Mass has two aspects: heaviness and inertia. An object's heaviness is the attribute which causes it to be attracted to the Earth, and indeed to all other objects in the Universe: its inertia makes it more or less difficult to move, or stop, or deflect if it is already moving. There was no particular reason to think that these two properties of matter were intimately related, still less that they should be quantitatively *the same*. This point was made by Galileo's famous (if probably apocryphal) demonstration from the leaning tower of Pisa that, if they are heavy enough for air resistance not to matter, objects fall to the ground with the same acceleration independently of their weight. (Try it, it always surprises me, a small coin and a heavy book dropped at the same time will hit the floor at the same time, near enough.) The point is that a more massive object is more difficult to get moving but has an exactly correspondingly stronger gravitational force acting on it.

There are two ways you might react to this. You might say that it is just one of those things, and that it emphasises the central importance of mass in physics, perhaps that mass is the most essential property of material things; even perhaps that it is the measure of matter. This was, I think, more or less the eighteenth-century view, and the gift to chemistry that I referred to.

The other reaction is to look for a reason. This was to be the attitude of Albert Einstein (1879–1955). His theory of gravitation of 1915, the general theory of relativity, was formulated to make the coincidence of heavy and inertial mass inevitable rather than just one of those things. This was in keeping with Einstein's earlier special theory of relativity, of 1905: to put it brutally, he had shown then that mass was not all it had been cracked up to be as the Great Fundamental. For one thing it was in principle interconvertible with energy. Even worse, the mass of an object changed according to how it was moving in relation to you. In any case Einstein had followed Ernst Mach (1838–1916) in supposing that the mass of an object depended on the total matter in the Universe, again suggesting that mass might be more an incidental than a fundamental measure.

All the same, there is no doubt that for the development of chemistry in the eighteenth and nineteenth centuries the equation of mass with 'amount of matter' was enormously fruitful. The Scottish physician, chemist and physicist Joseph Black (1728–1799)[1] paid particular attention to the weights of things taking part in chemical transformations. In 1754, as part of his work for an MD degree at Edinburgh, he became interested in what we now call carbonates. For example Black studied the effect of heat on *magnesia alba* (a basic magnesium carbonate) and found that it lost weight while giving off a gas which he called 'fixed air' (carbon dioxide) leaving a 'base' (magnesium oxide). This same gas bubbled off when *magnesia alba* was dissolved in acid with again the same proportional loss of weight. For Black this 'air' was not just some sort of vague effusion but a definite substance as real as any other substance: he measured this reality by showing that it had weight which persisted whether the gas was combined with the base in the form of *magnesia alba* or in the much more voluminous free form.

A similar quantitative approach was adopted by the great French lawyer and chemist, Antoine Lavoisier (1743–1794) in the 1770s when he embarked on a series of experiments showing that a number of pieces of received chemical wisdom were wrong. Lavoisier was to demonstrate repeatedly the general principle that mass is conserved through chemical reactions; that whatever else may happen in a reaction, whether heat is put in or light or heat comes out, for example, if you can collect all the material products then their total mass will turn out to be the same as the total mass of the materials you started with.

The principle of the conservation of mass was to become a critical article of faith for chemists in the late eighteenth century and throughout the nineteenth century. Nowhere was it more important than in helping to establish the modern atomic theory.

The atomic theory

There followed careful investigations, particularly in Germany and France, of the compositions of pure materials and it was soon discovered that, anyway for most simple materials, the proportion of elements was always the same. Copper carbonate, for example, was found always to have the same proportion of copper in it whether it was a natural mineral or prepared by synthesis[2]. Such work led to the idea, first put forward, unnoticed, in 1789 by the Irish chemist William Higgins (1766–1825)[3] and then by the English schoolmaster John Dalton (1766–1844) of a quantitative atomic theory. Suppose that the different elements each had atoms of characteristic mass and that in forming compounds these atoms joined together in simple fixed proportions. Dalton suggested, for example, that water was formed by the combination of a hydrogen and an oxygen atom – in his symbolism:

hydrogen   oxygen   water

This idea led to the prediction that when the same elements can form different compounds there should also be a simple relationship between the proportions of the elements in each case. For example element A might form two compounds (in modern symbolism) AB and AB_2 so that the mass of B combining with A would simply be double in the second case. Carbon monoxide and carbon dioxide would be examples of this. Several such cases were soon established.

Ancient atomism   Atomic theories were hardly new. In the fifth century BC the Greek philosophers Leucippus and Democritus had formulated and taught an entire system of the Universe based on the idea of atoms in perpetual motion in the void, explaining the continuity of material existence in terms of the immutability of the atoms and explaining change in terms of changing arrangements of the atoms.

The Roman poet and philosopher Lucretius wrote a book-length poem *On the Nature of Things* ('published' *ca.* 55 BC; one copy luckily survived). This is a wonderful piece of scientific speculation based on hard atomism. He had no qualms about bringing mind into his view of material things:

> A high pile of poppy seed can be disturbed by a light puff of breeze, so that it trickles down from the top, whereas a heap of stones or corn ears remains immovable. In proportion as objects are smaller and smoother, so much the more do they enjoy mobility; the greater their weight and roughness, the more firmly are they anchored. Since therefore, the substance of the mind has been found to be extraordi-

narily mobile, it must consist of particles exceptionally small and smooth and round[4].

Lucretius' masterpiece was first printed in 1473[5]. The engineer Hero of Alexandria (*ca.* AD 62–150), inventor of numerous mechanical and pneumatic devices, had a modern-sounding view of the nature of gases, insisting that gases consisted of minute particles only partly filling a vacuum. Hero's book *Pneumatics* appeared in translation in 1575.

Atomism as a doctrine   By the sixteenth century the doctrine of atomism was there to be picked up by the creators of modern science. And it *was* picked up: by Galileo, Descartes, Francis Bacon (1561–1626), Robert Boyle (1627–1691), Newton . . . Newton expressed his belief:

> All these things being considered, it seems probable to me, that God in the beginning formed matter in solid, massy, hard, impenetrable, movable particles, of such sizes and figures, and with such other properties, and in such proportion to space, as most conduced to the end for which he formed them; and that these primitive particles being solids, are incomparably harder than any porous bodies compounded of them; even so very hard, as never to wear or break in pieces; no ordinary power being able to divide what God himself made one in the first creation. While the particles continue entire, they may compose bodies of one and the same nature and texture in all ages: but should they wear away, or break in pieces, the nature of things depending on them would be changed. Water and earth, composed of old worn particles and fragments of particles, would not be of the same nature and texture now, with water and earth composed of entire particles in the beginning[6].

Magnificent, but hardly much of an advance on, say, Lucretius who also thought clearly and wrote beautifully. Indeed it is hard to find prominent non-believers in the atomic doctrine in Newton's own time. So what was new about Higgins's and Dalton's ideas coming on to the scene so late?

   Well, atomism had previously seemed to be *just* speculation about particles far too small to see. The very method of science, the Newtonian method indeed, depended on being able to alternate speculation with experiment. How could there be anything more to say about atoms until such speculations had been tested, and how can one run experiments on things which there is no hope of ever being able to see?

Relative mass of atoms What Dalton's theory suddenly made clear was that it might be possible, if not to know the masses of atoms, at least to know the relative masses of atoms: and that this should be quite good enough for most purposes.

It still is. Chemists now can tell you the absolute mass of a carbon atom (if you must know, it is about 0.00000000000000000000002 grams) or any other atom you ask them about; but they will have to do a quick calculation on the back of an envelope. What chemists carry in their heads are 'relative atomic masses' or 'atomic weights' of elements, that is to say the relative masses of the atoms of which those elements are composed. The relative atomic mass of chlorine, for example, is about 35.5, which is to say that chlorine atoms are (on average) about 35.5 times as heavy as hydrogen atoms. So if you want to make hydrogen chloride, which contains one atom of each, then for every gram of hydrogen you will need 35.5 grams of chlorine. Put the other way round, if you know the relative atomic masses of the elements you can determine the relative numbers of the different kinds of atoms in a substance by finding out what masses of the elements are required to make it with nothing left over.

Well, every senior school child knows this, also why I said that chlorine atoms were 35.5 times as heavy as hydrogen atoms on *average*. There are two kinds of atoms – isotopes – of chlorine with relative atomic masses of about 35 and 37. But isotopes were only recognised in the twentieth century. Fortunately for nineteenth-century chemistry, isotope ratios are almost constant for most elements so the averaged relative atomic masses of atoms will do for the purposes of calculation.

On the way to molecular models Dalton's picture was deficient in a number of ways, this only partly due to inadequate experimental data: but the essential general idea was correct. Actually it took quite a long time to clarify some important specific points – that water is in fact H_2O and not HO, for example, which meant that the atomic mass of oxygen was often wrong – and indeed organic chemistry in particular was in a muddle until the late 1850s.

Also, the idea of a *molecule* as a distinct spatial structure with atoms joined to each other in definite ways (through 'covalent bonds') was quite slow in coming; and that idea too was essential before organic chemistry could really get going. One distinguished chemist, Hermann Kolbe (1818–1884) simply would not believe that molecules had three-dimensional shapes that mattered. He got quite worked up on the subject:

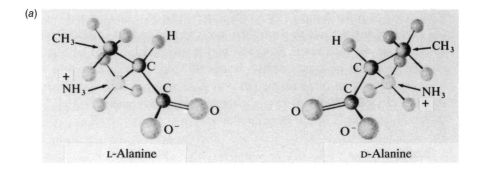

(a)

L-Alanine   D-Alanine

(b)

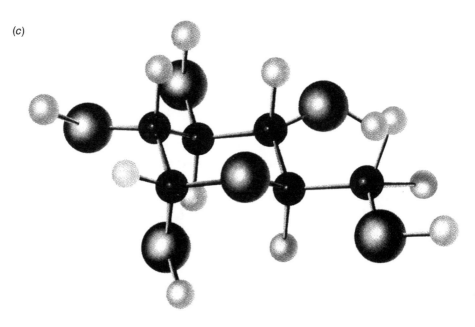

(c)

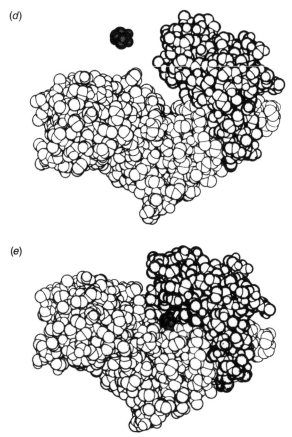

Figure 1.1. Models for molecules.

(a) Ball-and-stick representation of the amino acid alanine in its 'left-handed' and 'right-handed' forms. (Only L-alanine is used in making normal proteins.)

(b) Corresponding 'space-filling' models. In these models it is more difficult to see how the atoms are joined together but they can give a better impression of, say, how molecules might pack together in a crystal or fit together with another molecule (as in d and e).

(c) Ball-and-stick representation of the sugar glucose (one form of the natural 'right-handed' glucose: α D-glucose).

(d) Space-filling models of glucose and a protein molecule, the enzyme hexokinase. This enzyme attaches a phosphate group to glucose molecules.

(e) The glucose molecule is here bound to the enzyme, which has changed its shape somewhat to accommodate it. When it is released again, the glucose molecule will have a phosphate group attached to it.

Parts (a, b) from CHEMISTRY by Pauling & Pauling. Copyright © 1975 by Linus Pauling and Peter Pauling. Used with permission of W. H. Freeman and Company. Part (c) after Pauling & Pauling (1975); (d, e) from Bennett & Steitz (1980).

If this seems exaggerated one should read the writings of a Mr van't Hoff, full of bad tricks of the imagination, which I should prefer to ignore if a distinguished chemist [Wislicenus] had not given him his patronage. This Dr van't Hoff, employed in a veterinary school at Utrecht, takes no pleasure, it appears, in exact chemical research. He has found it more comfortable to mount a veterinary Pegasus and to announce how, in his mad flight through a chemical Parnassus, the atoms have appeared to him to be scattered in space[7].

He then goes on to say that poor Wislicenus too now 'excludes himself from the ranks of exact scientists' Well, Jacobus Hendricus van't Hoff (1852–1911) was to prove himself to be about as exact a chemist as you could wish for, and he had been explaining his idea (of 1874) of how organic molecules should often exist in forms that are mirror images of each other (figure 1.1a, b), clearing up in principle the problem of the 'optical activity' of many materials from biological sources whose solutions were known to twist light waves passing through them. Without this structural insight, arrived at independently in 1874 by Joseph Achille Le Bel (1847–1930), there would have been no hope of understanding biological molecules, and hence the fundamental processes of life. Figure 1.1 (a, b) shows 'right-handed' and 'left-handed' versions of one of the 20 amino acids that proteins are made from (only the 'left-handed' versions of these molecules are used in normal proteins). Figure 1.1c is a picture of a ball-and-spoke model of glucose (this time just one version: the normal 'right-handed' one). It is more easily drawn like this:[11]

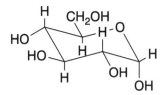

but if you look carefully you will see that it is the same structure even although the viewing angle is a little different and the representation somewhat more symbolic. Yet a third ('space-filling') representation of glucose is shown in figure 1.1d. The glucose is of course the smaller of the two molecules here. Even a glucose molecule is quite a complex structure with two dozen covalent bonds in it which have to be joined correctly. Now look at the other molecule in figure 1.1d – a protein – and try to imagine how complex this is: it too has all its thousands of covalent bonds made correctly. Protein molecules like these are highly sophisticated pieces of molecular machinery; they make up most of the most central machinery of life. The mid-twentieth-century discoveries of molecular biology would have been impossible without knowing in detail the spatial arrangements of atoms in molecules and thus being able to draw or build three-dimensional models of the sort illustrated in figure 1.1.

Atomic electricity

Another point which was not clearly made until quite late in the nineteenth century, but was inherent in a combination of Dalton's and Faraday's ideas, was that if matter was atomic and a definite amount of matter could be associated with a definite amount of electricity, as shown in electrolysis experiments, then electricity must be 'atomic', that is to say not infinitely subdivisible.

This point was made in 1874 by George Johnstone Stoney (1826–1911) and the ultimate indivisible unit of electricity, the ultimate charge, was given a name by him in 1891: *the electron*[8].

In 1897 J. J. Thomson (1856–1940) was studying the then mysterious smooth flow of electricity across space – between wires sealed into vessels from which virtually all air had been pumped – and found that this flow consisted of a stream of minute negatively charged particles, which *he* called electrons.

In some ways it is a pity that Thomson used Johnstone Stoney's term. Johnstone Stoney's electron was the ultimate unit of charge, which actually comes in two opposite sorts: Thomson gave the same name to a particle which happens to 'carry' one of these sorts of charge, but has other attributes as well. In particular it has mass, which seems a very different thing: as far as we know there is no ultimately smallest possible unit of mass, as touched on earlier, and it only seems to come in one sort. The fact that all masses attract, whereas only unlike charges do, further limits the analogy between gravitational and electrical action. For moving bodies there are further divergences: charges do not resist change of motion in a way at all similar to the inertia of mass.

The electromagnetic connection I have made no mention so far of what seemed to be a third form of action at a distance, magnetism, because it turned out that this was not so much a third kind of force as an indication that electric forces are more complicated than you might have thought. Magnetic effects result from moving charges. Our knowledge of how electric and magnetic forces are connected derives almost entirely from nineteenth-century studies, although Benjamin Franklin had already observed, in 1751, that iron needles could be magnetised by means of discharges of static electricity, and there had been other such indications.

The year 1820 saw the start of a consistent search for the electromagnetic connection. In this year the Danish physicist Hans Christian Oersted (1777–1851) discovered that if a wire carrying an electric current was placed parallel to a compass needle, the latter would be deflected in one direction, and then, if the current was reversed, in the opposite direction. Furthermore the force between a magnet and a current carrying wire appeared not to operate by attractive or repulsive pulling or pushing but in a circle. In the same year, in France, François Arago (1786–1853) showed that a coil of wire with a current flowing through it acted like a magnet, being able to pick up and hold iron filings so long as the current was flowing. At about the same time his compatriot, André Marie Ampère (1775–1836), made a systematic study of such effects and suggested in 1825 that magnetic materials have tiny perpetually circulating electric charges in their particles.

Fields of force   Faraday too was interested in space effects of currents in wires. His many researches here culminated in the discovery, in 1831, of electromagnetic induction, how one changing electric current can generate another via a changing magnetic 'field'. Better than anyone Faraday understood the connections between electricity and magnetism. The transformer and the dynamo were his inventions, crucial practical inventions, so it turned out, to shift electricity from a curiosity to the most useful form of energy since fire.

It may seem extraordinary to physicists today that Faraday was very weak at formal mathematics. His success seems to have depended on an intellectual inventiveness in elaborating pictures of what was going on. He made great use of the idea, not itself altogether new, of lines of force acting like invisible elastic threads connecting opposite charges or magnetic poles, or surrounding current-carrying wires. Such an imagery makes it quite as natural to comprehend forces that act in circles as in the pull or push-pull way of gravitational or electrostatic forces.

Faraday's lines of force were the descriptive elements of fields. These were not to be seen as additional coats and frocks to be added as an afterthought to the *really* real atoms in order to account for new phenomena as required. For Faraday it was atoms that were dubious. Writing in 1844:

> Thus, for instance, the weight or gravitation of a body depends upon a force which we call attraction; and this force is not something away or separate from the matter, nor the matter separate from the force; the force is an essential property or part of the matter and, to speak absurdly, the matter without the force would not be matter. Or, if we recognise matter by its hardness, what do we other than recognize by our sensations a force exerted by it[9].

Although today we cannot but believe in atoms, none of us are atomists any more, not in the Greek tradition. Newton had helped the trend away from the clear-cut atoms of Democritus, Lucretius and Descartes: he supposed that there were forces operating at a distance between atoms by analogy with the huge gravitational forces which seemed manifestly to operate across millions of miles of space. Since Newton we can no longer insist that anything has a clear location. Where is the moon? Out there a quarter of a million miles away? Well you might say that most of it is out there, but what sense is there in saying that the moon is in one place but has an influence here in raising the tides twice a day, because, oh yes, it has an attached gravitational field. (How is it attached – with stitching?) Is it not better to say, as Faraday did, that material things consist of fields, more intense in some places, less so in others? . . . (Discussion to be continued.)

Light

The great Scottish physicist James Clerk Maxwell (1831–1879) is often referred to in the same breath as Newton and Einstein. He sought to combine the accounts of electromagnetic phenomena that had been given by Faraday and, in mathematical form, by Ampère in France and Karl Friedrich Gauss (1777–1855) in Germany. In 1864 Maxwell wrote down a set of equations describing the dynamic effects of electric and magnetic fields on each other[10]. He had added an extra piece which went beyond the known facts: the idea of a 'displacement current'. This was not an electric current in the sense of a flow of electric charges in a wire. It was to be thought of rather as a momentary distortion or strain set up in an

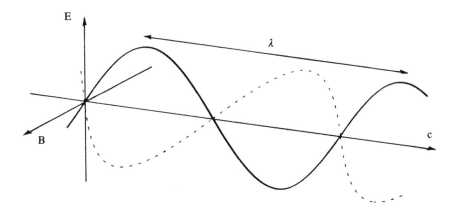

Figure 1.2. Propagation of an electromagnetic wave consists of oscillating electric and magnetic fields at right angles to each other – directions E and B in this figure – and at right angles to the direction of propagation, c. From Webster (1990).

electric field in space. Perhaps only if one saw fields as material things would one be likely to think like this.

In Faraday's transformer a changing electric current in one of two wires wrapped round a piece of iron creates a changing magnetic field in the iron which in turn induces another (changing) electric current in the second wire. The iron is not absolutely necessary although it helps to localise the magnetic fields to maximum effect. Maxwell realised that electromagnetic effects should be possible without any wires either.

Imagine jerking an electric charge: that is, not just moving it but quickly accelerating it and decelerating it again. This would create a momentary changing magnetic field. But why stop there? Changing magnetic fields surely produce changing electric fields even if there are no conducting wires around. So we are, as it were, back where we started with another effect, similar to the effect of the original jerked electric charge . . .

The result should be a pulse travelling through space, or if the charge is made to oscillate back and forth, a wave train with the changing electric and magnetic fields keeping each other going indefinitely. Maxwell was able to deduce how such oscillations of electric and magnetic field should propagate in space (figure 1.2) and how fast they should go.

This turned out to be about 300 000 kilometres per second, which was close to the best estimates for the velocity of *light*.

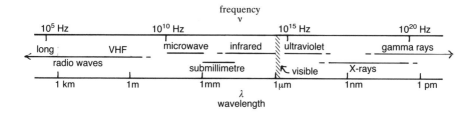

Figure 1.3. The electromagnetic spectrum.

It was a stunning discovery. The conclusion was irresistible. Light was to be identified with these hypothetical waves. And there was now a prediction sitting there, that there should be other forms of electromagnetic radiation corresponding to different oscillation rates (frequencies). Such were discovered between 1886 and 1888 by Heinrich Rudolph Hertz (1857–1894). Hertz demonstrated that oscillating currents set up in an electric circuit could produce similar oscillations in a (suitably tuned) circuit some distance away. Hertz had discovered radio waves, and was able to show that this form of electromagnetic radiation travelled at the same speed as light and had several other properties in common with light. Now we recognise visible light as but a small part of a much broader 'electromagnetic spectrum' which includes, for example, X-rays, ultraviolet rays, and infrared radiation (known also as 'radiant heat') (figure 1.3).

Heat

Francis Bacon thought that heat was a form of motion of particles in objects[11], and Newton used a similar idea when he attempted to explain how (radiant) heat could pass through a vacuum or how heat could pass directly from one body to another. His tentative explanation was in terms of of vibrations, in a medium 'exceedingly more rare and subtle than the air'[12]. But the prevailing view up until the mid-nineteenth century was that heat was some sort of fluid.

Maybe the weather had something to do with it, but whatever the reason the nature of *heat* was a particular preoccupation in Glasgow in the eighteenth and nineteenth centuries. It seems to have started with

William Cullen (1710–1790) whose work 'on the cold produced by evaporating fluids'[13] greatly influenced his pupil and successor Joseph Black, who in turn influenced his friend James Watt (1736–1819) and helped him develop his version of the steam engine[13]. The tradition was to continue in the nineteenth century with William Thomson, Lord Kelvin (1824–1907) who, among many other things, helped to develop the now classical science of energy: thermodynamics.

Between 1756 and 1766 Black established the more modest science of calorimetry. He distinguished clearly between the temperature of a body and the amount of heat in it. He discovered that materials differed in their capacity for heat. He introduced the idea of latent heat: the heat absorbed when a solid melts or a liquid evaporates. Yet Black did not know what heat was. He thought of it as a fluid.

Even classical thermodynamics, did not – and does not – actually require any particular commitment as to the nature of heat. Heat could be taken to be simply a form of energy that could flow from one place to another and could be interconverted with other forms of energy. Energy indeed had become a kind of stuff in that, like mass, it was apparently never destroyed, only redistributed. This principle of the conservation of energy was to be called the first law of thermodynamics. It was obviously analogous to Lavoisier's principle of the conservation of mass.

But latent heat in particular was to remain somewhat mysterious in the absence of any good ideas about what heat really was. And then another somewhat arcane quantity, entropy, was introduced in 1865 by Rudolph Clausius (1822–1888) to account for the brute facts of the operation of heat engines, such as steam engines. As the French engineer Sadi Carnot (1796–1831) had made clear, such engines can only work if there is a temperature difference being maintained: heat can only be (partly) converted to the useful mechanical energy of working machinery if there is a flow of heat from a heat source to a heat sink. This was a general limitation on the interconvertibility of energy. The principle of the conservation of energy was not enough to explain what was going on: in addition to energy being conserved there was another quantity, entropy, which tended to increase. There was a second law of thermodynamics.

Well, whatever entropy was it was a nuisance: but at least it could be measured and put into equations which allowed one to work out which physical and chemical processes might have a chance of actually working. Chemical (including biochemical) reactions are more likely to happen, for example, if entropy increases in the process. But what is entropy? It was to be another decade before a good answer emerged.

In the meantime a good answer to the question 'What is heat?' had been found.

The kinetic theory[14]

The Swiss mathematician Daniel Bernoulli (1700–1782) had a somewhat Democritean view of the nature of air: that it consisted of 'very minute corpuscles which are driven hither and thither with a very rapid motion' and pointed out that the pressure of air in an enclosed vessel could then be understood in terms of innumerable collisions of the particles with the walls of the vessel. It must all have sounded a bit far-fetched, and the general opinion was that gas pressure was due to repulsive forces operating between the particles. That is what Newton had thought, and Dalton was to adopt a similar idea.

In 1821, however, J. Herapath of Bristol was back with a kinetic view of gases:

> ... but after I had revolved the subject a few times in my mind, it struck me that if gases, instead of having their particles endued with repulsive forces subject to so curious a limitation as Newton proposed, were made up of particles, or atoms, mutually impinging on one another, and the sides of the vessel containing them, such a constitution of aeriform bodies would not only be more simple than repulsive powers, but, as far as I could perceive, would be consistent with phenomena in other respects, and would admit to an easy application of the theory of heat by intestine motion. Such bodies I easily saw possessed several of the properties of gases; for instance, they would expand, and, if the particles be vastly small, contract almost indefinitely; their elastic forces would increase by an increase of motion or temperature, and diminish by a diminution; they would conceive heat rapidly and conduct it slowly; would generate heat by sudden compression and destroy it by sudden rarefaction; and any two, having ever so small a communication, would quickly and equally intermix.[15]

'Herapath's hypothesis' became well known and by mid-century this kinetic theory of gases was gaining ground, Clausius himself becoming an adherent.

But it was Maxwell who really put the theory in place. It was in Maxwell's style for him to add some mathematical precision to the

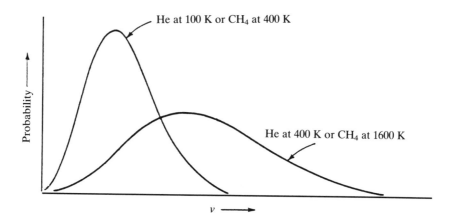

Figure 1.4. Maxwell distribution curves showing the spread of velocities for molecules in gases.
From GENERAL CHEMISTRY 3/E by Linus Pauling. Copyright © 1970 by Linus Pauling. Used with permission of W. H. Freeman and Company.

discussion, as well as new ideas of his own, in particular that the molecules of a gas would in general be travelling with different speeds; he worked out exactly what the distribution of speeds should be at different temperatures (see figure 1.4)[16].

The kinetic theory does not only apply to gases: molecules of liquids and solids are in motion also. And the motions are not only translational motions through space: molecules vibrate and rotate as well. And of course the kinetic theory of matter is, among other things, a general theory of heat. As Francis Bacon had suggested, heat, the heat of a body, *is* the inner motions of that body; or now to put it more precisely a distribution of kinetic energy (motion energy) among molecules.

Even in the late nineteenth and early twentieth century there were major scientists – Mach and the physical chemist Wilhelm Ostwald (1853–1932) were the most famous – who refused to accept not just the kinetic theory, but even the existence of atoms and molecules[17]. You might have thought that the successfully emerging science of organic chemistry, based as it was on detailed ideas of molecular structure, would have made such disbelief hard to maintain. And then there was a beautiful account of that hitherto mysterious quantity entropy which had been proposed by Ludwig Boltzmann (1844–1906) in 1877. It was an account in terms of molecules and based on the idea of distributions of energies between molecules.

It was Maxwell's and Boltzmann's critical realisation that although the molecule-by-molecule situation for a gas will be hopelessly unpredictable, with energy exchanges going on all the time, the overall distribution of energies – how many molecules will have such and such an energy – can be predicted statistically.

Let us think for a moment about a rough analogy. One can think of 'distributions' of the cards in a pack. For example 'alternating-black-and-red' or 'never-two-of-the-same-suit-next-to-each-other'. You would be lucky if a shuffled pack of cards just happened to have either of these distributions in spite of the fact that each is consistent with very large numbers of specific arrangements. (There are about 10^{51} ways of having an exactly 'colour-alternating' pack, and about 10^{60} ways of having perfect 'suit-antipathy'.) The point is that there is an even larger number of specific possible arrangements (about 10^{68}) in all and most of these would *not* have either a strict black–red alternation or escape having at least one case of two same-suit cards next to each other: so your chances of finding 'colour-alternation' in a shuffled pack are about 10^{-17} ($10^{51}/10^{68}$), that is to say one chance in a hundred thousand million million. The chances for 'suit-antipathy' are a bit better: one in a hundred million.

Well, since there are usually far more than 52 molecules in a sample of material (about 10^{23} in a teaspoonful of water) and more than 4 possible energies that each can have, you can imagine that the numbers for collections of molecules are even larger, with the result that

(i) odd distributions of energy (low entropy states) do not arise just by the random shuffling effects of thermal motions, and

(ii) given that there are ways of getting to odd distributions, some are going to be easier to arrive at than others.

So what has all this to do with things like steam engines? The first law of thermodynamics says that all forms of energy are in principle interconvertible. What this seems to suggest is that we ought to be able to use, say, heat in the air around us to drive a car: by sucking air in, converting some of its heat energy into mechanical energy and then blowing the now much colder air back into the surroundings. What we would have done would have been to slow up air molecules to speed up the car.

Figure 1.5 shows a design for the kind of power unit which looks as if it should do the trick. Using the latest techniques of microscopic engineering we put tiny trapdoors into a thin wall between two compartments, each containing air. The rapidly moving air molecules will get through

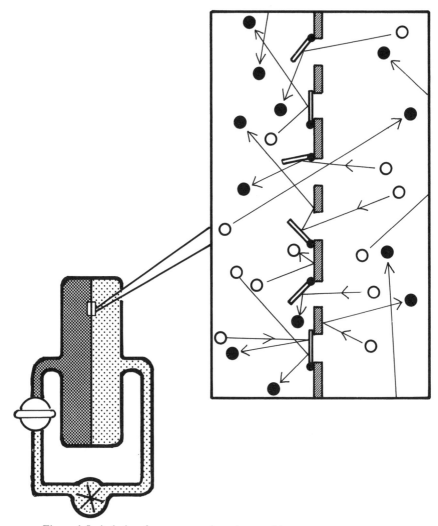

Figure 1.5. A design for a perpetual motion machine.

the trapdoors much more easily in one direction, as you can see. So pressure will build up between the two compartments and the pressure difference can be released through a turbine. A large enough battery of such devices working in parallel should soon get you under way (maybe a train might be a better idea than a car . . .).

I remember when I was a student at Edinburgh spending two or three days really thinking that such a device might work. It seemed to me that the reason why none had yet been invented was simply that no one had yet been able to do fine enough engineering. What convinced me that I was wrong was not that this idea defied the second law of thermodynamics, which I knew it did, but because if there was any such possible micromachinery it would surely have been discovered by organisms during the process of evolution. Organisms are experts at making micromachinery, yet they clearly use no such power systems[18].

I will leave the question hanging for the moment of why it is not possible to harness the energy of molecular motions. Gas molecules haphazardly colliding with one another will very soon 'shuffle' their energies so that the normal distribution of energies will be like that of a shuffled pack of cards: the most probable. Given the numbers involved, the tendency to this shuffled state must be powerful, this state being enormously more probable than any other. Now suppose you have two materials at different temperatures, say two gases separated by a thin heat–conducting wall. Why does the heat flow from the higher temperature to the lower? Not because of the first law of thermodynamics, nor because of 'heat pressure' because heat is not a fluid or a crowd of particles.

No, it is because such a set-up is analogous to one of our semi-arranged packs of cards, and because there is a Great Shuffler at work in the inescapable kinetic motion of the molecules which will re-distribute the energies of the molecules. How strong this tendency will be will depend on how much more probable the more fully shuffled state is than the more arranged state that you started with. Entropy is the degree of shuffledness. It is not energy but the tendency for entropy to increase that drives this process.

In general for physical and chemical – and biological – processes this tendency to increase entropy is one of two factors in determining which way processes, such as chemical reactions, will go. The other factor is in those forces operating between atoms and molecules. These may act in opposition to the shuffling tendency. When water freezes, for example, the attractive organising forces have the upper hand while at higher temperatures, where molecules are moving faster, the shuffling, disorganising tendency predominates.

What Boltzmann did was to quantify all this by showing how one could calculate what he called the 'thermodynamic probability' of different physical states of systems, more or less the number of conceivable arrangements for the energies of the molecules in different states, by analogy with our card game in which evidently the chances of getting a particular kind of distribution is directly related to the number of ways in which that kind of distribution can be realised. To save you a journey to Vienna to read it off Boltzmann's tombstone, I give you his key equation which expresses this idea more precisely:

$$S = k \log_e \omega$$

S is the entropy, ω the thermodynamic probability, and k is a universal constant, the same for all physical, chemical or biological systems whatever: Boltzmann's constant.

So why do molecular trapdoor engines not work?

The answer is because kinetic motion is inescapable[19]. It would apply not only to the air in the engine, but also to the dividing membrane, the trapdoors, their hinges ... Everything would be in a frantic rattling motion so that for as many molecules coming from the right, in figure 1.5, that would slam into the door to open it (and maybe get through) there would be others that would slip back the other way. There would be cases where the slamming door actually knocked molecules the other way: indeed if you think about it from this point of view you might even persuade yourself that the trapdoor would act as a kind of pump flapping the molecules preferentially to the left. Well, a full analysis is difficult but the conclusion is clear: if the system is in equilibrium (e.g. with the same pressure of air on either side at the same temperature, and with the distribution of energies between the molecules 'Maxwellian') then any molecular process that can happen in one direction can equally well happen in reverse. This is known as 'the principle of microscopic reversibility'. There is no avoiding it.

Kinetic motion is visible

In 1827 the Scottish botanist Robert Brown (1773–1858) noticed that very small particles he was examining under a microscope were in continuous haphazard motion, dithering about one way and then the other. This lively behaviour of all very small particles became known as Brownian motion. It seemed mysterious at the time[20].

Now we have a way of explaining Brownian motion. We can say that it is due to the suspended particles being bombarded by water molecules on all sides, *but not always evenly*. At one moment a few more water molecules might collide with one side of the particle than the other, giving it a momentary push one way or perhaps starting it spinning, only to be pushed or turned another way a moment later. No doubt this is happening, but a better way of putting it is to say that small suspended particles participate in the kinetic motion, like everything else. They are doing the same kind of thing as the water molecules, and have the same average kinetic energy as the water molecules. Of course if they are visible at all under an optical microscope they are much more massive than water molecules and therefore move more slowly, and with larger objects still the overall motion becomes imperceptible.

Not at first knowing anything about Brownian motion, Einstein[21] had come to the conclusion that the kinetic theory of matter implied that suspended microscopic particles ought to behave like this. He then produced a general theory of Brownian movement which he published in 1905 and in which he related the vigour of the movements of such particles to the sizes of molecules colliding with them. (You can see the idea: if the sizes of water molecules had been infinitesimal there would have been no effect . . .) Three years later the French physical chemist Jean Perrin (1870–1942) carried out a series of observations on suspended particles from which, using Einstein's theory, he managed to estimate the actual masses of atoms with considerable accuracy. The debate, it seemed, was over. Atoms and molecules exist and, yes, they are in perpetual motion. Ostwald conceded. Mach went quiet.

The '1900' revolution

Two things in particular had happened in the closing years of the nineteenth century to cast doubt on the fundamental Lavoisier–Dalton picture. One was the discovery of the electron, soon found to be a constituent of all matter and much lighter than a hydrogen atom, the lightest atom known.

Another was the discovery of the radioactivity of uranium in 1896 by Antoine Becquerel (1852–1909). There followed the discovery of other radioactive elements by Marie Curie (1867–1934), Pierre Curie (1859–1906) and others. By 1900, it was being realised that atoms could sometimes fall apart.

No doubt this seemed shocking at the time, but as it was soon to turn out it would still be possible to think in terms of ultimate units of matter, even if these were now to be seen as smaller units. Today every school child learns (with no shock at all) that atoms are made up of negatively charged electrons surrounding a tiny nucleus, and that this nucleus consists of positively charged protons and uncharged neutrons packed tightly together. The different kinds of atoms are different arrangements of these three 'fundamental particles'. A hydrogen atom, for example, has one proton in its nucleus, and there are heavier forms of hydrogen with either one or two neutrons as well. Helium has a nucleus containing always two protons and (usually) two neutrons. All the elements are defined by the number of protons in their nuclei and hence the number of electrons around the nucleus.

Well, for a few halcyon years in the 1930s protons, neutrons and electrons seemed to be the true 'atoms' out of which everything was made. The Daltonian principle, at least for the time being, was intact.

The situation rapidly became more complicated with the discovery of a plethora of new particles, produced mainly by high-energy collisions between the more familiar particles. Most of these would have disappointed Newton. They can hardly be said to be immutable. They last for less than a nanosecond, which is the time it takes for light to travel about 30 centimetres. Also it is now clear that the forces that keep the protons and neutrons together inside the nuclei of atoms are different from either of the classical kinds (gravitational or electromagnetic).

Even protons and neutrons are not 'fundamental' it seems, each being made up of three smaller bits called quarks, although the forces holding quarks together are so strong – and get *stronger*, to begin with, with distance – that quarks have not yet been found on their own.

The whole idea of matter as ultimately wee and sandy seems to be wearing a bit thin. Apart from anything else every time wee sandy things of any sort turn out to be made of still wee-er sandy things, we are faced with questions of how the grains stick together and, as Faraday would have said, it seems to be these forces that are the more fundamental forms of existence . . .

A more serious undermining of nineteenth-century atomism came in 1905 when Einstein (you know, the Brownian motion man) published his special theory of relativity and gave to the world a new equation as important and as stunningly simple as Boltzmann's, but which *everyone* has heard of:

$$E = mc^2,$$

which is to say that energy (E) and mass (m) are equivalent and in principle fully interconvertible. The constant c^2 in the equation, the square of the velocity of light, is so huge that a great deal of energy corresponds to very little mass. This explains why Lavoisier's principle of the conservation of mass had seemed to be true: chemical reactions never make or use enough energy for the mass of that energy to be perceptible. The new principle, the new first law of thermodynamics, is of the conservation of mass-energy. Mass-energy, or more conveniently *energy*, could be seen as the fundamental stuff of the world, the various particles being different ways of parcelling it up.

There have since been innumerable confirmations of Einstein's equation. For example if you compare the mass of an atom with the total mass of its separate constituent electrons, protons and neutrons you will find that the figures do not match. Lavoisier's law does not hold: atoms are always a bit lighter than the sum of their constituent parts. This is because in forming, say, a carbon atom from lighter constituents (as happens in some stars) a great deal of energy is lost (as starlight), which is to say that a little mass is lost. Another confirmation is that our sun has been able to shine for so long, in this case mainly by building helium from hydrogen. And then there is the nuclear industry, the hydrogen bomb . . .

The quantum shock

But the *real* bomb that was thrown into physics and chemistry at the turn of the twentieth century was neither the electron nor radioactivity nor relativity: it was Planck's constant.

I ask you to imagine the scene. It is the 14th of December 1900, and we are at a meeting of the Berlin Physical Society. Enter Max Planck in a heavy cloak concealing a black spherical object with a smouldering string coming out of it. To everyone's amazement he casually rolls his bomb down the aisle right into the heart of Physics. Some feeble attempts are made to avert catastrophe but – too late! – the bomb goes off. There is great destruction and there are many injuries. When the smoke finally clears a single letter has mysteriously appeared on the blackboard:

$$h$$

Try as they may, no one can rub it out. Among the injured is Herr Professor Planck himself. Later in hospital he is to tell reporters that he had thought his bomb was 'just a toy' . . .

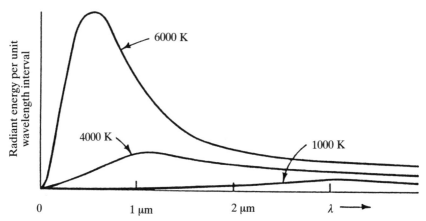

Figure 1.6. Distribution of wavelengths of electromagnetic radiation from a black body or cavity at different absolute temperatures. (Absolute zero, the lowest temperature possible, is about −273 °C, so an absolute temperature of, say, 600 K corresponds to 6273 °C.)
From GENERAL CHEMISTRY 3/E by Linus Pauling. Copyright © 1970 by Linus Pauling. Used with permission of W. H. Freeman and Company.

Max Planck (1858–1947) had been describing to the Berlin Physical Society his latest ideas on why things like metals, coals and so on glow in the way they do when they get hot: more strictly he was concerned with so called black body or cavity radiation.

If you heat up a piece of iron it will glow red to yellow to white to bluish, in the usual way, but in general different materials do not behave in exactly the same way. However, if you drill out a cavity in a block of metal then the radiation from the cavity will not only be somewhat brighter but will always have the same characteristics whatever the metal (or other material) you have used. Here is the place to look, it seems, for general laws relating temperature with electromagnetic radiation.

The superficial reason for the colour changes on heating was well known. It could be seen by analysing the wavelengths of radiations coming off at different temperatures: shorter-wavelength, that is, higher-frequency and bluer, radiation becomes more dominant at higher temperatures (figure 1.6). But what were the deeper reasons for these curves? The next step had been to find some mathematical relationship that would describe their characteristic shapes: to look for an equation, a rule that would generate curves that were similar to the observed curves. Planck himself had at last succeeded in doing this some months earlier, although his equation was rather complicated.

Atomic oscillators Now Planck was trying to go deeper and explain the equation, by developing a theory of what in detail was going on when objects emit or absorb radiation. His idea was that the atoms in the radiating material were tiny electromagnetic oscillators. This idea worked, but only if he supposed that such an atomic oscillator had two rather odd properties.

The first was that it could only have certain energies (E) which depended on its characteristic frequency (ν) such that:

$$E = nh\nu$$

n being a whole number and h a constant.

To see the oddness of this think of a more familiar oscillator, a sounding piano string. It too has a characteristic frequency, its note, but one is not aware of any rules limiting the degree of loudness or softness with which one can play a note on the piano. The score may advise 'forte' or 'double forte' but there is no implication that these are distinct levels and that you are not able to have anything in between. But for atoms there seemed indeed to be distinct levels for the 'loudness' (more correctly energy) of their characteristic 'notes'.

The second odd thing about Planck's hypothetical oscillators was that they did not radiate or absorb their energy continuously, but in jumps or 'quanta', corresponding to changes from one energy level to another. The energy, then, for a single such quantum jump would be given by:

$$E = h\nu$$

The corresponding piano string would be very odd indeed, as it would vibrate silently for most of the time – even when in its 'double forte' mode, – only emitting a sudden audible note if it changed to a lower energy. A 'Planck piano' using such strings would be especially irritating to play as you would never quite know when its vibrating strings were going to emit their notes. It would also be difficult to play for another reason. Just as energy could only come out of a string in quanta, so it could only go in. To get a string into a higher energy state (so that it was set to emit a note some time or other) you would need to hit the key with exactly the right amount of force: the string would only accept an appropriate quantum. Worse still the different notes would have different energy requirements: you would have to hit the top notes a bit harder to get them going. The conclusion seems clear: don't buy one of these pianos.

All along Planck had supposed that his assumptions were strictly for the purposes of calculation. It is a common device, in engineering calculations particularly, to pretend that something which is continuous is made up of little pieces or elements, and then to think about what will happen when the elements become indefinitely small. But Planck's constant did not seem to be like this. Ominously, his new equation would only fit the experimental curves if h had a definite value, a small value admittedly (6.626×10^{-34} joule sec) but not infinitely small. This was no toy.

Quanta are to be taken seriously   It was yet another 1905 paper of Einstein's that was to remove any doubt about the reality of the quantisation of energy. This was a paper on the the photoelectric effect: light shining on a metal surface can knock electrons out of the metal. The puzzling thing was that it seemed that blue light was better at doing this than red light. One could adjust the conditions so that a red light, however bright, was incapable of ejecting electrons while even a feeble blue light was effective, but there would be no way of getting the opposite effect: blue light was in some intrinsic sense more powerful. Einstein's interpretation of this was that light consists of packets (later to be called photons) whose energy is dictated by Planck's equation:

$$E = h\nu$$

Since h is a constant this means that high-frequency photons have more energy in them than low-frequency ones. The photons of blue light, for example, will have about twice the energy of the photons of red light. So the idea was that electrons are ejected from the metal by individual photons and that they require a minimum amount of energy to do this . . .

A more familiar example of a difference in the intrinsic energy of photons is in the well-known destructive effects of ultraviolet light. The sun produces relatively little of this – over 90% of its power output being in the visible and infrared regions of the electromagnetic spectrum – and only a small proportion of ultraviolet gets through the atmosphere anyway. But these photons can be like bullets. The higher-energy ones can break the bonds that hold atoms together in molecules: including molecules in your skin, for example.

Waves are to be taken seriously too   In the early years of the nineteenth century the physician Thomas Young (1773–1829) in England and the civil engineer Augustin Jean Fresnel (1788–1827) in France had demonstrated to almost everyone's satisfaction that light must be a form of wave motion[22], long before Maxwell was to show what kind of waves they were.

The classic demonstration of the wave nature of light is Young's experiment of 1801, which in modified form is illustrated in figure 1.7. The fact that light passing though very small holes or slits spreads out beyond them was already a sign that light might be better described as a train of waves than a hail of bullets, but Young's experiment does better than this. The set-up in figure 1.7 consists of a compact primary light source – a lamp behind a fine slit – and a pair of slits in another barrier placed between this and a screen. What appears on the screen is a whole series of bright and dark bands.

This phenomenon has a ready explanation in terms of interference between two wave trains. Except right in the middle of the screen the light will have to travel slightly different distances according to whether it goes through the top slit or the bottom slit. The result will be that the two wave trains arriving at the screen will do so either with their troughs and peaks in synchrony, in which case they will produce extra strong light, or in opposition where they will produce nothing (darkness). The wave trains will alternate between being 'in phase' and 'out of phase' like this at arrival points further away from the centre of the screen. Hence the succession of bright and dark bands. It is very difficult to explain such 'interference patterns' except on a wave theory.

Quanta *and* waves are more serious still   How can the photoelectric effect, which cries out for an explanation of light in terms of particles, be reconciled with Young's convincing demonstration that light must be a form of wave motion. Can light somehow be both?

It seems so. The particle character of electromagnetic radiation can indeed be made to show up in Young-type experiments. Suppose you could to do Young's experiment with a very faint light source such that (in particle language) it only produced a photon every few seconds. And let us say that you can see single photons using a supersensitive screen which twinkles every time a photon hits it. Well the first photon duly arrives and shows that indeed it is behaving like a bullet in that it hits the screen at a definite spot and delivers up all its energy there. Likewise the next photon ... You might be beginning to think that the bullet theory had won outright.

But then you turn up the light intensity so that, as is usual for lamps,

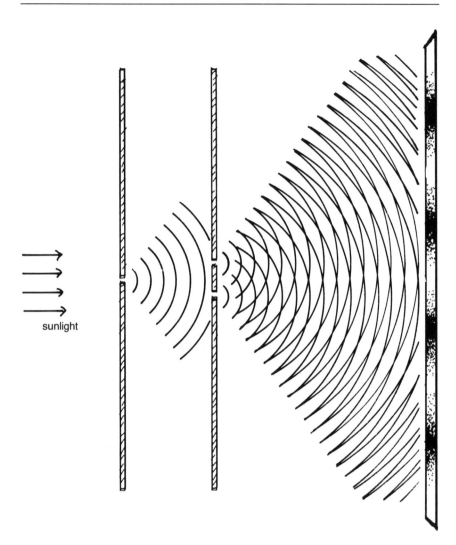

Figure 1.7. A set-up for repeating Young's experiment of 1801 to show that light is a form of wave motion. (The experiment was originally done with pinholes, but very fine slits are now more common.) Light passing through a single slit on the left acts as a compact source from which its waves spread out, making two secondary sources at the double slit in the second screen. Waves from these secondary sources interfere so that if a screen is placed at a suitable distance it will show a sequence of light and dark bands. The light bands appear where the two sets of waves are in phase with each other, where their crests and troughs coincide and reinforce each other, as at the centre of the screen. The dark bands in between result from waves arriving from the two sources being out of phase. Here crests and troughs cancel

billions of billions of photons are pouring out. Now instead of the very occasional twinkle the whole screen is ablaze. Under these conditions the wave theory seems to be true after all, because now you are simply repeating Young's experiment, and of course you get interference bands as before.

To see both aspects at once you put the lamp intensity knob back to a low but intermediate position: to produce, say, about 100 flashes a second on the screen. Then you will see at once what is going on. The flashes will be most frequent at the positions of the light bands in the Young pattern, least frequent in the dark bands . . .

Nothing seems to be forcing the photons to go anywhere in particular. Each one picks its own place to arrive, so to speak. But there are preferred destinations. The light regions are where photons are most likely to arrive, the dark ones where they are least likely to arrive. Indeed in an ideal experiment they would *never* arrive at the exact centres of the dark bands, the points of stillness (nodes) according to the wave description.

Which slit did the photon go through?   It might be reasonable to suggest perhaps that a flash seen on the lower half of the screen would have been caused (or would be more likely to have been caused) by a photon that had gone through the bottom slit, and *vice versa* for flashes higher up. Yet that does not seem to be so. If you close one of the slits the banding tendency for the arrival points will go away and you will be left with a single broad brightish band. The two-ness of the slits is essential. If the photon needs both slits, then it looks as if somehow it goes through both slits to produce the effects observed.

Coherence   Another more general consideration seems to lead to the same paradox. Interference patterns usually depend upon there being a single original light source illuminating the two slits, although it might have seemed that two separate light sources, say two thin glowing filaments, would have been just as good as a pair of slits illuminated from behind. Why not? A picture similar in its essentials to that of figure 1.7 can be drawn with this simpler arrangement.

Ordinary light, such as sunlight or lamplight is not a single mammoth wave train but a haphazard collection of what can be thought of as short strands resulting from the haphazard way in which the light is usually produced from hot matter. The worst bit about this from the point of view of interference experiments is that the strands are not generally speaking in phase with each other. The waves are not all going up and down in unison. So it is necessary to have two mutually coherent light sources for interference experiments that is to say two light sources which, if they are each a jumble of strands are at least the *same* jumble of strands, so that each strand individually is represented in each light source. In that way the formal diagram of figure 1.7 will correspond to any one strand. The easiest way to achieve such a mutual coherence is to do what Young did: derive the two light sources – the pair of slits – from a single source behind them.

Now we can guess why light waves produced in, say, a glowing filament are not 'in unison'. It is presumably because the light results from more or less individual quantum events. By a 'strand' in the above discussion, then, we should probably mean just one photon. So it looks as if Young's experiment worked, with his clever set-up, because every individual photon was given the chance to go through both slits, and took it.

Of course, you may say, the whole thing is insane. Surely if one is going to say that a photon is an indivisible particle you cannot then say that it can go through both slits: that is simply to give and deny it particleness in the same breath.

I agree. But what cannot be denied, I think, is that there is a waviness of some sort, a probability-of-turning-up wave and that *that* goes through the slits and self-interferes in the manner of any self-respecting wave. Whether one should say that the quantum of energy goes through the slits at all is less clear: all we seem to know is that a quantum of energy started in a hot filament and ended on a screen. What it was doing in between is anyone's guess, if indeed it makes sense to say that it was anywhere, or doing anything, or that it kept its identity between times . . . but I will leave these deeper mysteries until chapter seven.

In the meantime let us just do what most people do in such discussions: settle on adjectives and say that light has particulate and wavelike properties, and discuss any particular phenomena using whichever analogy seems a good idea at the time. Such a policy is ragged, but it works remarkably well.

Matter waves

In 1924 the French aristocrat Prince Louis de Broglie (1892–1987) realised that particle- and wave-like aspects of matter were unavoidably implied by Planck's equation, which was by now being used in describing the behaviour of atoms as well as light. It was perfectly logical (in an insane sort of way) to suppose that if electromagnetic waves could also be particles then electrons should also be waves (well, I mean, why not?). Indeed de Broglie was able to work out what the 'associated wavelength' of matter waves of any sort should be. If the momentum (mass times velocity) of the individual particles in a stream of particles is p, then the wavelength, λ (the distance between successive crests in the 'matter waves') should be given by

$$\lambda = h/p$$

This turned out to be exactly the case: a stream of electrons shows interference patterns and from these patterns the 'associated wavelengths' of electron beams can easily be calculated. These always turned out to be as de Broglie predicted. The effect has since been confirmed with other particles as well, neutrons for example[23].

Standing waves   We have been talking about wave trains, waves moving through space like waves in the sea, going on and on. But there is another familiar kind of wave motion, the standing-still waves in a sounding piano string or a ringing bell.

A piano string indeed provides one of the simplest examples of a standing wave of this sort. Its note is determined by its fundamental mode of vibration:

Here the string is moving everywhere except at its two ends. If that was *all* that a sounding piano string was doing it would have rather a boring tone. In fact, as with all ringing objects, it is vibrating in other ways too. A piano string can also vibrate like this:

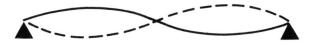

Here in addition to the end points there is another point in the string which is not moving – another 'node' point as it is called – right at the middle. This vibration mode is ringing at an octave above the first one, making its sound by pushing and pulling the air around it with twice the frequency of the fundamental mode. Then as you might imagine there are higher such 'harmonics' too, e.g.:

which has two nodes, and so on. A piano string manages to vibrate in many such ways at once so that the actual sound you get is a superimposition of the fundamental and harmonic modes in a proportion that gives the characteristic piano sound (other instruments create sounds that have different mixes of harmonics).

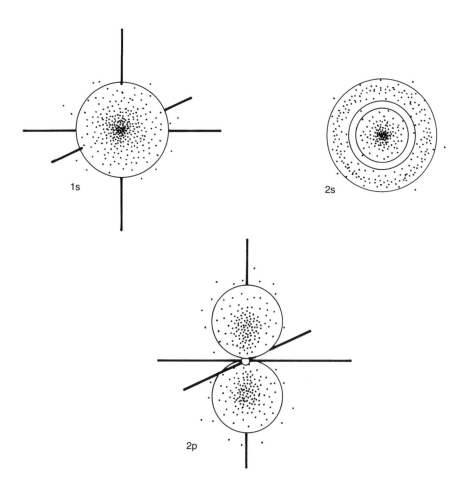

Well, then, electrons in an atom are held in place, in the vicinity of the positive nucleus, by their negative charges: if electrons in general are waves, then perhaps electrons in atoms should ring like bells: perhaps electrons in atoms are standing waves. What a wonderful idea!

In 1926 Erwin Schrödinger (1887–1961) published an equation describing how de Broglie's waves should evolve (change) in space and time, and this provided a means of calculating the arrangements of electrons in atoms.

Like the photons arriving at the screen in Young's experiment, electrons (if you are thinking of them as particles) have only a *chance* of being in any particular place within an atom, but a bigger chance in some places than others. Like the photons in Young's experiment these chances vary in a wavy way, but here in a way analogous to standing-wave effects rather

Figure 1.8. Dot maps indicating where (in some imaginary experiment) an electron would be most likely to be found when it is in different 'orbitals' in an atom. The s-orbitals are spherically symmetrical and if an electron is in the most stable (lowest-energy) kind of these, designated 1s, then the most likely place for it would be right at the centre, at the nucleus. Then the probability of finding it would simply tail off as you went away from the centre. (The circle is not a boundary, but represents a sphere within which there is some definite chance, say 95%, that the electron would be found, in the imaginary experiment).

There is only 'room' for two electrons in the 1s state so for an atom with more than two electrons higher-energy orbitals will be occupied. The next up is another s orbital, the 2s. The top right picture is an imaginary cross-section of a 2s orbital. Again it is spherically symmetrical but the probability of finding the electron drops to zero and then rises again as you go away from the nucleus – before falling off as before. This is analogous to a string vibrating in its first harmonic, where there will be a nodal point in the middle which is still. In higher harmonics of s orbitals, 3s, 4s. . .there are successively more of these spherical 'still' regions.

The lower picture shows a different style, that of the p orbitals. The lowest energy of these is designated 2p. If an electron is in a p orbital there is no chance of finding it at the nucleus. Instead there is a pair of regions of high probability some distance north and south, as it were. p Orbital like these come in threes because they can be orientated along the y-axis as shown, but also along the x- and z-axes. Thus between them the 2p orbitals can accommodate six electrons. Higher harmonics, 3p, 4p. . .have increasing numbers of regions of 'stillness' within their paired lobes, and each type can accommodate six electrons. Then there are still further styles with increasing numbers of lobes: d orbitals and f-orbitals. . .but let's leave it at that.

than simple interference effects. Now, if one wants to know where an electron is likely to be in an atom, if one wants to make a map, say, with levels of shading to indicate high- and low-risk areas (sorry, *volumes*) then one has to work out its standing wave modes using Schrödinger's equation.

Pictures of standing wave modes for a piano string fit a one-dimensional case, but an electron in an atom – say the one electron in a hydrogen atom – is more complicated to the extent that here its wave is in three dimensions. (It is more like a bell in this respect.) Figure 1.8 shows some of the standing wave modes for electrons in atoms calculated from Schrödinger's equation. The 1s mode, for example, can be compared with the fundamental mode of vibration of a string – there are no nodes – while the 2s is a first harmonic with one node (not a nodal point, but a nodal plane . . .). In deference to the outdated idea that electrons move in orbits around the nucleus like planets round the sun, the electrons are said to occupy 'orbitals', i.e. of the kind shown in figure 1.8.

A new piano The last quantum piano we looked at had

M. PLANCK – BERLIN 1900

inscribed in inlaid gold letters above the keyboard, and it behaved strangely. Now we can push on the new

E. SCHRÖDINGER – ZURICH 1926

model. It is just as odd but at least we can open the lid of this one and get a better look at the works. Again, as with the Planck model, the strings 'ring silently' most of the time, emitting or absorbing energy only in well-defined packets when abruptly changing from one energy level to another. The main new feature which we can now see is that these distinct allowed energy levels are alternative standing wave modes.

In the piano corresponding to an iron atom there are 26 vibrating strings: 26 electrons. Most of these are arranged in pairs, and the pairs into groups vibrating in the different ways such as indicated in figure 1.8.

Is there anything corresponding to a non-vibrating string – an electron having a rest?

The answer is no: to talk of a 'string' with no amplitude of vibration is to say as much as there is no electron there: no amplitude is no chance of finding an electron. The electron *is* (the totality of) the vibration of the 'string'. (The bad news is that, really, there is no 'string'.)

There is, all the same, an important class of non-electrons in atoms. These are the so called 'vacant orbitals': standing wave modes which are possible but are not being used. This may seem a very esoteric kind of 'thing', but perhaps not if you are an office worker: vacant orbitals are like slots or pigeon holes, 'places' where electrons might be. The possible standing wave modes – the orbitals, occupied or vacant – have this kind of reality.

This point is emphasised by a powerful restriction, a kind of office rule about the use of pigeon holes. I can see a tired looking notice:

No more than two electrons per pigeon hole please!

(And then perhaps there is another scribbled note to say that two in the same pigeon hole are only allowed if they have opposite spins; what *that* means I will leave till Chapter 7.)

It was indeed another surprise that electrons in atoms have this rule that no two of them can be in exactly the same state. This rule, called the Pauli exclusion principle, has a counterpart in our large-scale world: no two things can be in the same place at the same time. But what 'place' means for electrons does not seem to be quite the same as what we usually mean. Yes, the p-orbital shown in figure 1.8 seems to 'occupy space' in much the same way as a balloon of that double-lobed shape would: but then in another sense the electrons hardly seem to worry about space at all: the more different kinds of orbitals are just superimposed.

To get a sense of the sheer complexity possible you might like to think of a gold atom. This has 79 electrons with standing wave modes as follows.

Starting with the fundamental mode – labelled the 1s (figure 1.8) – two electrons can have this simple style of standing wave; then there can be two more with the (2s) higher harmonic version, the more complicated type with a nodal surface inside it; then six ringing in the 2p dumb-bell modes, two electrons in each of the three double-lobe forms arranged at right angles to each other ('north–south', 'east–west' and 'up–down'); then another two in the next harmonic up of the spherical s style (3s); ditto another six for 3p, which now has a 2s-like doubleness in each of its lobes, i.e. nodal surfaces inside the lobes where there is zero chance of finding the electron; then two more in the 4s mode; then *ten* in a new, more lobey and complicated 3d mode; then still higher harmonics in 4p, 5s, 4d, 6s similarly 'filled'; and then in case you were getting bored *fourteen* ringing in a still fancier set of seven multi-lobe modes (4f); and finally 6s and 5d providing twelve slots between them for the eleven electrons left. A crowded place, a gold atom.

Forces between atoms

You might say that the exclusion principle compels atoms to be interestingly different from each other: each kind of atom is required do something at least slightly different with its electrons. For chemistry, it is the so-called outer electrons – those that are stuck with the highest-energy standing wave modes – that matter most since they determine most directly how an atom is likely to interact with other atoms. In gold, for example, these are the electrons in the 6s and 5d modes.

Atoms have a tendency to stick firmly to each other, because these outer electrons often interact with other atoms. For example, a metal atom will have one or two of its outermost electrons more loosely held than usual: hence the tendency for metals to exist as positive ions in solution. On the other hand there are atoms which can stabilise their electron organisation by adding electrons (if they can find any). The chlorine atom, for example, is usually found as its negative ion Cl^-.

Two kinds of chemical bonding result from such effects. As touched on earlier, salts such as NaCl consist simply of positively and negatively charged ions packed together through their mutual electrostatic attraction. Then again a solid metal owes its strength to the cohesion between its positive metal ions and a 'sea' of negative electrons: a kind of glue consisting of electrons which are no longer particularly tied to any atom.

Covalent bonds   For organic chemistry, and hence for biochemistry, by far the most important form of chemical bonding is covalent. These are the forces responsible for making specific molecules by joining atoms together in specific ways, as can be represented by ball and stick models such as those in figure 1.1. Covalent bonds depend on electron sharing. To take the simplest example two hydrogen atoms can create a 'better' (lower-energy) standing wave pattern if they share their electrons, so that now a pair of electrons is being held by both hydrogen nuclei which are themselves held together. Such a sharing of a pair of electrons is a covalent bond – one of the little sticks in the models. We would say that the 'atomic orbitals' of separate hydrogen atoms have fused to create a 'molecular orbital':

A bond between (say) two carbon atoms is formed similarly, except that in this case there are four 'outer' electrons available to make four covalent bonds with other atoms, making it useful for molecule building, especially as carbon atoms can form bonds with other carbon atoms without limit. Nitrogen has similarly the potential to make (normally) three and oxygen two covalent bonds, although here the capacity for like-bonding (oxygen–oxygen or nitrogen–nitrogen) is far more limited. They can, however, join up with carbon atoms to give the almost endless variety of molecules that are the special domain of organic chemistry (of which biochemistry is a small subdomain which we get to in the next chapter).

Even the directionality of covalent bonds – the effect that van't Hoff had understood and which Kolbe had been so scathing about – can be accounted for qualitatively in terms of the directionality of most of the vibration modes of the electrons in atoms (plus, a further analogy with piano strings, that different modes can 'mix' somewhat).

In all, the electronic theory of valency (whose origins go back at least to Humphrey Davy) was the third great theory of modern chemistry, after the modern atomic and the kinetic theories of matter. At last it was reasonably clear how atoms stuck together – if you were prepared to forget about deeper mysteries, anyway.

The unreasonable effectiveness of ball-and-stick models[24]

The good news in all this for organic chemists and biochemists seems to be that we can all just go back to our ball-and-stick (and similar) models of the sort shown in figure 1.1.

I suppose that most chemists would say that in the van't Hoff affair Kolbe made a wonderful fool of himself. Well, Kolbe was rude and he was wrong, but he was no fool. He had been wrong in supposing that simple spatial considerations could never apply to tiny things like molecules: but he was only *just* wrong. It is a gift from Nature to the organic chemist that familiar spatial ideas still work at the molecular level. We should be thankful because at just one level lower they do *not* work. As we saw, electrons do not 'fill space' within atoms in anything like the same straightforward way that, say, molecules seem to in crystals.

Like all models, the organic chemist's ones have some clear limitations. There are important, if weak, attractive forces which always exist between different molecules, and between different parts of the same molecule, depending on some mobility of electrons within all atoms and molecules. Other somewhat stronger forces between molecules are caused by the electrons being somewhat displaced within molecules so that some parts may have permanent small negative charges while other parts are slightly positively charged. Generally these so-called secondary forces are not so easily represented in simple molecular models. Then again, in line with Faraday's remarks (page 17), there are no hard boundaries to molecules, just an increasing repulsive force when they get too near to each other and the fuzzy clouds of probability-of-finding-an-electron begin to overlap.

We can draw a hydrogen molecule as two hydrogen atoms joined by a little stick to represent the shared pair of electrons which constitutes the covalent bond between them:

$$H—H$$

But do not enquire too deeply where these electrons are. Electrons do not *have* definite positions within covalent bonds. We say that electrons are always to some extent 'delocalised' even if a little stick for a pair of them may be quite a good symbol to represent roughly where they are and what they are doing.

More serious limitations of stick models are common. They are very obvious in molecules such as benzene. A benzene molecule is a ring of six carbon atoms with one hydrogen atom attached to each. As carbon is 4-valent – makes four bonds with surrounding atoms – one might have expected an alternation of double and single bonds:

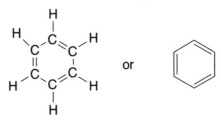

In fact all the bonds are the same length: in between the normal double and single lengths. This is one of many indications that benzene cannot be fully represented by any one such drawing. A pair of drawings is sometimes used:

The double-headed arrow does not say that the molecule is jumping between the alternative ways of arranging the electrons in the double bonds, but is intended to mean that the real structure is a sort of blend or superposition of (mainly) these two. The double bond electrons are delocalised in molecular orbitals spread over all the carbon atoms.

Graphite is a material made up from enormous numbers of benzene rings fused together like wire netting. A piece of graphite consists of stacks of huge flat molecules containing billions and billions of benzene rings. Here there are electrons delocalised from one end of the piece of graphite to the other; this is why graphite conducts electricity.

A piece of metal conducts electricity even better. Here again those 'loose' electrons which hold the metal ions together are delocalised, effectively throughout the piece of metal: they are no longer in such restricted 'pigeon holes'.

More dramatic still is the phenomenon of superconductivity which some metals, such as lead, show at near the absolute zero of temperature (*ca.* −273 °C): zero on Kelvin's scale. Suddenly at below 4K all resistance disappears. At that temperature a current started in a ring of lead will continue to flow for ever.

Such phenomena – and I will be coming back to discuss them again in later chapters – are called 'macroquantum effects'. Yet, really, effects like this just rub our noses in what was implicit in Young's experiment, Planck's bomb, Einstein's interpretation of light, de Broglie's insight, Schrödinger's equation, and for that matter the whole of chemistry. As the Yorkshireman *might* have said: there's nowt so queer as stuff.

And to make *that* point is one of my three intentions for this chapter. Another is to provide, or provide reminders of, some school chemistry which will be needed shortly, in the next chapter. My third purpose is to provide some examples and start us thinking in general about what a scientific theory is, and of the uses and failings of *models* in this context.

Then when we come to it later we will be able to see what we should expect, and what we need not expect, of a theory of consciousness. So a page or two more to finish on that.

Models and analogies

Good analogies are *like* in some respects that are clearly understood; and *unlike* in other respects that are clear also. The organic chemist's models, for example, are thought to correspond to real molecules with respect to distances between atoms and so on, but not literally in all respects, and usually the distinctions are clear enough. Maybe the little sticks are made of steel and they go rusty, but there is no danger at all of this being taken as a blinding new insight about the nature of molecules.

Yet, as Mary Hesse[25] has said, a good scientific model should have a third aspect apart from evident likeness and unlikeness to the reality it refers to. It should have a certain 'open texture', giving scope for further exploration: it should not merely seek to summarise what is known. Then it can be a research tool as well as a teaching aid. The model itself can be studied for *its* properties and this may suggest new possibilities (or impossibilities) and raise new questions.

An example of the use of a model for exploring possibilities was in the discovery of the double helical structure of DNA where building a real physical model out of wire helped to provide the critical insights.

Then again a ball–and–stick model may raise the question of whether the sticks are rigid or bendable and if so whether elastic or plastic, to set one wondering if there is a correspondence with Nature here. There is. Indeed ball–and–stick molecular models can be improved, for some purposes, by having compactly coiled springs instead of sticks, to represent a feature of covalent bonds that they can be bent (fairly easily) and (with more difficulty) stretched or compressed. We know these details mainly from studying the absorption of infrared light by molecules. If you pass infrared light through a material it will pick out just those photons which it can use to set its molecules vibrating, usually in very many different ways: so you look for which photons went missing on the way through . . .

If a little spring is a wonderful model for a covalent bond this is among other things because nobody thinks that a covalent bond really is a little spring. Of course you should never *believe* models, they only have an 'as if ' status and they are likely to let you down any time. Here the shock comes when you learn that the bonds can only vibrate with certain discrete amplitudes (it's Planck's piano again). *That's* not like steel springs at all, and it should make us extra cautious.

Indeed although we might be inclined to say that Mach and Ostwald were a bit extreme in their skepticism, there were good reasons at the time to be wary of the kinetic theory and the statistical form of thermodynamics which was its extension. Boltzmann's explanation for entropy was certainly one of the high points of nineteenth-century science and powerful support for a kinetic theory of some sort. It may have seemed to support, too, a billiard ball model of atoms and molecules, but actually it contained within it some seeds of trouble: the development as a whole showed that a billiard ball model could go surprisingly far, but also that there were clear bounds to its power.

For example it turns out that the capacity of a gas to store heat depends on how many atoms it has in its molecules. If it has only one atom, like helium, then it holds all its heat in a translational form, that is to say its heat consists simply of the flying about in all directions of its molecules. On the other hand nitrogen with two atoms, and imagined to have a dumb-bell shape, can also rotate (as well as fly about) and so it has a greater capacity for heat. Now the calculations only work out to give observed heat capacities if you assume that nitrogen is not able to rotate along its axis. Why not, why can the nitrogen molecule not spin like a top? It may seem a small point, but it is one of many cracks that were already beginning to show even before Planck and the black body affair.

Molecular models are of a rather literal kind, toy models I will call them, like model trains or aeroplanes, only scaled up instead of scaled down. But many models used in science are more abstract kinds of analogies.

An example here would be Newton's use of the idea of a gravitational force. Force is a familiar notion, but already an abstraction in so far as it is one removed from the source of our ideas about force, derived from memories of heavy suitcases, sweating horses, grunting wrestlers, or whatever. We all know what force means, so it will do as the starting point for the gravitational model. All objects in the Universe behave *as if* there was a force acting between them across space. Furthermore if m_1 and m_2 are the masses of two such objects and d the distance between them this force can be worked out from Newton's equation:

$$F = G \, \frac{m_1 \cdot m_2}{d^2}$$

where G is a universal constant, like Boltzmann's or Planck's always the same everywhere.

This brings us to another characteristic of models in science, that they can often be expressed in mathematical terms, allowing among other things quantitative predictions so that the 'truth' of the model can be checked in detail.

We can say indeed that what corresponds to the organic chemist's toy models in Newton's gravitational theory *is* his equation. Just as you can see what kinds of new substances might be possible by means of toy models (or more often more conveniently by drawing structural formulae) so too can physicists play with their mathematical representations of reality.

Not only the gravitational force idea but Newton's equation itself is still an analogy: what he is saying is that there is an analogy between aspects of the behaviour of newly detached apples, planetary motions, tides, etc. and the behaviour of this equation. Yes, equations can be said to 'behave'. In the above example F changes if you change any or all of m_1, m_2, or d, whatever these symbols might stand for: here in ways that may be qualitatively obvious, but which you would want a calculator to explore in detail. For other equations, such as Maxwell's or Schrödinger's, the behaviour may not even be qualitatively obvious. Then again most calculations in physics use combinations of equations in deriving new ones, so that again results are not necessarily at all obvious. Major 'discoveries' can be made with pencil and paper. Such is the value of play.

The organic chemist's toy models can also be used in combination: it is an exceptional issue of of the weekly *Nature*, these days, that does not have a (computer-generated) model of a protein molecule showing how it interacts with something else (I have one here; see figure 1.1d, e on page 13). Molecular biology simply cannot do without such models, any more than physics can do without its highly developed system of mathematical analogies.

Cheshire cat syndrome   The mathematical constructs of physics are so beautiful and effective that it is a particular hazard of the trade to suppose that they *are* the reality. (If only equations would go rusty sometimes, it might help to diminish this risk.)

An often quoted (but innocent) remark of Hertz – that 'Maxwell's theory is Maxwell's system of equations'[26] – may have helped to start a trend towards the ultimately incoherent idea that 'everything is in the mathematics'. I hasten to add that neither Maxwell nor Hertz would have said any such thing. (Of course the mathematics must be *about* something in physics, the Pure Mathematics department is next door.) But faced with the inscrutability of matter[27] seen now at its sharpest in the modern (quantum) theory, together with the uncanny accuracy of that theory, the temptation is to take up a pragmatic position, to stick with what we know works and ask no questions – and to say that matter theory is quantum theory's system of equations.

Why is that such a bad idea? Surely, if it works . . .?

Well, there is a preliminary objection that in practice mathematical models are unobtainable, or hopelessly unwieldy, in many of the most interesting areas of science (e.g. most of molecular biology).

But the deeper objection is, as I said, that it is a fundamental mistake ever to identify a model with reality. We may set up our chess board with a restricted number of pieces operating under a restricted set of rules. And we may have fun for a time and gain new insights; but sooner or later, if history is anything to go by, we will lose touch with the game that Nature is playing.

Force, field, charge, mass, energy, cause, effect, possibility, probability, actuality, substance, form, place, space, event, motion, spin, time, sequence, particle, wave, quantum . . . there are plenty of pieces to play with. And at least we know now for sure that we do not know at all what matter is. It is not even clear any more where we should draw the line around a set of phenomena and say 'these are to do with material things'. There is just 'world stuff', *Weltstoff*, as Julian Huxley[28] said we should call it. Are Lucretius's atoms of the mind in there, smooth and round? That sounds like the wee sandy stuff again: perhaps we can find something better.

Let us move to biology.

General References

History of Science: Mason (1956/1962); Singer (1959); Crossland (1971).
History of Chemistry: Toulmin & Goodfield (1962); Leicester (1956/1971); Partington (1960).

Notes

1 Kent (1950) on Joseph Black and his times.

2 Proust (1799).

3 Atkinson (1940); Leicester (1956/1971), p. 153.

4 Latham (1951).

5 Stones (1928).

6 From Newton's *Opticks: or, a treatise of the Reflections, Refractions, Inflections, and colours of light* (4th ed., corrected, London 1730), Book III, Question 31. Quoted in Thayer (1953), p. 175; and in Crossland (1971), p. 76.

7 Kolbe (1877). Quoted in Crossland (1971), p. 268.

8 Johnstone Stoney (1891).

9 Faraday (1844). Quoted in Crossland (1971), p. 216.

10 Maxwell's paper 'A dynamical theory of the electromagnetic field' was presented to the Royal Society on October 27th 1864 and published in the *Philosophical Transactions* the following year. It has recently been reprinted with an excellent Introduction on Maxwell's approach to science and his debt to Faraday (Torrance, 1983, pp. 1–27).

11 Russell (1946), p. 565.

12 Opticks: Query No. 18 (see note 6). Quoted in Thayer (1953), pp. 141–2.

13 Cullen's paper 'On the cold produced by evaporating fluids' was the first publication of Glasgow University's Chemistry Department, which had been founded in 1747 with Cullen's appointment as lecturer. See Kent (1950).

14 See Crossland (1971), pp. 229–36.

15 Herapath (1821), quoted in Crossland (1971), p. 231; Stones (1928).

16 Maxwell's paper *On the dynamical theory of gases* was read to the Royal Society on May 31st 1866 and appeared in the *Philosophical Transactions* the following year.

17 Ostwald (1904), Faraday Lecture to the Chemical Society.

18 Maxwell himself made the most celebrated thought experiment along these lines, imagining a shutter separating two compartments but which was so light that it could be slid open with no energy by a tiny Demon, who could see the fast molecules when they approached from one side and quickly open and close the shutter to let them through. This way a temperature and pressure difference would be built up between the two sides and hence a means of harnessing pure heat . . . Kelvin considered the possibility of

such mechanisms being present in living things. See Ehrenberg (1967); Bennett (1987); Maddox (1990).

[19] Bennett (1987).

[20] Brown (1828). There has been some discussion recently as to whether Brown really saw Brownian motion. Cadée (1991) thinks he did.

[21] To be found in Einstein's *Autobiographical Notes*, reprinted 1979.

[22] For example, in his 1801 Bakerian Lecture to the Royal Society, and a subsequent note, Young accounts for the colours produced by such things as soap bubbles and surface scratches in terms of the interference of wave trains (Young 1802).

[23] The reason it does not work with tennis balls is, among other things, that their momentum is *so* much bigger than the tiny quantity h that the associated wavelength is far too small for any wavey properties to show up.

[24] Refers to Wigner's famous title 'The unreasonable effectiveness of mathematics in the physical sciences' (Wigner, 1960).

[25] Hesse (1961).

[26] Hertz (1884).

[27] John Foster's term, used also by Lockwood (1989) as a chapter title.

[28] Julian Huxley (1962) on p. 167.

2

Life

Aristotle said that man has three kinds of soul: a 'rational soul' (this was his special one); an 'animal soul' (to do with sensation and self-movement); and then a 'vegetative soul' which all living things have and by virtue of which they reproduce, absorb nutrients, grow, and decay.

The vegetative soul was the essential attribute of life, a controlling principle or integrating factor. Around 1820 Coleridge defined life similarly as 'the power which unites a given all into a whole that is presupposed by all its parts' and Ruskin (1860) too when he wrote that 'The power which causes the several portions of the plant to help each other we call life . . .' and compared this to the way in which the elements of a fine painting are unified in the whole.

Let us change the language, but hang onto the idea that what distinguishes organisms from other natural systems is their complex integrity. To maintain that integrity the parts, ultimately the molecules, must in some sense 'know about each other'. I do not say that every molecule in your body is directly in touch with every other: no organisation needs, or could cope with, total communication; but indirectly the members of that changing society of molecules and crystals which is your body must in some sense be 'in touch' if the society is to have a chance of lasting ten minutes, never mind its allotted span. A major theme of this chapter is molecular communication. I start with some general remarks on the commodity of communication: information.

Information and surprise   A message only conveys information to us if it tells us something we did not already know; and you might say that the more it surprises us the more information it contains. The statement 'It rained yesterday in Fort William' would contain little information for those who have ever had a holiday there; but it might be real news for a foreign visitor.

This example illustrates the difficulty of measuring information, but at the same time suggests that it *can* be measured if somehow you can arrive at an estimate of the 'improbability' of a message.

By convention an amount of information, I (measured in 'bits'), is said to be related to a probability, p (measured in odds), by the expression:

$$I = \log_2 (1/p)$$

(i.e. bits of information = $\log_2$ 'improbability'), so that on being informed of one of two equally likely outcomes, for example the outcome of tossing a coin, you acquire precisely one unit – one bit – of information. If you plan to toss a coin 100 times you will have very much less of an idea about the total outcome, this being one out of 2^{100} equally likely possible sequences of heads and tails. Such a sequence would convey 100 bits ($\log_2[2^{100}] = 100$) and similarly any random looking 100-long binary string such as

0010100101110101110101010101100101101011110100001011101011010101
0101100010101111011111011010101010101010111000

is said to convey 100 bits of information whether or not the string has any further significance: this kind of bone-dry 'information' just *is* the sequence.

Of course it might also contain information in the more usual sense of the word – it might be a cryptogram for example – but if we start thinking of information at this level we are back with the Fort William problem. (What if when we decipher the message it turns out to be banal, or an obvious lie . . .?) The virtue of thinking of the information as being the uninterpreted symbol sequence itself is that such 'information' is relatively easily measured (by counting the number of symbols and the number of kinds of symbols and knowing their relative frequencies). This is not the warm-blooded information of real life, where quality matters most and the quantity usually vague (as in 'there was little information to be had from his presentation' or 'her book has a lot of information about the lesser wines of the Gironde'). In biology both kinds are of interest: I will use the terms 'formal information' or 'information capacity' when I am talking about information of the bone-dry, easily measurable sort.

Two further comments. First, quite small amounts of formal information correspond to gigantic improbabilities: for example a particular sequence holding a mere 100 bits is one possibility out of more than a million million million million million. That is not the kind of thing you just hit on by chance.

Second, the special part of biochemistry called molecular biology can be said to have started (about the middle of this century) with the realisation that molecules can hold information. By analogy with binary strings, strings of letters on a page, and so on, we can see what kinds of molecules are likely to be efficient in this way. They should consist of strings of units, for convenience of a limited number of different sorts, but which can be freely arranged – permuted – in a vast number of ways. That is what the nucleic acids, DNA and RNA, are like: they are long strings of 4 kinds of symbol. It is also what proteins are like: they are strings of 20 kinds of symbol (see figure 2.1).

Nature's engineer

We do not now think that organisms must defy the laws of physics, any more than a great work of literature must defy the rules of grammar. Life is a way of *obeying* the laws of physics. But it is a very special way, as great works of literature are special.

We have indeed plenty of other examples of this kind of thing in human artefacts. No one suspects the least violation of the laws of physics in the workings of a motor car; but then no one expects that the laws of physics alone can *explain* a motor car either. A machine is explained in terms of physics and chemistry plus (at least) an engineer. An organism is explained in terms of physics and chemistry plus (at least) evolution through natural selection.

This means that, whatever else, organisms in general are machines that can evolve, which means that they must in general be able to reproduce and pass on characteristics to their offspring. The mechanism for evolution which Charles Darwin (1809–1882) and Alfred Wallace (1823–1913) presented in 1858 requires that such inheritable characteristics should nevertheless be subject to variation; so that rather as, say, a farmer may improve his cattle in terms of characteristics such as milk production by deliberately choosing to breed from high-yielding individuals, so Nature without any question of deliberate intent must inevitably tend to 'select' variants which are more successful in the struggle for survival and the competition for reproductive success. Rabbit variants in any generation which can run faster, or build a better burrow, or hear or see a little better, or have stronger sexual drives . . . will on the whole tend to leave more offspring. In so far as they pass on to their offspring their

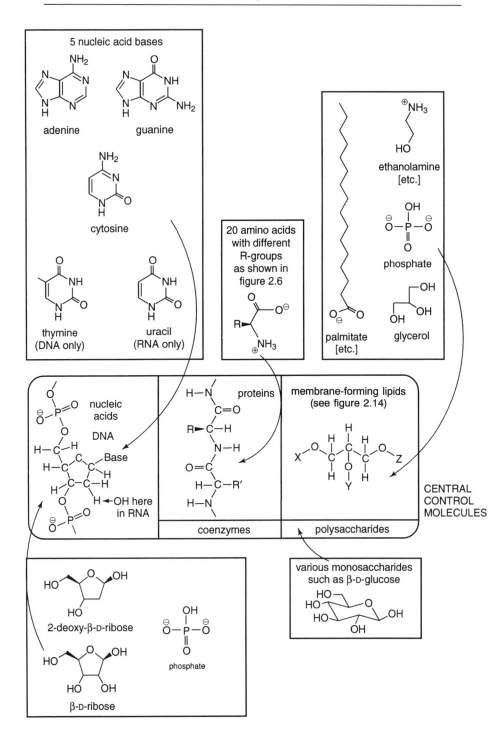

5 nucleic acid bases

adenine guanine

cytosine

thymine (DNA only) uracil (RNA only)

ethanolamine [etc.]

phosphate

palmitate [etc.] glycerol

20 amino acids with different R-groups as shown in figure 2.6

nucleic acids

DNA

Base

H←OH here in RNA

proteins

coenzymes

membrane-forming lipids (see figure 2.14)

polysaccharides

CENTRAL CONTROL MOLECULES

2-deoxy-β-ᴅ-ribose

phosphate

β-ᴅ-ribose

various monosaccharides such as β-ᴅ-glucose

characteristics, then as time goes on (and to the distress of farmers) rabbits will tend to become better adapted to the situation in which they live.

The whole idea is so simple and so sensible that one might wonder why it took so long to catch on (although actually it is far more subtle than I have made out[1]). But catch on it did, and this idea, evolution through natural selection, is now the central idea of biology[2], expressed in Dobzhansky's famous rumpty-tumpty aphorism: 'Nothing in biology makes sense except in the light of evolution'[3]

The genetic theory of organisms

We come then to the crucial question of heredity: how can organisms reproduce and pass on specific characteristics to their offspring; what is the mechanism of *that*? Darwin and Wallace had little idea, although unknown to them Gregor Mendel (1822–1884) had hit on the essential part of what is now the modern theory.

Mendel distinguished the outward characteristics of an organism (now called phenotypes) from inherent determinants of these characteristics (now called genes). An organism is now said to consist of two bits: The Phenotype (that is the sum of all its characteristics, from its molecules to

Figure 2.1. A Potted Molecular Biology.

A set of molecular control devices are made by joining 100 or more kinds of 'building blocks' indicated in the outer boxes.

DNA, one of the two nucleic acids, holds the genetic messages that are passed on between parents and offspring. These are written in the form of long sequences of 'bases'. The other nucleic acid, **RNA** helps to 'translate' DNA messages into protein molecules.

Proteins make up most of the innumerable molecular machines on which life depends. Much of this machinery is situated in membranes, which enclose living cells and are also found within cells. These membranes are made from proteins and special **lipids**, (fats).

Coenzymes are assistants to proteins. They are quite complex, middle-sized molecules generally made from RNA components together with other specialised parts. ATP is the most famous example (see figure 2.3).

Polysaccharides are (often complex) arrangements of small sugar molecules. When attached to outer membranes they help cells to assemble into more complex structures.

From Cairns-Smith (1982).

its visible features) and The Genotype (its collection of determinant genes). Now the key idea was that what is passed on between generations is not characteristics as such but their determinants. Rabbity character-istics reappear in every generation of rabbits because the things which cause these characteristics – genes – are passed on in sperms and egg cells. Thus it is only genes which are reproduced in the sense of having direct copies made of them, although phenotypes are re-produced in the sense of being produced again and again under the control of genes.

A modification Maynard Smith's diagram[4]:

$$P \qquad P \qquad P' \qquad P'$$
$$\nearrow \qquad \nearrow \qquad \nearrow \qquad \nearrow$$
$$\rightarrow \quad G \quad \rightarrow \quad G \quad \rightarrow \quad G' \quad \rightarrow \quad G' \quad \rightarrow$$

gives the idea, and indicates the source of inheritable variations.

Genes are messages   There are two essential things about genes: they must be replicable (indicated by the G → G arrows) and they must be capable of controlling (in combination) the production of a phenotype (indicated by the G → P arrows). The twentieth-century insight that genes are messages (written in DNA molecules) allows us to understand in a general way how this can be so. After all, messages can be reprinted indefinitely; and they can be used to control processes (think of an auto-matic machine in a factory controlled by a magnetic tape).

The source of variations   For evolution to be possible genes must (a) sometimes change so as to produce modified copies (as indicated by G → G' in the diagram) which (b) continue to replicate in the modified form and which (c) can produce altered phenotypes which (d) can affect chances of survival and reproduction.

The critical point about (a) is that the changes in the genetic infor-mation can be effectively random.

We now understand that in sexually reproducing organisms there are two kinds of randomness about the genetic information present in off-spring: first, in the particular mix of genes inherited from the parents, but second, and in the long run more significant, in *mutations* which from time to time arise. These are changes in the gene messages themselves, usually caused by mistakes in copying. 'Big mistakes' leading to very sig-nificant changes in phenotype are most unlikely to be advantageous; they are very likely to be 'selected against'. But among the smaller of these random modifications some few will confer a significant 'selective advantage'. Such mutated genes, if they are not lost early on by chance, have a good prospect of eventually replacing the original versions within a breeding population[5].

The idea that variations could be random was particularly shocking to many of Darwin's contemporaries, and there are still people who reject Darwin's mechanism for evolution because they 'cannot believe that life is a product of random chance' (or words to that effect): what Dawkins hilariously calls The Argument from Personal Incredulity[6]. It is not a strong argument. Selection, not chance, is the creative force of evolution (see above or, better, read Dawkins): the role of chance, here, is more or less to provide for each generation a small spread of minor design modifications which are then subject to selection. Random variations do not cause evolution. They allow it[7].

Cells and their molecules

A gene is useless on its own. It needs very special, very protected, very helpful surroundings to work in, to be replicated and to produce its phenotypic effects; and these surroundings are provided by the effects of other genes. The true 'unit of life' is not a gene but a certain minimal collection of genes plus their phenotypic products. For example there is a 'Xerox machine' (needed to replicate *any* gene) which is the phenotypic product of *many* genes, and all of this (and much more besides) must be part of the 'minimal collection' required in the effective unit of life: the cell.

There are some provisos for higher organisms like ourselves, but the essential self-sufficiency of cells is demonstrated by the fact that most organisms on the Earth are microorganisms consisting of only one cell. There are two types of these: bacteria and eukaryotes (such as yeasts).

Since we and our brains are huge communities of eukaryotic cells I will be concentrating attention on this type (see figure 2.2)

Over 99.99% of the genetic information is stored in the nucleus: the Main Library of the cell. The mitochondria are smallish numerous organelles which manufacture the convenience fuel ATP (see figure 2.3). They have the rest of the information[8] in the form of a few small 'books'. In humans, for example, the (nuclear) genetic information is held in the form of 46 enormous molecules of DNA, providing a total formal

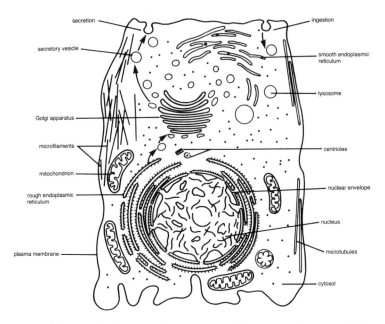

Figure 2.2. An animal eukaryotic cell: some of its parts and some of their functions.

The 'plasma membrane' is the main frontier of the cell. It consists of a double layer of lipid molecules with embedded proteins (see figure 2.15, p. 87).

The 'endoplasmic reticulum' is a convoluted internal membrane, which helps to segregate and transport protein molecules. Ribosomes (the small dots in the picture) are the centres of protein manufacture. 'Rough' endoplasmic reticulum has ribosomes embedded in it.

A 'mitochondrion' is a machine for manufacturing the universal fuel ATP (see figure 2.3 opposite).

The cell contains many membrane-bound vesicles which may take part in 'secretion' or 'ingestion' (see also figure 3.2 on p. 95). 'Lysosomes' are special vesicles which digest large molecules.

The 'Golgi apparatus' is part of the protein transport machinery.

'Centrioles' are organising centres of microtubules, which are part of the cytoskeleton of the cell, as are 'microfilaments' of actin (see figures 2.11 and 2.12 on pp. 80–1).

The 'nucleus' (as opposed to the 'cytoplasm', which is the rest of the internal contents of the cell) contains almost all the DNA.

The 'cytosol' is that part of the cell volume (about half) not occupied by membrane-bounded organelles such as the nucleus, mitochondria, lysosomes etc.

From Green et al. (1990).

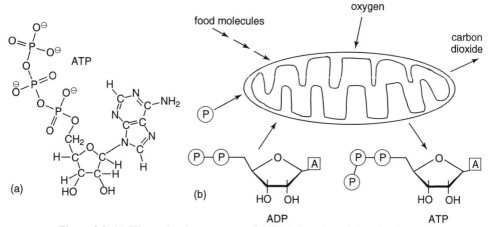

Figure 2.3. (a) The molecular structure of ATP (adenosine triphosphate).
(b) In the cell ATP is a 'wound-up' molecule made (largely in mitochondria) from ADP and phosphate using energy derived from foods. Energy
can be obtained quickly by letting ATP 'wind down' again to ADP and
phosphate.

information capacity of about 10^{10} bits, written in its 4-symbol language.
If these symbols were actually to be written out (and within a decade it
may be possible to do just that) it would fill a book of about a million
pages. These DNA molecules, together with the spools on which they
are wound and other associated molecules, constitute the chromosomes.
Before a cell divides in two all this information is replicated so that each
of the progeny gets a complete copy. Skin cells, liver cells, brain cells . . .
each have the same 'million pages'.

Gene replication   The 'Xeroxing' process through which a new copies
of DNA messages are made (for the G → G legs in the diagram on page
58) is illustrated in figure 2.4 (a). This starts with the double DNA molecule being partly unzipped into single strands, with new 'letters' then
locking into place almost as soon as the single strands become exposed.
It is a templating process depending on a specific fitting between the four
bases such that A (a big one and a 'socket') always goes with T (a small
one and a 'plug'): see figure 2.4 (b). Similarly G (a big one and a 'plug')
goes with C (a small one and a 'socket').

Hydrogen bonds   Base pairing depends on those secondary forces
between molecules which we touched on in the last chapter, especially

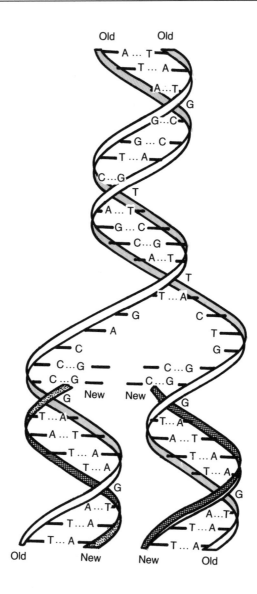

Figure 2.4. (a) Replication of DNA.
From Molecular Biology of the Gene, vol. I, 4th ed., by Watson *et al.* Copyright © 1987 by James D. Watson. Published by the Benjamin/Cummings Publishing Company. Reprinted by permission.

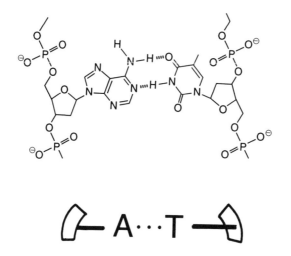

(b) Close-up of an A. . .T base pair.

on one of the strongest of such forces, 'the hydrogen bond'. I will expand a little on this here.

Recall that secondary forces are much less definite than covalent bonds, they are more like a mild stickiness than a definite linkage. The stronger kinds of secondary force arise from permanently slightly unbalanced charges within molecules. For example, covalent bonds between unlike atoms are usually 'polar', that is to say one of the two atoms in the liaison has a slight excess of electron density in relation to the positive nuclei of the atoms while the other has a slight deficit. A water molecule, for example, has a somewhat uneven electron distribution with the (particularly electron-hungry) oxygen atom having more than its fair share of the negative charge. The oxygen's excess of negative charge is furthermore concentrated in two 'lone pairs' of electrons, which point into space in much the same way as the O—H bonds do. The result is that water molecules stick together as illustrated in figure 2.5 through electrostatic attraction with O—H bonds and lone pairs lining up.

These polar interactions are stronger than most because the charge displacement is relatively high with oxygen, and because the uniquely small hydrogen atom allows a close approach. Only three kinds of such 'hydrogen bonds' need concern us:

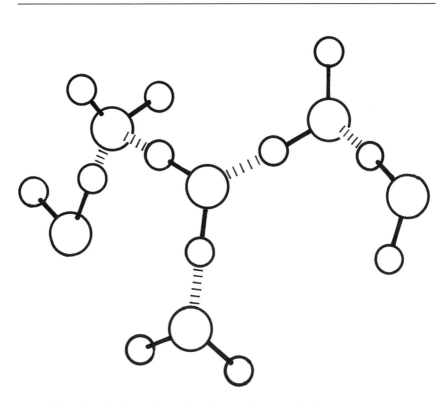

Figure 2.5. Hydrogen bonds in a cluster of water molecules.

$$O\text{---}H\text{- - -}O \quad \text{(in water especially)}$$
$$N\text{---}H\text{- - -}O \quad \text{(in proteins and nucleic acids)}$$
$$\text{and } N\text{---}H\text{- - -}N \quad \text{(in nucleic acids especially)}$$

Hydrogen bonds are about a tenth of the strength of a covalent bond (other secondary forces are more like a hundredth).

Gene expression   If gene replication requires much 'Xerox machinery' to help bring it about, that is as nothing compared to what is needed for 'gene expression', the G → P legs in the diagram on page 58, the processes through which DNA messages cause the construction of things like wall-flower petals, rabbits' ears or human brains.

Nevertheless at least one critical early part of the technique, making protein molecules, is quite well understood now. The gist of it is that parts of DNA sequences are first 'transcribed' in the cell's nucleus into 'offprints' written in RNA molecules (which are very similar to DNA;

see figure 2.1). These new message tapes then move to ribosomes (the little dots in figure 2.2), most of which are outside the nucleus. Although small in relation to other cell components shown in figure 2.2, a ribosome is nevertheless a highly complex piece of equipment. It is the place where the genetic messages are 'translated' into long specific sequences of amino acids: protein molecules. A message written in 4-symbol RNA language is thus translated into a message in a different language: a 20-symbol protein language (figure 2.6).

Next question: What can such messages mean?

Folding reveals an immediate meaning

Both RNA molecules and protein molecules have a most extraordinary property. If they have the right messages in them they may fold up into tiny machines, and there are many thousands of different kinds of such machines in cells. That is not like any message I have ever seen (if you except pop-up birthday cards, which have perhaps some glimmer of a resemblance).

These submicroscopic machines include the enzymes which control all the chemical transformations going on inside us. Each of these tiny sub-components is what it is, does what it does, by virtue of its own particular message, the particular paragraph of the genetic information that it contains and which determines the shape it will fold into, and how it will behave.

Protein folding Most of the most critical cell machinery is protein. This should not perhaps surprise us, because proteins have a very high information capacity. To see what I mean by this imagine you are building up an arbitrary protein chain, as in figure 2.6. Every three atoms along the main chain there is a side group and you have a free choice from 20 alternatives as to which it should be. With, say, 100 side groups (a small protein) the total number of possible sequences would be 20^{100} – a number far exceeding the number of particles in the observable Universe. This gives one a sense of just how much *engineering* is possible in principle for these molecules, how much scope there is for finding and adjusting a sequence for some particular purpose.

Now let us consider how such sequences (often called primary structures) are able to fit particular purposes: how they can fold themselves

Figure 2.6 A ball-and-stick model-building kit for
proteins.

To make a protein model one might start by building
its repetitive main chain or backbone. Only the first six
such main chain units are shown in (a). (For a typical
protein the chain might be some 200 units long.) One
would then attach amino acid side groups to the (α)
carbon atoms of the main chain as indicated by the
arrows, choosing from the set of 20 shown in (b) (and
attaching through the β atoms of these side groups). As
with, say, typing a sequence of letters where there is no
restriction as to which letter can in principle be put next,
the side groups in the model could be inserted in any
order. In fact the total number of possible sequences 200
long (20^{200}) *far* exceeds the number of atoms in the
known Universe, yet our biochemical systems contrive
to specify such sequences exactly using the information
in DNA molecules, which constitute the genes, which
are passed on between generations.

Protein molecules in living cells are incredibly tiny
pieces of machinery. What they do and how they work
depends on how the long chain folds up – and *that*
depends on the amino–acid sequence. There is as yet no
way of knowing for sure how most sequences will fold
up. It depends on a complex balance of factors. But two
general principles of folding have been noticed repeatedly. One is that the main chain tends to stick to itself,
to form stretches of helix or places where parts of the
chain lie more or less parallel to each other (regions of
'secondary structure'; see figures 2.7 and 2.8). Another
general feature is that the chain tends to fold in such a
way that side groups that are made from carbon and
hydrogen atoms only, and are thus not able to form
hydrogen bonds with water, keep away from the water.
These 'hydrophobic' side groups tend to form the core
of the protein molecule. On the other hand polar groups,
especially those with net electric charges, are more likely
to be on the outside in contact with the surrounding
water molecules.

Part (b) from PROTEINS by Creighton. Copyright
© 1993 by W. H. Freeman and Company. Used with
permission.

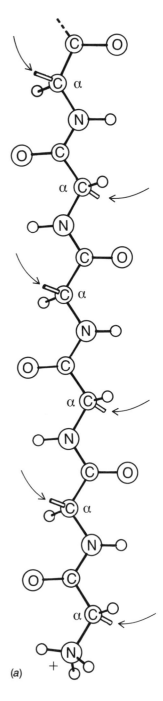

(a)

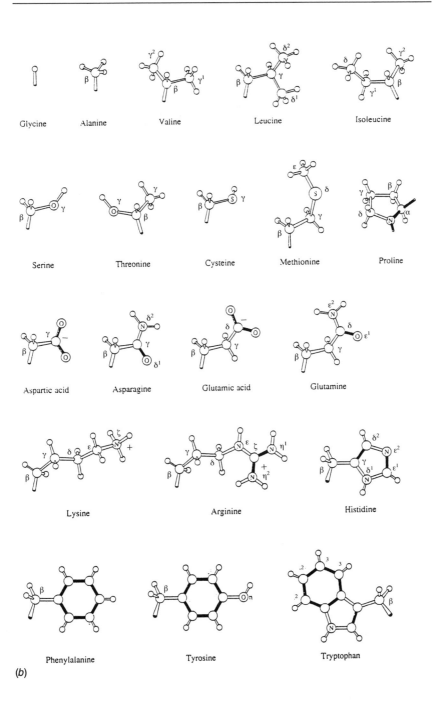

(b)

(a)

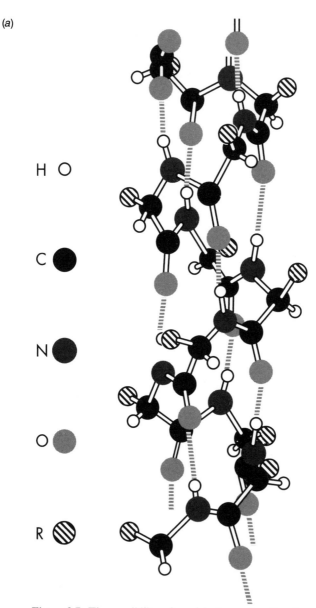

H ○

C ●

N ●

O ●

R ⊘

Figure 2.7. The possibility of good hydrogen bonding between N—H and C=O groups in the main chain of a protein (compare figure 2.6a) means that (a) the chain may form into a helix – the 'α-helix' – or (b) different parts of the chain may line up more or less parallel to each other to make a region of 'β-sheet'.

From Green *et al.* (1990).

(b)

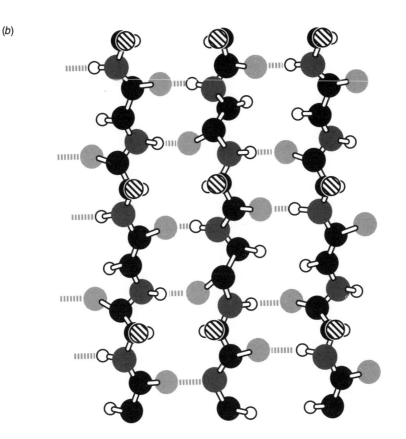

into actual machines. In such folding they are said to develop secondary and tertiary structures.

Secondary structure The amino acid units in a protein chain are held together by amide links:

which are thus repeated again and again along the chain (figure 2.6(a)). Now NH groups are good hydrogen bond 'donors' and the oxygens are good hydrogen bond 'acceptors' so you can see that, given that it is quite flexible, a protein chain might tend to form N—H $\cdots$ O=C hydrogen bonds between different parts of itself: that it might be 'self-cohesive' in a more general if less predictable way than RNA. There are indeed two such folding modes that are commonly found in proteins, the so-called α- and β-structures. In the α-structure (figure 2.7a) the molecule is coiled into a helix: in the β-structure (figure 2.7b) hydrogen bonds are formed between different parts of the chain lying more or less parallel to each other, and running either in the same or in opposite directions.

Tertiary structure   In the event a protein molecule may have α-structure but no β-structure, or *vice versa*; but in the typical case there will be both α- and β-structure there (figure 2.8). It is seldom easy to predict which of these folding modes any piece of a protein chain will adopt; or indeed whether it will fold in a regular way at all. One reason for this is that good N—H $\cdots$ O and C=O $\cdots$ H—O hydrogen bonds can also be formed between peptide links and water molecules. The whole thing is a delicate balance between tendencies: to form α- or β-structure or to become clustered with water molecules, or to do something else.

And then the side groups have *their* tendencies: to associate with each other, or with water molecules, or for that matter with peptide links. In the end it is the sequence of the side groups that decides the matter, and here their sheer variety is crucial.

The different kinds of side groups are shown in figure 2.6(b). They are indeed a varied lot. Some, at the top of the figure, are definitely water haters (well, the term is 'hydrophobic' but that is literally what it means). Such side groups are 'oily': they are non-polar and unable to form hydrogen bonds with water, and they tend to cluster together.

Hydrophobicity   Actually it is not so much that hydrophobic side groups or molecules hate water as that water hates them. The main reason why oil does not dissolve in water is because the presence of such a molecule in water is a nuisance to the water molecules: they cannot form hydrogen bonds with this interloper so they have (as it were) to take great pains to arrange themselves so that they can still hydrogen bond fully to each other. 'Great pains' here is 'low entropy' in more respectable language: in the presence of a hydrophobic molecule there are fewer ways in which the water molecules surrounding it can be arranged and still be completely hydrogen bonded.

So oil and water don't mix, and you can be pretty sure also that however a protein chain folds up it will do so with most of the hydrophobic side

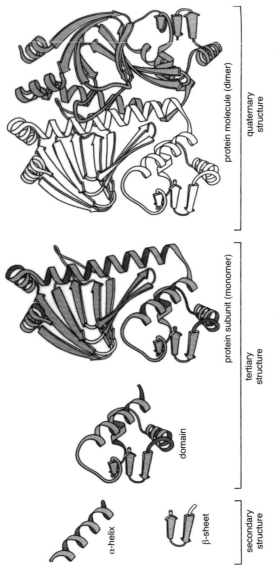

Figure 2.8. Representing a protein molecule by showing just how its (two) main chains are folded. Sections of α- and β-structure (secondary structure) are shown on the far left. Next along is a more or less distinct coherent region of the protein known as a domain, and then how one whole chain folds (tertiary structure). On the far right there is the still higher (quaternary) structure: the actual protein molecule consists here of two identical chains, which fit together neatly and are held together by non-covalent forces.

From Alberts et al. (1989), courtesy of Jane Richardson.

groups buried inside the molecule away from the water. Indeed we can go further than this. The groups will not just be bundled in there like carelessly packed luggage: the chain will (as far as possible) fold to allow the inner side groups to pack neatly for much the same reason as the molecules in a crystal pack neatly: because they too are under the influence of secondary forces tending to bring them closely together.

At the other extreme to the hydrophobic there are the 'hydrophilic' side groups. They 'love' water, especially those that carry an electric charge. Water molecules cluster strongly around such groups, pointing their hydrogens towards negative charges and forming particularly strong hydrogen bonds, or likewise pointing the lone pair electrons of their oxygens towards positive charges. So we can predict that there will be a tendency for protein molecules to fold so as to leave charged groups on the outside. By and large they do.

The compromise is a machine   The net effect of all these tendencies is a decision: a protein molecule with a given sequence in given surroundings folds in a given way. It is a compromise, a balancing act between energy and entropy effects: to keep the energy as *low* as possible (to give in as far as possible to attractive forces, to avoid repulsive forces due to poor packing, and so on) while keeping the entropy (especially of the surrounding water molecules) reasonably high. There is often one best general way of doing this, although all proteins are continually shifting about between slightly different folding arrangements ('conformations'), and some flip about between substantially different conformations in a balance which may depend sensitively on the surroundings. We will be coming back to this shortly.

Our best computers cannot yet predict how a protein molecule with such and such a sequence will fold up. The only computer we know of which can do this is the protein itself: it usually finds its own best compromise in seconds[9].

Thus one piece of genetic information – one gene to be precise – is 'expressed' in the form of some tiny piece of machinery.

Molecular recognition

Nucleic acid molecules have an exceedingly efficient recognition system in the way in which molecules with complementary sequences will

mate up with each other. This is the fundamental mode of communication for nucleic acids But nucleic acids are only good at recognising
other nucleic acids. Proteins have a much more general ability. A
protein can recognise more or less any molecule if it has been con-
structed to do so. This is the main *raison d'être* of protein, and it lies
at the centre of most of the communication systems within cells. How
do they do it?

The quick answer is with sockets, an idea easily expressed in terms of
a jig-saw model:

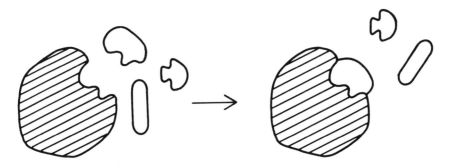

Remember that molecules, particularly smallish molecules, move with
fantastic speeds. They will traverse the short distances in cells very
quickly indeed. For example an ATP molecule (figure 2.3), or any
molecule of similar size, will cross a cell (a distance of about 10 μm,
a hundredth of a millimetre) every fifth of a second or so[10]. So all a
protein has to do is wait there with its highly selective jaws open. All
the molecular fish in the cell will swim in sooner or later; and the
right one will stick.

So given a selection of molecules in its surroundings a protein will bind
to molecules ('ligands') which have a complementary shape to some part
of the protein. The more detailed the shape correspondence, the stronger
will this binding tend to be.

But there are other factors. A protein surface can be type-selective as
well as shape-selective. For example, a molecule might have polar, ionic
and hydrophobic regions, then the protein surface will have corresponding
regions, with charges, hydrogen bonding groups, hydrophobic clefts and
so on, suitably arranged.

Then again the 'jaws' need not always be open. A protein molecule
is a highly dynamic object. What we call its secondary and tertiary

structure has usually been discovered by studying crystals of the protein (using X-rays) and is a kind of average or preferred structure under these conditions. In reality, in solution, its parts are continually flipping about between slightly different – occasionally between very different – folding modes. And some of these may let in a molecule which can then be bound inside: so that a 'jaws' analogy is better here than a simple socket.

Why should *this* happen? It is interesting to think it through. In the end it goes back to the idea that the folding of a protein chain in water is a compromise. It is not perfect. If it were perfect a protein would never bind anything (except water). When a protein binds a molecule it was designed by natural selection to bind, the combination becomes more stable than before. This is the sense in which we can say that a binding protein 'knows' about its ligand. It has a 'yearning' for it. The energy–entropy balance which determines the folding arrangement (given the sequence) is improved given *also* the ligand bound appropriately to the protein. It is a way of speaking that I will make use of to say that a bound ligand has become *part* of the secondary–tertiary structure, in much the same way as innumerable bound water molecules are.

So when I use the word 'socket', or have a drawing of one, this is what I mean: yes, it might be literally something like a socket, but it need not be. 'Socket' is a short-hand term, or a useful image (anyway it avoids my having to try to draw a yearning).

Protein as catalyst   An enzyme is a protein molecule with a yearning of a more subtle sort. It is stabilised a little by binding its substrate(s) (the molecule or molecules which are to react); but really its yearning is for a half-way stage of the reaction which it catalyses. It is time for another aside.

Energy barriers which make life possible   Consider a reaction making one covalent bond between two molecules, call them A and B:

$$A \qquad B \quad \rightarrow \quad A\cdots B \quad \rightarrow \quad A\text{—}B$$

If such a reaction is not actually an explosion then we know (from the normal frequencies of collisions between molecules) that the vast majority of the collisions between A and B do not lead to any reaction. It is indeed the crucial feature of covalent bonds that they are not continually being made or broken like this. What keeps them safe are energy barriers which have to be overcome. In our example, as A and B approach they will normally *repel* each other to begin with as their regions of increasing electron probability begin to overlap. Where a covalent bond can form, however, this repulsion does not continue to grow but reaches a maximum at some intermediate arrangement – indicated by the A · · · · · B state – after which it becomes an attraction, as a new kind of collaborative harmony for the electron standing wave patterns is discovered. The critical intermediate state is called the 'transition state' for the reaction. If they get that far the job is more or less done.

For an ordinary chemical reaction, even one taking place at quite high temperatures, only a few fastest molecules, at the top end of the Maxwell–Boltzmann distribution (Chapter 1, page 22), will have enough energy to reach a critical transition state when they collide, and even then only some will collide suitably oriented. At ordinary temperatures the energy needed to make and break the main covalent bonds in biological molecules in this haphazard way is hardly every achieved, which is just as well.

So how is it that enzymes can overcome such protecting barriers and arrange things so that from the countless reactions that *might* happen they selectively encourage just *their* reactions?

Partly they do it by binding their 'substrates' in such a way that they and their reactive parts are close together: but mainly they do it by effectively removing the energy barrier – they stabilise a transition state for *their* reaction[11].

Recall why any protein ever binds anything: because that way it stabilises its secondary – tertiary structure, or as I more fancifully put it, it has a yearning for a particular ligand. Now think of what will happen if the protein's yearning is for the transition state of a reaction, the critical A · · · · · B arrangement for example. Just binding the substrates even in the right orientation is not quite good enough: the fit will be more perfect if the substrates move towards the transition state (if A and B are pushed together in our example). That may not be what the substrate wants (in a manner of speaking) but it is what the enzyme 'wants'. It has more to gain from the resulting stabilisation of its secondary–tertiary structure than the substrate has to lose from being distorted into an arrangement which is admittedly rather unstable.

Yet it is not all happiness for the enzyme: its yearning may be satisfied a thousand times a second, but it is as often frustrated. No sooner has it clasped its substrates to itself and in the process distorted them to a transition state than the reaction goes all the way. The products are no longer so good a fit. They escape.

Protein as computer: allosteric effects   Then there is another thing. One protein socket designed to bind one kind of molecule (or transition state) may be affected by whether another socket somewhere else on the protein has some other, perhaps quite different, molecule bound in it or not. Thus an enzyme with one catalytic socket and another simple binding socket may be turned on by a control molecule (figure 2.9). You will see that a control molecule by altering the shape of an enzyme could as easily switch it off, *prevent* it from operating.

Again there is the idea that the secondary–tertiary structure of a protein is not solely determined by its primary structure. Other molecules may join in to influence the overall folding, even sometimes to tip the balance between substantially different folding arrangements[12].

It is hard to exaggerate the importance of such 'allosteric' phenomena, described by Jacques Monod as the second secret of life (after the DNA structure)[13]. Through them protein molecules can make contrived causal connections, of the sort that are the basis of computing and control mechanisms generally (*if* this input *then* that output). We will come to several examples of such clever protein switchgear when talking about how cells sense their surroundings, and how cells, especially nerve cells, communicate with each other.

The fine adjustment screws   How can proteins be so clever? I gave a general answer in terms of their information density – that they have the potential: but how is it achieved through natural selection?

Consider a simple and common kind of mutation that has the effect of changing just one amino acid in a protein chain. Many of these may have no perceptible effect on function[14]: if they are far away from the active sockets, for example. Others, which alter amino acids in the active sockets themselves, are likely to be disastrous. Others again will be in between, causing some small adjustment to the shapes etc of the critical sockets. It is like an instrument which has both coarse and fine adjustment screws (and idlers): high performance depends on the ability to make fine adjustments. Natural selection operating on 'in between' mutations can do just that.

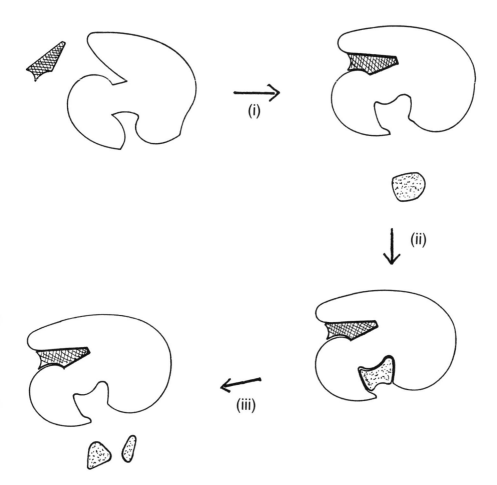

Figure 2.9. An allosteric enzyme at work.
(i) A control molecule (top left) interacts with an enzyme to alter its shape.
(ii) The enzyme can now bind to its substrate. In doing this the enzyme
engineers the microenvironment of the substrate (and may significantly dis-
tort the substrate) so as to encourage it to react in a particular way (iii).

Higher-order molecular structure

The element of self-assembly A dew drop, a soap bubble, or a sugar
crystal are familiar examples of self-assembled objects: they are higher-
order structures whose molecules have come together (in a more or less

organised way) and hold together (more or less firmly) under the combined influence of kinetic motion and secondary forces. This is not like the construction procedures of human engineering; at least I have not heard of machines being put together just by shaking up pre-made components. Usually the assembly of components needs, well, manipulation: more of the same kinds of contrivance and external control that went into the manufacture of the components themselves.

Self-assembly is the 'hands off' part of the construction system of cells. The secondary – tertiary folding of a protein chain is an excellent example of it: this folding occurs more or less spontaneously without detailed external control[15]. By contrast the welding together of the primary chain is 'hands on'. This is manipulation needing, again and again, inputs of energy and information. It is not something which just happens on its own.

Of course you may say that even a self-assembly does not just happen on its own: general conditions have to be right – the temperature, concentration and so on – and *they* may have to be contrived. Yes indeed; and all three elements – self-assembly, molecule-manipulation and 'pre-arrangement' – are to be found in a close collaboration in the construction systems of cells[16]. But let us think now about a rather pure form of self-assembly, a still higher level of protein structure.

The quaternary level of structure Many protein molecules consist of several subunits. – individual protein chains – held together through secondary forces (see figure 2.8d). Haemoglobin is the classical example: its molecules are clusters of four subunits[17]. But in fact most enzymes are 'multimers', one effect of this arrangement being to sharpen allosteric responses[18].

Polymers Imagine a protein molecule with two opposite surfaces which are complementary to each other fitting together like jig-saw pieces:

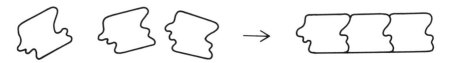

If the two complementary surfaces are arbitrarily placed (in a three-dimensional model) the usual result will be a helix. Actin, one of the most common proteins in eukaryotic cells, polymerises like this (figure 2.10), forming actin filaments.

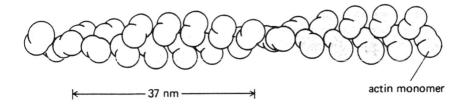

Figure 2.10. Helical arrangement of actin molecules in an actin filament.
From Alberts *et al.* (1989).

This is one of the many proteins that form a kind of scaffolding in cells, a 'cytoskeleton' which among other things helps to keep cells in shape (figure 2.11).

Microtubules are another major component of the cytoskeleton. These are polymers of two closely related proteins, the so called α- and β- tubulins (figure 2.12).

Energy and control   Once appropriate conditions have been set up for a self-assembly no additional energy is needed, in principle, to make it happen; but in practice more energy is often put in to modify the spontaneity of the process: to exert control. This is nicely illustrated in the case of cytoskeleton proteins which must not only polymerise, but do so in the right places, to the right extent, and at the right times.

Actin is present in relatively high concentration in cells with about half of it polymerised into actin filaments at any one time. Actin units are directional and their polymers retain the directionality, having two different kinds of ends 'plus' and 'minus':

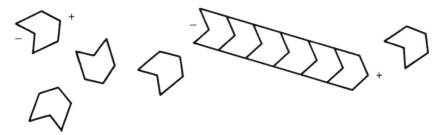

One can imagine units adding and subtracting at each end with addition going faster to begin with until the concentration of free actin molecules falls to a point at which the rate of addition equals the rate of subtraction and a dynamic equilibrium is attained (as happens for example with ice in contact

microvillus   plasma membrane

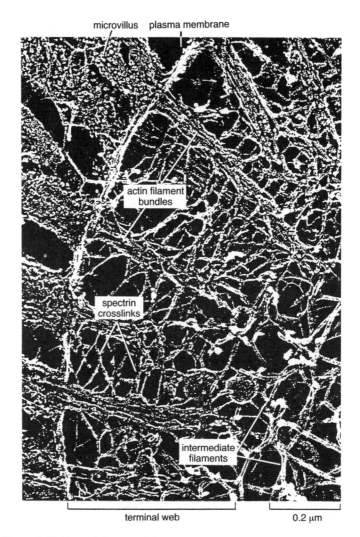

actin filament
bundles

spectrin
crosslinks

intermediate
filaments

terminal web   0.2 μm

Figure 2.11. Part of the cytoskeleton of an intestinal cell, showing how the cytoskeleton can help to maintain a highly non-spherical shape for a cell. In this case bundles of actin filaments help to maintain finger-like extensions of the plasma membrane so as to increase the surface area of the cell. Also shown are two other cytoskeletal proteins: spectrin rods form links between actin bundles, and deeper into the cell 'intermediate filaments' are made of a fibrous protein.

Reproduced from Hirokawa & Heuser, *Journal of Cell Biology*, 1981, **91**: 404, by copyright permission of the Rockefeller University Press.

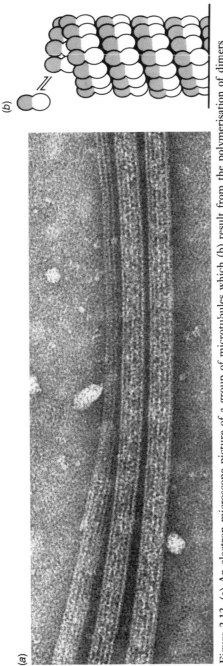

Figure 2.12. (a) An electron microscope picture of a group of microtubules which (b) result from the polymerisation of dimers of α- and β-tubulin.

(a) Photo by Dr A. V. Grimstone; (b) from Alberts et al. (1989).

with water at 0 °C: crystallisation and dissolution are both going on but at equal rates). This is the kind of thing you would expect for a simple physical system, but actin molecules in cells are more subtle than this.

Although units do indeed come and go from both ends, the plus end grows faster. Well, there might be some 'kinetic' reason for this, which is to say that one end might be easier to join to than the other, perhaps due to some change of shape that takes place when the units polymerise which 'blunts' one or other of the ends. Even so, you would not expect *net* growth to be faster at one end than the other once the dynamic equilibrium is attained. The principle of microscopic reversibility discussed in the previous chapter which prevents 'trap-door' and other such perpetual motion machines is quite clear on the matter: if (at equilibrium) it grows faster at one end then it must dissolve faster at that end too. Otherwise there will be a serious infringement of the second law of thermodynamics: you could have vast numbers of molecules lined up and growing exclusively in one direction, and use that to drive a perpetual motion machine . . .

Yet actin filaments *do* add at one end and subtract at the other: 'treadmilling', it's called. It goes on all the time in cells. Through it cells can change shape and move about[19]. So what are they up to?

Not to keep you in suspense any longer the 'self-assembly' of actin filaments is not quite what it seems. The units that go on at one end are not the same as the units that come off at the other.

The actin subunits in solution have a molecule of ATP (see figure 2.3) tightly bound to them. When an ATP-containing subunit joins up to an actin filament its resulting shape change encourages the hydrolysis of the ATP to a (still tightly bound) ADP and like this the unit is no longer held so firmly. Now the plus end can grow faster *and* the minus end dissolve faster without any infringement of the second law, because the one process is no longer simply the reverse of the other: the system is not in equilibrium but is consuming energy all the time. ATP molecules are needed and are being 'unwound' to ADP, and these will have to go back to the mitochondria or in some other way be 'wound up' again. This is a typical price to be paid for molecular control. And it is a wonderful example of the seemingly magical things which can happen when protein molecular machinery is powered by a molecular fuel. When we come to discuss how the brain works, even when discussing the physical origins of consciousness, we will come across more examples, both established and conjectured, of just this sort of 'magic'.

Covalent alterations   We have been discussing how the binding of a ligand can alter the properties of a protein. More crudely, a protein's function can be altered, or switched on or off, by having things attached to it through covalent bonds. Phosphate groups are favourites here because, I suppose, ATP is a highly available molecule and phosphate groups, being strongly negatively charged, can easily affect the way a protein folds. So this is a common kind of reaction:

$$ATP + protein \rightarrow ADP + protein\text{-}phosphate$$

Motor proteins   Individual protein molecules may be able to move consistently in one direction, if they are designed to do so and if they are supplied with ATP or some other source of energy. Figure 2.13 is a hypothetical example of a protein which can exist in alternative folding states: 'bunched', or 'stretched' with either 'back end sticky' or 'front end sticky'. By going through the states shown in the order shown the protein could caterpillar its way across a surface. But would it?

Well, no. There is nothing in principle wrong with the idea of a protein molecule being able to flip between alternative folding modes with different shapes and different cohesive properties for some surface. Recall the delicate balance of factors that determines the secondary–tertiary structure of a protein chain: it can very well be that a number of substantially different 'solutions' will have very similar energies, so that the protein will arbitrarily flip about between the alternatives as part of its kinetic motion. But the protein caterpillar in figure 2.13 still will not work just like that. For a protein subject simply to kinetic motion each step will be reversible (left-hand scheme). Our caterpillar would simply dither about – it's the principle of microscopic reversibility again – at each step as likely to go one way as the other. How could it be made to go through its folding states in the appropriate order?

The trick would be to make one of the steps irreversible (more than one if you like, but one will do, and it does not matter which). In the right-hand scheme of figure 2.13 there is a small difference. One of the steps is irreversible. I chose to make this the seemingly trivial 'shifting of stickiness' step, but any would have done to provide the necessary ratchet effect. We might suppose that B $\rightarrow$ C can only happen if an ATP molecule is hydrolysed to ADP at the same time.

Although detailed mechanisms are not known it seems clear that shape changes and adhesion changes are involved in the action of real

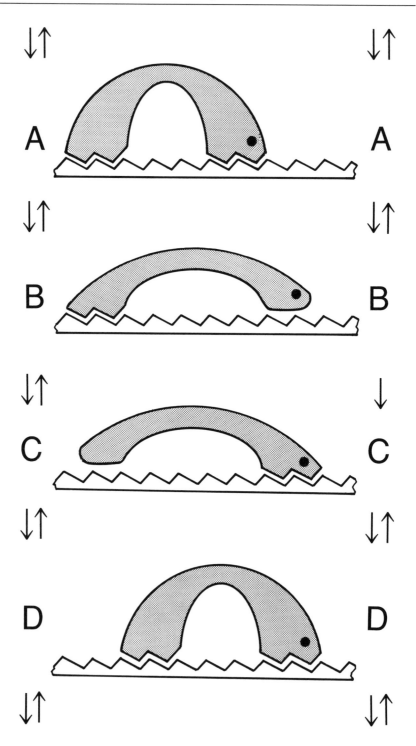

motor proteins: certainly molecules such as ATP are needed for proteins that produce mechanical movement at many different levels. For
example, they are part of the 'Xerox' machinery for replicating DNA,
where the unzipping process (figure 2.4) has to be driven continuously
in one direction. Then again they can move particles within cells along
microtubules[20]. At least two classes of proteins can act like motorised
roller skates so that a microtubule can guide the transport of different
things in opposite directions according to which of the kinds of roller
skates are fitted[21]. Motor proteins held between microtubules can cause
them to slide past each other[22], or in other cases to make a bundle of
microtubules flex back and forth: the basis of the action of (for
example) a sperm's whip-like swimming engine. Then again another
class of motor proteins attached as part of one set of fibres (myosin)
interleaved with another set (actin) causes the two sets to slide in
relation to each other – when supplied with ATP and a controlling
signal – and this is the basis of the force exerted by muscles and
hence of all the large-scale movements of animals . . .[23].

Membranes   The membranes of eukaryotic cells are made of a special
class of lipid molecules together with protein molecules. An example
of a membrane-forming lipid is shown in figure 2.14. As you can see
these have a hydrophilic head group attached to a pair of fairly long
hydrophobic tails. (The tails are made only from hydrogen and carbon
atoms; as discussed earlier, structures like this are unable to form
hydrogen bonds with water and have a strong tendency to keep away
from the water.) Furthermore these molecules are of such a shape that
they can self-assemble into double sheet structures as shown in figure
2.15. This is an ideal way for the molecules to keep their hydrophobic

Figure 2.13. A protein molecule which, switched between different conformations (owing to its kinetic or 'Brownian' motion), might be imagined walking across a surface if (say as above) the conformational changes took place
in order (A → B → C → D). However, they would generally not take place
in an appropriate order if each step was reversible (left-hand scheme). The
molecular caterpillar would dither about, going backwards and forwards.
This problem could be overcome by making one (or more) of the steps
irreversible (right-hand scheme) but that would only be possible if energy
was being supplied from outside: for example, if the step B → C depended
on the hydrolysis of an ATP molecule.

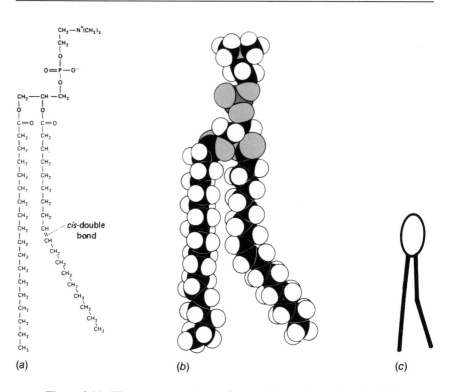

Figure 2.14. Three representations of a typical membrane-forming lipid molecule: (a) the structural formula, (b) a space-filling model (c) a thumbnail sketch. The molecule consists of a 'head' region, which has a strong affinity for water: by itself it would be highly soluble in water. The double 'tail' region is, by contrast, like liquid paraffin or paraffin wax, highly insoluble in water. The paraffin chains may be of somewhat different lengths and are fairly flexible. They often have one or more double bonds in them, which produce local kinks in the molecules.
From Alberts et al. (1989).

regions out of contact with the water. Also indicated in the figure are protein molecules floating in the membrane (see figure 2.15 and its legend).

Membrane proteins like these, which have a hydrophilic hole through them, can form more or less selective pores which allow certain molecules or ions to diffuse back and forth. There are also various pumps which drive particular molecules or ions one way through a membrane.

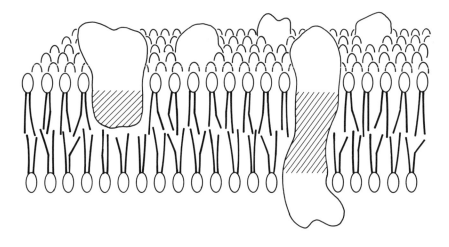

Figure 2.15. When put into water, lipid molecules of the kind shown in figure 2.14 tend to assemble themselves into membranes with their paraffin tails clustered together inside (out of contact with the water) and the head groups on the outside. A biological membrane also has protein molecules in it, as indicated here. The way these proteins 'float' in the membrane will depend on the distribution of *their* hydrophilic and hydrophobic groups (see figure 2.6). Hydrophilic regions are more likely to be sticking into the water, whereas regions with hydrophobic groups on the outside of the protein (hatched) tend to be buried well within the membrane. Proteins that cross from one side of a membrane to the other are very common. Some of these may take the form of hollow cylinders with *hydrophilic* interior surfaces, which may selectively allow certain ions to diffuse through. A still more ingenious membrane-crossing protein is illustrated in figure 2.16. Examples of proteins transmitting information from one side of a membrane to the other are discussed in chapter 3 in relation to one of Nature's simplest forms of intelligence.

This is another kind of motor which, unlike a simple pore, requires energy. Figure 2.16 is a formal view of such a piece of machinery. Then again other proteins allow special messages to pass through the cell's outer membrane. We will have much more to say about such proteins.

We know now what Aristotle's vegetative soul *is*. It is software, in computer terminology, the software that makes and controls an organism's

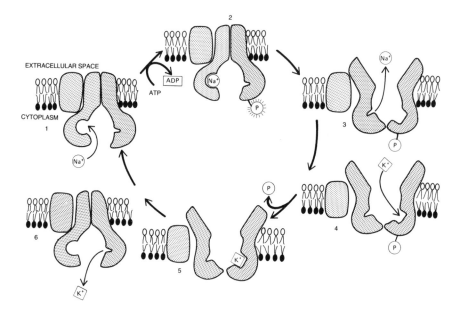

Figure 2.16. The sodium–potassium pump uses ATP energy to push Na⁺
ions out of cells and K⁺ ions in. This diagram illustrates the essence of how
it is thought to work.

1. A sodium ion binds to part of the protein surface exposed to the inside of
the cell. 2. A phosphate group has been 'forcibly' attached from an ATP
molecule, which leaves the protein in a strained state. 3. The protein
undergoes a change of conformation to release the strain – and which also
releases the sodium ion to the other side of the membrane and creates a good
binding site for potassium. 4. A potassium ion duly binds. 5. The phosphate
group is lost to give a new strained state. This strain is released by the
protein molecule flipping back to the original conformation and the potassium is released on the inside of the cell.
From Alberts *et al.* (1989).

machinery. The vegetative soul is, precisely, genetic information. In the
long run this is all that is passed on between generations[4], so what else
could it have been?

Now as we move to higher levels of organisation perhaps we will find
that the sensitive, wilful, animal soul – the consciousness – is also a kind
of information. Is it *just* the software of the brain? Many people seem to
think so. I am not among them.

General References

Watson *et al* (1987); Alberts *et al* (1989).

Notes

[1] See any good book on evolution: for example Darwin (1859), Maynard Smith (1975); Dobzhansky et al (1977); Bendall (1983); Kimura (1983); Dawkins (1986); Gould (1989); Ridley (1993) . . .

[2] Introducing a series of symposia on biological theory Waddington (1968) wrote: '. . . living things do not merely synthesize specific structures out of simpler molecules; it is an equally important fact that they reproduce themselves and indeed it might be claimed that the most important fact about them is that they take part in the long-term processes of evolution'. It was as near to a definition of life as Waddington was prepared to go.

[3] Dobzhansky (1973).

[4] Maynard Smith (1975) p. 67. Cell machinery as well as genes are passed on to offspring – in animals this is in the egg cells – but all this machinery is eventually 'diluted out'. Like everything else it has to be replaced under the control of the only things that are inherited over the long term: the genes.

[5] Haldane in a series of papers (e.g. 1927), Fisher especially with his book (1930) and Wright (e.g. 1931) introduced this way of talking – and also some mathematics.

[6] Dawkins (1986), p. 38.

[7] Earlier in the century, before Haldane, Fisher and Wright reintroduced the idea that evolution goes through an accumulation of small effects (operating in parallel as well as successively), 'mutationists' had become dominant, believing that the direction of evolution is determined by which (big) mutations happen to happen. This still seems to be what creationists and other laymen *think* evolutionary biologists are saying, but they hardly ever are. No doubt there *is* a strong element of chance in evolution, but as I have discussed elsewhere (1971, 1982) that is not so much because mutations are chancy – they would always have provided much the same sort of background of 'noise' – but because physical environments and circumstances generally are unpredictable.

[8] Actually there are only 16 569 base pairs in human mitochondrial DNA compared with *ca.* 3 000 000 000 in the nuclear DNA (Grivell, 1983).

[9] It takes about 2 seconds for the protein barnase to fold up completely (Bycroft *et al.*, 1990) but both ribonuclease (Udgaonkar & Baldwin, 1988)

and cytochrome c (Roder, Elöve & Englander, 1988) take more than 10
seconds. In each case some secondary structure appears to be formed
rapidly, on a millisecond time scale or less. See also Baldwin (1990).
Special proteins ('chaperones') often speed up the folding process
(Frydman et al., 1994).

[10] Alberts et al. (1989), p. 92.

[11] Factors responsible for enzyme catalysis are discussed in Fersht (1985):
transition state stabilisation especially in chapter 12.

[12] See, for example, Schirmer & Evans (1990); Schlichting et al., (1990).

[13] Perutz (1990) in the first sentence of his book on allosteric regulation.

[14] Kimura (1983) has argued convincingly that most mutations which lead to
changes in protein primary structure are 'neutral' like this, which is not at
all to say that amino acid sequences are not the principal determinants of
protein function, only that what a protein 'means' is often little affected by
a single 'misprint'.

[15] Although 'chaperones' often speed up the folding process (note 9) they
probably do not determine how the molecule will fold.

[16] I discussed these three elements of the cellular construction system at
greater length elsewhere (1985), pp. 67–73.

[17] Perutz (1964; 1990).

[18] Perutz (1990).

[19] Abercrombie (1980).

[20] Allen (1987).

[21] Scholey (1990).

[22] Johnson (1985); Brokaw (1986).

[23] Amos (1985); Bement & Mooseker (1993).

3

Forms of intelligence

According to Victor Serebriakoff's broad view of it, *Intelligence* should be seen simply as 'optimising behaviour in the light of information', without prejudice as to how this is achieved, whether consciously or automatically, or whether there is a lot of it or a little. On this view the word intelligence should not be restricted to discussions of organisms with big brains: not if we want to understand intelligence – its nature, its biological rôle, its technological future. I go along with that[1].

Even my refrigerator, which knows when it has to switch its cooling motor on and off, is a tiny bit intelligent on that score: about as much so as an allosteric enzyme which will switch off when enough of its product has been made and on again when more is needed. And whole cells are *bright*. They are able to cope wonderfully, to respond appropriately to threats and opportunities, to keep conditions inside right for near-optimum performance . . .

A germ of intelligence

Consider the case of that most studied of animals, the bacterium *E. coli*. To keep its internal conditions right it needs food and it goes and looks for it.

Among their many evolutionary achievements *E. coli*'s ancestors invented the wheel. *E. coli* has a set of rotating flagella held in bearings running through its cell membrane and outer coat (all made of protein as you might imagine) and driven by an in-flow of hydrogen ions through (in effect) turbines, whirring round at about 100 revolutions a second. (Charging pumps elsewhere in the cell membrane push hydrogen ions out to maintain the potential.) An *E. coli* has two ways of moving according to the direction of rotation of its flagella: if clockwise each flagellum operates more or less independently and the bacterium tumbles about; if anticlockwise many of the flagella clump together into a unit and the bacterium then swims in one direction. Unstimulated, the bacterium switches between swimming and tumbling every few seconds. This is its Standard Performance in randomly exploring its surroundings. Not very intelligent, you might say, but wait.

Imagine you are watching an *E. coli* under a microscope and you add some sugar to its little pond. The bacterium will now spend longer swimming, less time tumbling. The sugar has stimulated its swimming, but that is not the whole story. In a few minutes the bacterium would be back to swimming and tumbling in the same proportion as when there had been no sugar: it would be back to its Standard Performance. What stimulates the altered behaviour, to spending more of the time swimming, was the *change* in sugar concentration. If you were to change it the other way, by diluting the sugar, there would now be be more tumbling, less swimming, but again only for a time: in a few minutes your *E. coli* would be back again to its Standard Performance.

Now think of an *E. coli* in the wild and you will see what sensible behaviour this is. The idea is to swim from places which have low concentrations of food molecules to places which have higher concentrations. Striking out at random on one of its Standard Performance swims our *E. coli* happens to move, let us say, into a region of increasing sugar concentration. This puts it into its keep-swimming-longer mode. If after the next tumble it shoots off in the opposite direction it will switch to tumble-again-sooner, restricting its movement in that direction. . . Eventually in its 'biased random swim' it might reach a region of high but uniform concentration. There it would revert to its Standard Performance, which would keep it more or less in the same place. An exactly analogous but opposite behaviour is set in train by the presence of noxious substances.

Much is known about the molecular details of how *E. coli*'s search and avoidance behaviour is controlled. The details are complex, but I will stick to essentials (figure 3.1).

The key sensing structures are allosteric proteins, embedded in and crossing the main cell membrane (the plasma membrane), which have a binding socket on the outside and a catalytic socket on the inside. There are several kinds sensitive to different external ligands: attractants or repellents. In some the outer binding socket can directly fit an active ligand; others work via a receptor protein which then binds. In either case the catalytic socket on the inside is allosterically affected by whether

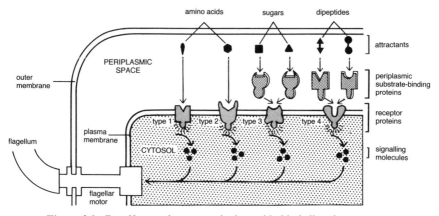

Figure 3.1. *E. coli*'s search system. Amino acids bind directly to receptor–enzyme proteins in the plasma membrane of the bacterium, which then produce signal molecules inside. These in turn control the direction of the rotation of numerous flagella and hence how it will swim. Other food molecules such as sugars and dipeptides act indirectly via other proteins. Essentially the same system, but sending opposite internal messages, helps *E. coli* to avoid noxious substances.
From Alberts *et al.* (1989).

the outer binding socket is occupied or not. The catalytic socket is a phosphate-transferring enzyme which operates on special signal molecules within the cell. These are proteins which transmit a 'yes' or 'no' message according to whether or not they have a phosphate group attached. On diffusing to the flagellar turbines they bind there to affect which way the turbines rotate.

We have here three essential elements of any control device: a sensor, a channel of communication and an effector. But there are also two other computer elements.

There is, in effect, an adding machine to arrive at an overall decision about which way to go. The different sensors add or subtract their effects, voting 'yes' or 'no', as it were, with the more active or numerous having a greater say.

Then there are timer mechanisms. As we saw, the changes in behaviour must only be temporary for the gradient-sensing systems to work. The several types of catalytic sockets controlling the signal molecules are themselves acted upon by other slower-working 'spoiler' enzymes, which over a period of time cancel the effect of binding (or losing) a ligand. These 'spoiler' enzymes are of two kinds, which add or remove methyl (CH_3-) groups. For example if a catalytic socket alters so as to start producing tumbling signals (because the outer socket has bound a repellent or lost a food, depending on which kind of sensor it is) this alteration in shape also encourages the attention of a methyl-removing enzyme which can act on it better, perhaps because the altered shape exposes the methyl groups. Over a minute or so this spoiler enzyme cancels the changed behaviour, in this case because catalytic sockets with fewer methyl groups attached are less good at sending out the tumble messages. So the catalytic socket goes back to voting for a Standard Performance and waits for the next item of news.

To control many cells   If *E. coli*'s behaviour is a sign of a higher intelligence than my refrigerator's this is because it has more information to handle, and more than just wires between sensors and effectors. There is a computer. There are judgements to be made on the basis of information from several sensory inputs and available for optimising behaviour. There are several 'if–then' components inserted in the channels of communication. Let us now move on to chemical control techniques of eukaryotic cells living, as only eukaryotic cells can, in large organised communities – communities of cells like you and me.

Adjacent, proximate, and distant techniques   Often there are little holes, 'gap junctions', directly connecting adjacent cells. These are produced by special pore proteins that go through the two cell membranes and allow chemical signals to pass between cells in contact. Another example of a contact control device is where cells stick to each other via protein-plus-sugar molecules sitting in the cell membranes waving their sugary flags: whole cells can recognise each other this way[2].

Then again cells may send out soluble chemical signals to others in their vicinity, as when histamine is produced as a local alert in the case of injury or infection to increase the flow in nearby blood vessels and get them to leak out some immunological defence troops . . .

In addition to this kind of local 'paracrine' signalling there are long range 'endocrine' signals: hormones. These are high-level controllers – or rather agents of a high-level control system – and they are put into the blood stream by special cells, often in discrete glands. Their effects are typically widespread stimulating or suppressing the activities of many different types of cell throughout the body. Insulin, thyroxine, and the male

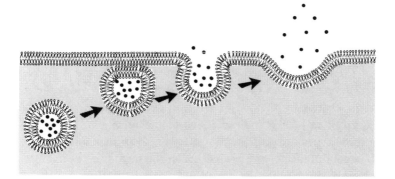

Figure 3.2. Molecules may be transported within cells in membrane-bound vesicles. Such molecules may be exported from the cell if the vesicle membrane joins with the plasma membrane of the cell as shown.

and female sex hormones are familiar examples. How are chemical signals transmitted, received and understood?

Transmission   Eukaryotic cells have to have elaborate arrangements for transporting molecules between organelles. A typical human cell has some ten billion protein molecules in it of perhaps ten thousand different kinds. These are not always made where they are needed and, along with other things, have to be put in their proper places. I will not even begin to discuss the ticketing arrangements involved except to say that a British Airways desk at Heathrow at the start of a bank holiday weekend would be forlornly quiet in comparison. The baggage handling procedure involves making transport vehicles, little bags called vesicles each with a lipid membrane similar to the main cell membrane[3].

Now much the same procedure is used to export proteins and other molecules out of the cell altogether (see figure 3.2), and this is a major technique for cells specialising in hormone production to deliver their goods to the blood stream – as it is in nerve cell signalling, as we will see shortly.

Reception   In some cases the signal receptors are membrane-crossing proteins similar to *E. coli*'s sensors, which when they bind a signal molecule on the outside change their shape on the inside and as a result change the catalytic activity of that part of the protein which is in contact with the cell interior. Usually the immediate effect is, again, to attach phosphate groups to protein molecules – sometimes to itself – and so set in train a succession of events through the altered catalytic or other activity of the phosphorylated protein molecules.

A common technique for eukaryotes introduces further links in the chain of events taking place at the cell membrane (figure 3.3). Here the cell-surface receptor and the enzyme catalyst which provides the internal signal are separate, with a go-between or 'G protein', so called because it binds GDP and GTP molecules (close analogues of ADP and ATP[4]).

The three types of component – receptor, G protein and enzyme catalyst – can communicate with each other in the membrane. First a receptor is switched on by binding its ligand (e.g. either the right or left receptor in figure 3.3). In this state it can now bind to and temporarily modify – 'switch on' – several G proteins. These in turn either switch on or switch off the enzyme that produces the signal molecules inside the cell.

One of the internal signals shown in figure 3.3 (left-hand side) is cyclic AMP (see figure 3.4). This is a common 'second messenger' as such molecules are sometimes called. As we saw, *E. coli* has such messenger molecules: soluble phosphorylated proteins in this case. But AMP has the advantage of being small, so that it moves fast, and of being easily made from an abundant starting material, and being as easily destroyed (figure 3.4).

Another similar train of events can lead instead to the release of calcium, Ca^{2+}, ions. These are even faster movers and the other major kind of second messenger molecule (figure 3.3, right-hand side).

These same two messengers, cyclic AMP and Ca^{2+}, can have totally different effects in different specialist cells: 'Do your thing' (or don't) is more or less the message these office boys relay from the management. The cell already knows what that is.

Timing devices are important in eukaryotic signalling, as they are for *E. coli*: not so much to sense gradients but simply to react to changes in the concentration of the external signal molecules. Usually a change is the *real* signal. Here again a relatively slow covalent modification of the receptor proteins or the G proteins seem to be involved very often – this time phosphorylation rather than methylation.

Cancelling mechanisms are a related need in all forms of chemical signalling. If you want to say ACT NOW and then a little later STOP AT ONCE it is no good if your messages are just left lying around to be inappropriately acted upon. Chemical signals of all sorts have to be swept up and disposed of promptly if they are going to provide up-to-date

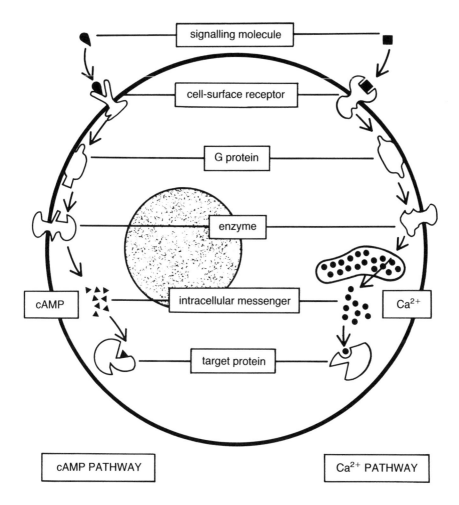

Figure 3.3. Two ways in which external chemical signals can switch on functions inside cells. The sequence of events on the left-hand side of the picture
causes an enzyme to produce an internal signal – a 'second messenger' – in
the form of cyclic AMP (see figure 3.4). The route on the right-hand side
leads to production by an enzyme of a substance that helps to release calcium
ions from storage sites within the cell. These then act as alternative internal
signals.
From Alberts *et al.* (1989).

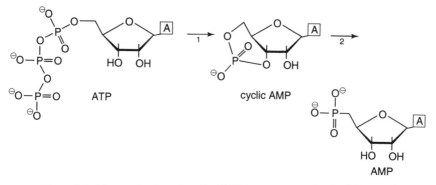

Figure 3.4. The production of cyclic AMP is a common signal within a cell that some particular molecule has attached itself to the outside of the cell's membrane. Cyclic AMP is easily produced (by reaction 1). Quite as important for a signal molecule, it is easily removed too (through reaction 2).

information. The active go–between G proteins have bound GTP molecules to keep them switched on[5]. This provides a built-in cancelling mechanism: their GTP molecules self-destruct (they hydrolyse after a time). Likewise with second messengers produced inside cells: cyclic AMP molecules are being hydrolysed continuously and Ca^{2+} ions are being continuously swept up.

Neuronal control

A new idea: long-distance telegraphy   In the endocrine and paracrine techniques of control, signals are broadcast. In the nervous system signals are also sent by cable to cells that are suitably connected up. This is the new idea. Signalling then becomes more rapid. It does not need such sensitive and discerning receivers: great masses of signals can be handled in close proximity without interference. Complex, compact computing becomes possible.

Such simple-minded remarks refer mainly to what I will call the Standard Neuron. There are other kinds of neurons that do indeed broadcast and help to interconnect the neuronal and endocrine control systems. We will come to these later. Even Standard Neurons send and receive chemical signals ('neurotransmitters') at their points of connection ('synapses') although these chemical signals only travel over minute distances to well-defined targets: most of the signalling is electrochemical, within insulated

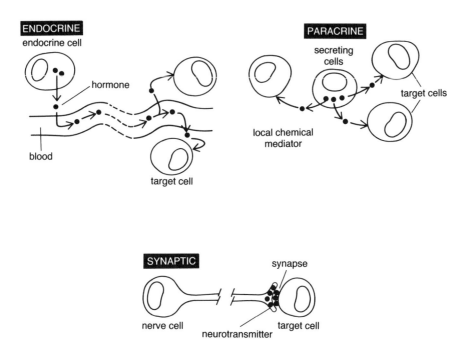

Figure 3.5. Three ways in which signals can be sent between cells.
From Alberts *et al.* (1989).

neuronal 'wires'. Figure 3.5 illustrates similarities and differences between the endocrine – paracrine approach and the neuronal technique of communication between cells.

Figure 3.6(a) shows the Standard Neuron and its parts. Figure 3.6(b) is more realistic, but still fails to get over some of the more staggering facts about these central components of nerve and brain. It has been estimated that there are about a hundred billion (10^{11}) neurons in the human brain altogether. Many are *huge* in the sense that their main cables ('axons') often make connections over tens of centimetres between different parts of the brain. Owing to this, and to the richness of their connections (see figure 3.7), it seems likely that any brain cell is in touch with any other through no more than six or seven intermediates[6].

In fact neurons constitute only some 10% of our brain cells. The others are known collectively as 'glial cells' ('glue cells'). These are present in nervous tissue generally, but in many more ways than being merely glue[7]. One type of 'oligodendrocytes' wrap themselves round axons to provide electrical insulation ('myelin sheaths'; see figure 3.8)[8]. The commonest

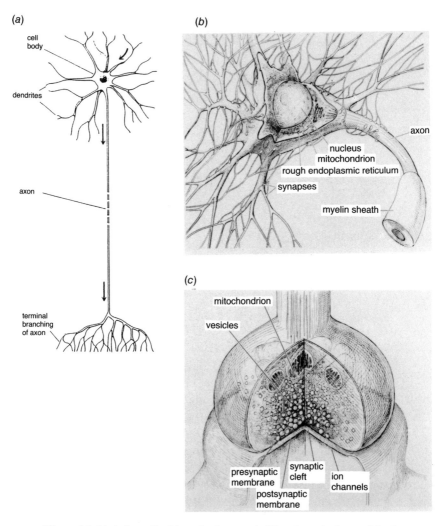

Figure 3.6 (a) A formalised 'standard neuron'; (b) a closer look at cell body region; (c) a synapse.
Part (a) from Alberts *et al.* (1989); (b, c) from Stevens, *The Neuron*. Copyright © (1979) by Scientific American, Inc. All rights reserved.

are 'astrocytes' (figure 3.9). These are small, star-shaped, and have many little feet which they place on both neurons and blood capillaries. It has recently been become a bit clearer what they may be up to. They seem to run a sort of valet service for neurons, mopping up neurotransmitters

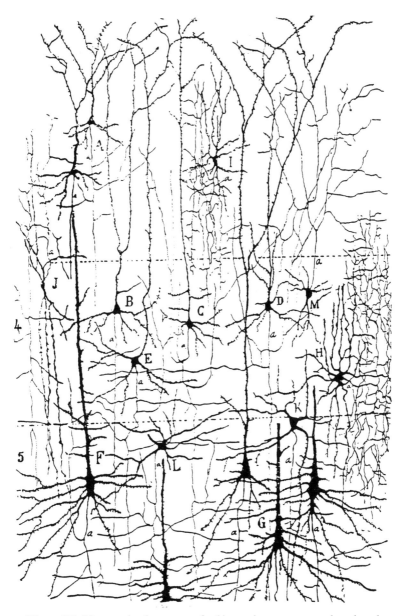

Figure 3.7. Neurons in the cortex of a kitten. Axons are smoother threads labelled 'a'; the others are dendrites. This drawing by Ramón y Cajal was of a section which had been stained by the Golgi method before being examined under the microscope. This technique has the effect of staining completely a very small proportion of the cells, so this picture greatly understates the true density of neurons in the brain.

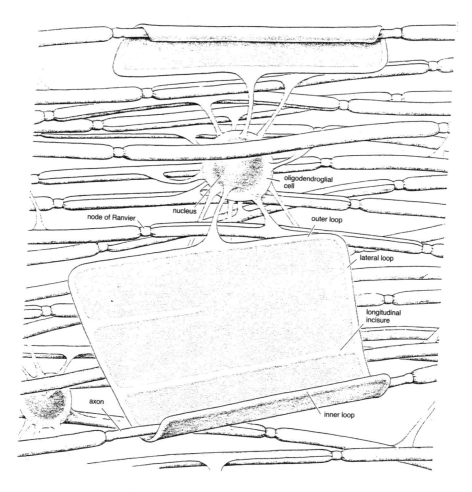

Figure 3.8. Myelination of axons.
From Morell & Norton, *Myelin*. Copyright © (1980) by Scientific American, Inc. All rights reserved.

transporting other molecules to them, and generally maintaining a suitable molecular and ionic environment for the neurons to work in[9]. Now it looks as if astrocytes may also form some sort of communication network in their own right[10].

Then of course the local blood circulation with its rich profusion of tiny capillaries is itself a crucial attendant subsystem. Brains use a lot of energy[11]. Oxygen and glucose in particular have always to be within easy

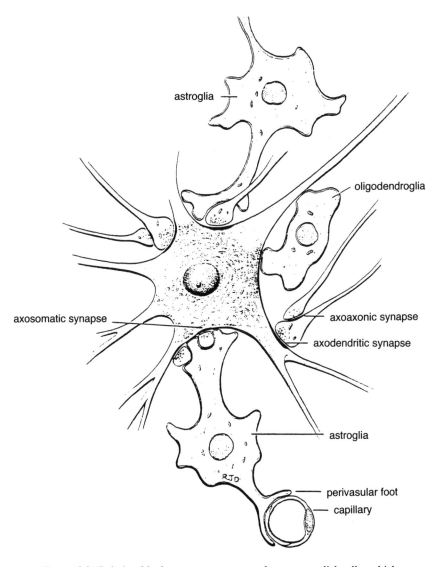

Figure 3.9. Relationship between a neuron and astrocyte glial cells, which
have processes extending to neurons and capillaries. Also shown are oligodendrocytes and nerve terminals, which synapse on dendrites, cell body and
axons.
From Noback *et al.*, *The Human Nervous System*, 4th ed., © Williams &
Wilkins 1991.

reach of all parts of nerve cells in the brain, as do other nutrients such as small molecules needed for making neurotransmitters[12].

Returning to neurons, we can think of them as just ordinary eukaryotic cells with some exaggerations. The most obvious are their shapes (some example are shown in figure 3.7). These are caused and maintained by the cytoskeleton[13].

The neuron's great length creates problems of supply, especially for such large objects as protein molecules or whole mitochondria. The cell body is the main production centre for such things, but it may be very far off from (say) the transmitters at the ends of the axon which need them. So how is the heavy baggage got from the factory to points of use which may be many centimetres away?

It goes by rail. Proteins and other molecules are packaged into the kinds of lipid-bound vesicles which we talked about earlier in this chapter. Along with mitochondria and other objects these run along the microtubules on those (kinesin) protein motor 'roller skates' touched on towards the end of the previous chapter. Then to avoid a build-up of material at the extremities there is also a counter-flow: materials are transported back for re-processing, suitably packaged and, would you believe it, fitted with the other (dynein) motors moving in the opposite direction on the same rails. (Actually it is an old eukaryotic trick[14].)

None of these 'axonal transport' processes is fast enough to account for the rate at which nerve messages are passed. A typical 'fast' transport rate is about 4 centimetres a day. If, say, the nerves to and from our fingers really worked at this sort of rate it would take several years to drink a cup of tea, and piano playing would be, well, different. Clearly axonal transport is just part of a general preparation for action: for the release of a pulse of neurotransmitters. The signal to do this rushes along the axons at speeds of up to 100 metres per second.

Galvani had thought that nerve actions were electrical, and he was right, but there is more to it than that. It is time for an electrochemical aside before coming to consider what sort of thing a nerve impulse really is.

The membrane potential

A thought experiment Suppose you have a small vessel full of water in a beaker of water. The small vessel also contains

(1) large molecules with negative charges which are balanced by
(2) small molecules which have positive charges and
(3) the vessel has little holes in its walls which allow the small positive
    but not the large negative molecules to get through.

QUESTION: Would the positive molecules go through the holes?

ANSWER: Of course they would: they are, after all, moving at random
and some will soon find some of the holes. Once in the big wide world
of the beaker they will be much less likely to find their way back. This
is just a familiar kind of entropy effect – solutions at high concentrations
always 'want' to become more dilute – but:
ANSWER (part 2):   There would be another effect. As the positive molecules began to escape this would produce an electrostatic potential – the
inside of the vessel would begin to develop a negative charge and the
outside a positive charge – and *that* would mean that further escapes
would be more difficult and escapees would indeed now be attracted back.
Sooner or later (in fact very soon) a dynamic balance would be reached
and the whole system would settle down to a compromise with a permanent voltage between the outside and the inside. This would not, incidentally, be the kind of voltage that you could make any use of, because it
would be in a settled-down, equilibrium state.

    Well, I have been more or less talking about a cell, or rather a feature
of the electrochemistry of cells. The negative molecules are things like
nucleic acid and protein molecules, molecules with phosphate groups
attached and so on. The positive molecules in our thought experiment
are potasium, K^+, ions. The holes are pores in the cell membrane which
particularly allow K^+ ions to leak through. Cells usually have an excess
negative charge inside – a negative 'membrane potential' – and most of
it is due to this effect[15].

The action potential

A priming pump   Virtually all animal cells have ATP-driven pumps
in their membranes which push sodium ions, Na^+, out of the cell into
the surrounding fluids, and K^+ ions the other way (see figure 2.16 on
page 88). The effect of this pump is to create an instantly usable store
of energy in the form of a sodium ion potential between the outside and

the inside, similar to the hydrogen ion potential that *E. coli* uses to drive its flagellar turbines[16]. Perhaps as much as two thirds of the ATP energy of an active neuron is used in driving these pumps[17].

A voltage-sensitive gate for Na$^+$ Consider now part of the axon of a neuron in its so-called 'resting state'. (It is 'resting' in the sort of way you might say a cat poised to pounce is 'resting'; really it is wound up like the rest of the cell by the Na$^+$–K$^+$ pumps.) The axon's membrane contains other crucial pieces of equipment: what are called 'voltage-gated sodium channels'. These open up if the normal membrane potential of around −0.07 volts is increased sufficiently (i.e. becomes sufficiently less negative)[15]. If this happens then Na$^+$ ions rush in, further reducing the negative charge inside, leading to still more opening up in a spasm of activity spreading in both directions along the axon. The patch of reversed potential near the original disturbance will cause local currents to flow inside and outside the axon, spreading the effect rapidly sideways (see figure 3.10a). Normally this 'action potential' is initiated in the stretch of axon next to the cell body, and so the nerve impulse travels along the axon towards its transmitter ends.

Two refinements. First, and in keeping with what we have come across before, there is a rapid self-cancelling mechanism here: in rather less than a thousandth of a second a voltage-gated Na$^+$ channel clams up no matter what the voltage has become. At about the same time some big K$^+$ channels wake up (also voltage-sensitive but taking longer to be roused). That starts a major outward flow of positive charges, quickly bringing the membrane potential back to around −0.07 volts, ready for the next spasm of activity. (A moderately fast axon can fit in some thousand separate impulses a second.)

Another refinement is that most axons are insulated (myelinated) along most of their length (figure 3.8) with small bare patches, or nodes, every half millimetre or so where the voltage-gated channels are concentrated[8]. This has the effect of allowing the nerve impulse to jump from node to node (figure 3.10(b)), increasing propagation speeds and using less energy.

Some further comments We have been talking about the Standard Neuron (doing its Standard Thing); what we know about this comes largely from the study of big nerves outside the brain. Over short distances brain cells have the means to communicate without necessarily generating impulses[18]. The effect of a synaptic potential travels within a tree of dendrites by simple conduction, by the kind of voltage spreading which is part of the more active impulse mechanisms as shown in figure 3.10. And

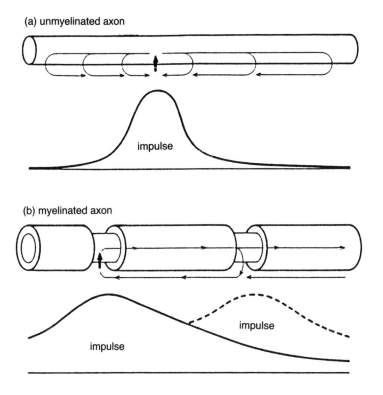

Figure 3.10. The spreading of an action potential along (a) unmyelinated and (b) myelinated axons. (See text.)
From *Neurobiology*, G. M. Shepherd, © 1988 Oxford University Press.

it happens between cells too, especially at gap junctions between neurons.

Although sending signals along 'wires' may be the new idea of neuronal control, none of the elements is new. Voltage-gated channels are found elsewhere, and signalling through impulses of changed membrane potential takes place in other kinds of cells, for example some plant cells[18].

Westinghouse signals

In one important respect the axon is the exact opposite of a wire. Here we might use an analogy with George Westinghouse's design for air brakes used particularly in railways and heavy road vehicles.

When I slam my foot on the brake of my car it is a positive action: the signal travels in the same direction and at the same time as the energy required to implement it. In this case 'brakes on' is a high-energy state. The key Westinghouse idea was to make 'brakes off' the high-energy state. Air has to be pumped into the brake mechanism, where it must operate against heavy pressure to release the brake. In principle then no energy is needed to *apply* Westinghouse brakes (in practice of course a little: to open an air valve).

Well, sending a message along a wire is normally like applying my car brake. The message goes along with the energy expended. But a signal in a nerve axon is definitely 'Westinghouse': the nerve is all the time primed up. The 'action potential' is really a pulse of relaxation (not a letting out of air of course, but a letting in of sodium ions). Here, contrary to our intuitions perhaps, no energy has to pass along the axon with the signal. What energy is expended flows at right angles to the signal propagation, and recharging is for the benefit of the next signal. Information flow and energy flow have been separated.

Synaptic affairs

When we come to talk of the *effect* of an action potential we are back to chemical signalling. The effect of an impulse arriving at a synapse is to release a pulse of neurotransmitter molecules from the 'presynaptic membrane' (i.e. the piece of membrane at the very tip of the axon terminal) to be picked up almost at once by receptors in the nearby 'postsynaptic membrane' – the directly opposing patch of membrane of the receiver cell.

Neurotransmitters are stored in the synaptic terminal knobs in crowds of vesicles ready to fuse with the presynaptic membrane and deliver their goods, in a typical eukaryotic way (figure 3.2 on page 95). The immediate stimulus for *this* is a sudden infusion of calcium ions into the axon terminal caused by the arrival of the impulse. Quite how Ca^{2+} stimulates vesicle fusion is not clear. What is much clearer is how the calcium ions get in: there are yet other voltage-sensitive gates, which are present in the membranes of axon terminals, and which open for calcium[19].

Suppose that a nerve impulse has arrived at an axon terminal and a few vesicles have released a pulse of their neurotransmitter signal molecules. Quickly these diffuse across the twenty or so millionths of a millimetre to the postsynaptic membrane. There they bind to an array of receptors which in turn open up channels that let through small ions. This now changes the local membrane potential of the receiver cell to encourage or discourage it to set in train an action potential of its own. Following these events the neurotransmitter molecules are rapidly removed from the synaptic space (reabsorbed, destroyed, *anything*, but it has to be done quickly: the next impulse may be on its way . . .).

Fast, slow, yes, no The fastest-acting membrane receptors are ion channels which are directly opened by neurotransmitters. These are 'ligand-gated ion channels'. They are relatively insensitive to the membrane potential, but open when they bind their specific neurotransmitter key. Figure 3.11a illustrates the classical 'excitatory' synapse which uses only ligand-gated channels.

Figure 3.11b shows a slower-acting synapse which works via separate receptors, G proteins, membrane catalysts and secondary messengers, etc., along the lines of the hormone receptor systems which we discussed earlier (see figure 3.3 on page 97). But the neurotransmitter has the same kind of effect – to open (or sometimes to close) ion channels – although its indirect mode of action lets it do other things too. For example, the secondary messenger in this system may set in train processes that operate on other proteins in the cell, creating longer-term effects so that the cell may remember something of the signal that had passed . . .

Figure 3.11c is yet another kind of synapse, this one 'inhibitory' and fast, although it also has a slower G protein-mediated system acting in parallel. In addition, in all three examples in figure 3.11, there are *pre*-synaptic receptors. These act as sensors to control the neurotransmitter concentration in the synaptic gap, usually reducing further release as this concentration builds up ('negative feedback'). Some have the opposite effect, though, and encourage still more neurotransmitter to be released. Such complications are typical, and there are many variations on the themes illustrated in figure 3.11.

Sensors, effectors, and computing Our sense organs convert the stimuli to which they are tuned into nerve signals. Each kind of sense organ has in it cells that make the critical conversion, and which we can think of as 'half neurons' since while their inputs are various forms of energy their outputs are much the same as the outputs of neurons

(a)

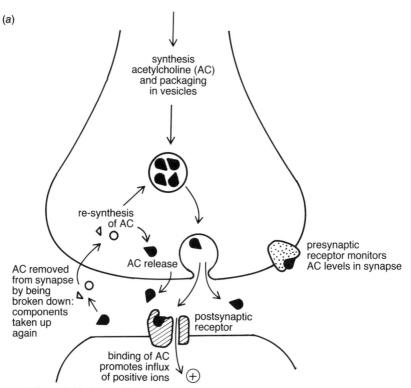

Figure 3.11. Three kinds of synapse.

(a) Fast, excitatory: using acetylcholine as neurotransmitter acting directly on cation channels.

(b) Slow, excitatory: using noradrenaline as neurotransmitter acting indirectly on cation channels.

(c) Fast, inhibitory: using γ-aminobutyric acid as neurotransmitter acting directly on anion channels. There is also a slower indirect action on cation channels.

Modified from Shepherd (1988).

generally: they open (or perversely in the case of rods and cones in the retina close) ion channels, thus altering local membrane potentials. . .

At the effector end of the system there are other 'half-neurons': muscle cells, for example. These receive neurotransmitter signals in very much the same way as any neuron would, with changes in membrane potential leading to an action potential which spreads over

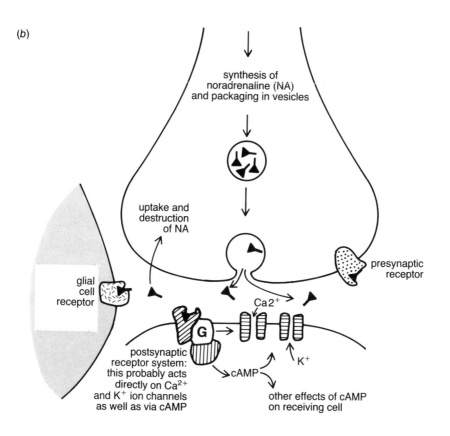

the muscle cell's membrane and may lead at last to behaviour unlike a neuron: contraction . . .[20].

In between, between great bundles of sensory nerve fibres coming in and the motor nerves going out, there is The Great Computer. Its intelligence is a distinct advance on *E. coli*'s, but still very much cell-based.

The computers within The Computer   Let us concentrate attention now on the dendrite or cell body end of a neuron, say a brain neuron. This might have many thousand axons from other cells attached to it. The arrival down just one of them of an action potential is unlikely to trip the receiving cell into action itself. For that to happen there must be a certain minimal level of stimulation: enough 'yes' votes coming in fast enough to set the whole cell off.

(c)

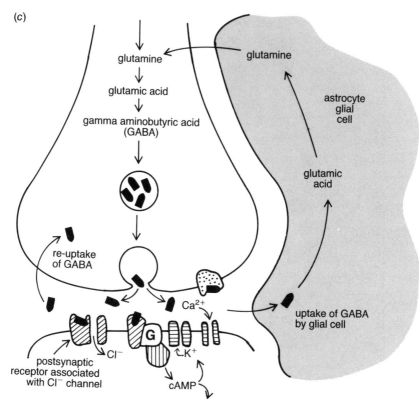

Figure 3.11(c). For caption see p. 110.

A 'yes' vote is registered when, for example, calcium or sodium channels are opened in the receiver cell so that positive charge flows into it. The effect would spread from the immediate vicinity of the synapse by local currents without producing any self-propagating action potential. This is because there are relatively few of the required voltage-gated Na$^+$ channels in dendrites and cell bodies.

Like *E. coli*, the neuron can both add and subtract in coming to its decisions. As we saw, many synapses are inhibitory, always voting 'no'. They may do this by opening channels that let in (appropriately enough) negative ions (Cl$^-$) to damp down the enthusiasm, although increasing an outward K$^+$ flow has a similar effect.

Yet the neuron is not a ballot box. It arrives at its decisions in a way that is somewhat more like the procedure at, say, an open air Union Meeting where members shout YE–EEES! or NO–OOOH!, and where some have stronger and some have longer voices – and some are nearer

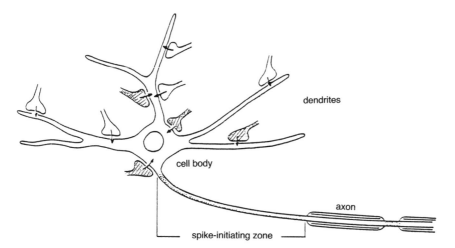

Figure 3.12. Diagram of a motor neuron from the spinal cord of a cat, showing excitatory (open) and inhibitory (shaded) synapses and the location of
the part of the axon in which the nerve impulse is generated.
From *Neurobiology*, G. M. Shepherd, © 1988 Oxford University Press.

the chairman's table. We might call this (still oversimplified) view 'a
Union Meeting model of the neuron' or more briefly 'a Union neuron'.

The net result of addings and subtractings over time and space is a
general membrane voltage level in the cell body, in particular in the region
where the axon emerges from it. The first short stretch of axon is
especially packed with voltage-gated ion channels; it is thus especially set
up for initiating action potentials. This is where the decision to fire or not
to fire is implemented (see figure 3.12), and then, if affirmative, the further
decision on how long to wait before firing again. How fast the pulses
follow each other depends on how 'excited' the transmitting cell is.

So there has to be a minimal level of enthusiasm to get a 'yes'; and
levels of enthusiasm are registered by the rate at which impulses follow
each other along the axon.

Then of course, as in all voting systems, 'yes' may mean 'no'. It depends
how the motion is framed. You know the kind of thing: 'Ladies and
gentlemen we will now move to a vote on whether to try to prevent
Colonel Hagshaw from extending his bungalow in the direction of the
new school'. Where the receiving neuron is an inhibitory one it is some
such yes-means-no motion that it is voting on.

Now one might imagine that what ought to happen is that each neuron should come to its collective decision on the basis of the inputs from other collective decisions of other neurons, and then pass *that* decision on to the myriad of other neurons to which it happens to be connected through its output cable: its axon. But *dendrites* are often in direct touch with each other (no great surprise; see figure 3.7 for example) so that quite a lot of 'off the record' communication can take place without action potentials being set off. Indeed there are neurons (in the retina for example) which never produce impulses at all[21] . . .

One, two, three – many

Some marine polyps and sea anemones seem to have only one neuron (or neuron-like) cell in their nervous systems. With a behaviour repertoire consisting of a single if–then response, say contracting one muscle if touched, one neuron coupled to an appropriate touch sensor is probably enough. We ourselves have control subsystems which in a real sense depend on only a few neurons. Spinal reflexes, for example the automatic drawing of the finger away from a hot-plate, may be understood in terms of only a few neurons connected together, even if many such subsystems operate in parallel.

With the invention of the modern computer in the 1930s and 1940s it was realised that neurons, even on the Ballot Box model, might serve as the basis of a neural computing system in much the same way as, say, radio valves. The great insight had been that exceedingly complex logical operations can be performed by combining together exceedingly simple logical elements based on simple if–then devices.

I have no doubt that the brain, whatever else it might be, is some sort of computer, but its dissimilarities from most present man made computers have recently been becoming more obvious.

The neuronal computers in organisms were never really there to do arithmetic, but to serve as controllers. The ancestor of the brain was more like a thermostat than an abacus. There was, as it were, a difference of intention from the outset. Then again the underlying devices, the neurons, are *far* more complex than transistors. They are eukaryotic cells no less, each of their millions of protein molecules a highly sophisticated machine. These are if–then–unless–but–however–remember . . . structures – at least.

Well, some of the latest ideas for computer design *are* a bit more 'neuronal'[22] if not yet remotely eukaryotic, which gives me an idea for a story.

It is set a few years into the future when artificial neurons – let us say Union neurons – can be purchased from the local ironmonger.

Harry is a publican. In an attempt to increase sales without taking on extra staff he invents 'Harry's Magic Beer Mat'. The customer simply places his empty glass on the mat and it gets refilled. Harry's first design was a spring-loaded platform – rather like the platform on bathroom scales – with the dendrites of an artificial neuron attached to the spring, to act as a stretch detector, and the axon ends attached to an effector. (We have such sensor neurons on all our muscles so that we know, for example, how our limbs are disposed without having to look.) A beer glass placed on the mat generates enough impulses to register 'yes' (a peanut doesn't) and the Beer Dispensing Effector comes into action: an L-shaped filler tube swings into place, a pump switches on, and the Customer is delighted.

At least that was the idea. But the first customer's shoes were beginning to fill with beer before Harry realised the value of inhibitory neurons. His Mark II design ingeniously incorporated a non-overspill mechanism without needing any additional sensor – like this:

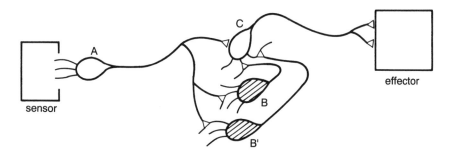

Neuron A fires when an empty glass is put on the mat and C fires in turn. As the glass fills up A's output impulse frequency increases to the point at which it sets off the inhibitory neurons B and B', which combine to cancel A's positive signal at C.

I am told by a psychic friend that Harry went on to invent Harry's Magic Bar Stool incorporating Customer Weight Sensors and, through a more complex network of neurons processing information from several springs in the seat, a Customer Stability Sensor; and he was thus able to arrange that only lemonade would be served to children and drunks.

Well, I *think* he could have done all that with Union neurons, but knowing Harry I am sure he will want to do more for his customers. Perhaps he will invent a machine that can come to recognise regulars (by noting characteristics of weight and wobbliness perhaps?) and serve them their favourite drinks. For this he is going to need systems that can remember, indeed which can learn like Pavlov's dogs: systems that have an associative memory. I know he is going to find that no amount of wiring together of Union neurons will work. He is going to need other pieces of hardware. He will have two options open to him: either throw in the neuronal towel and use special memory hardware, based on a floppy disc or something, or go and look for some decent neurons, not those Union ones but something more like the real thing.

You see, Nature is at her best when designing microscopic, molecular, machinery: after all she has to do that before she can do anything else. So given the option, supposing there had been one, she would go for microscopic memory systems, where the memories are in among the cells and their molecules. Anyway, nothing like a notebook or a floppy disc has been found in the skull.

Most likely there are a number ways in which our thoughts and experiences get written down, and most likely too we have only thought of some of them. All the same the evidence is accumulating that at least part of the memory mechanism is somewhat below the neuronal level of organisation[23].

E. coli has to be able to remember if it is to know, at any moment, whether its swimming is making things better or worse. And of course its mechanisms are necessarily subcellular. As we saw *E. coli* shows a form of adaptation, a very general property of control systems in cells. Neurons too tend to stop responding to repeated stimuli: not just out of exhaustion, but as part of the general cellular strategy of being tuned to respond to change. Here is how one of the forms of neuronal adaptation works.

The section of the axon nearest the cell body which initiates action potentials has among its numerous voltage-sensitive gates a set that let through Ca^{2+}: it also has some Ca^{2+}-gated K^+ channels, which can only be opened from the inside. So when an axon has been firing repeatedly its internal Ca^{2+} builds up and begins to open these K^+ channels, letting K^+ escape more easily and so making the cell more difficult to activate.

There are also longer-term effects which seem to depend, among other things, on more persistent changes in cell proteins. Such changes could be brought about by the 'slow' hormone-like neurotransmitter receptors as discussed earlier (figure 3.11b, c).

'Long-term potentiation' is one such phenomenon in which signals become *easier* to pass between neurons (on a time scale of, perhaps, weeks) and seems to provide a basis for associative learning[24]. Let us consider an example in more detail.

The hippocampus is part of the brain known to be involved in forming memories. Synapses here can be 'potentiated', that is to say repetitive impulses through a particular synapse may have the effect of increasing subsequent response by a receiver cell at that synapse, but not at other (quiet) synapses of the same cell. However, if even a single impulse (normally quite insufficient to have any potentiating effect) goes through a second synapse *at the same time* as a strong train of impulses are going through another synapse of the same cell then that single impulse will be effective: both synapses will become potentiated. This is an if–then device with a memory. A connection becomes reinforced as a result of an association, like a minimal version of Pavlov's dogs that would salivate when they heard a bell because they had previously learned to associate the sound of the bell with meal time. (As a matter of fact you don't have to be a dog to notice such things.)

This sort of 'long-term potentiation' in neurons seems to depend on some especially clever protein molecule, present among the ion channels of the postsynaptic membranes of these cells. We have discussed ligand-gated ion channels and we have discussed voltage-gated channels. Well, these proteins are both. They are 'and' gates in computer terminology: they open to let through Ca^{2+} ions if *both* their neurotransmitter is bound (which could be due to a single impulse) *and* at the same moment there is a general voltage rise (due to a strong train of impulses through at least one nearby synapse)[25].

We cannot yet say that memories *consist* of patterns of preferred connectivity between neurons, an idea put forward by Donald Hebb many years ago[26]; but it has been shown that networks of artificial 'neurons' with such properties can indeed form the basis of computer systems that can learn.

Not to forget forgetting, there is also an opposite effect, through which associations can be undone: apparently when voltage levels are above resting potential but not sufficient to open the doubly gated Ca^{2+} channels[27].

Neurotransmitters galore

Figure 3.13A, B shows the commonest of the 'fast' neurotransmitters: ones that can act directly on ligand gated ion channels (see also figure 3.11a, c on pages 110, 112). Most people know that the hormone adrenalin is put into our bloodstream by the adrenal glands to prepare us for dicey situations. It works by acting on a variety of cells (increasing blood pressure, speeding up the heart, releasing glucose from the liver . . .). In the brain, however, adrenalin is a specialised neurotransmitter doing such quiet things as helping to process taste information from the tongue[28], although even here adrenalin has a somewhat hormone-like action, in common with all the 'monoamine' group of neurotransmitters shown in figure 3.13c in that its receptors are of the relatively slow kind mediated by G proteins (see figure 3.11b on page 111.

And then there is a paracrine strand in the activities of at least some monoamine neurotransmitters: they may diffuse to adjacent synapses, creating a general activation or inhibition of several neurons in a neighbourhood of perhaps several millimetres[29]. Such local broadcasting would seem to be an economical approach to activating or inhibiting like-minded neurons (if you will pardon the expression): if they are physically close to each other they are likely to be concerned with a similar function.

Noradrenalin, another monoamine transmitter, is found especially in a wonderfully small central region of the brain called the 'locus ceruleus' consisting of only a few hundred neurons. These sparingly send their branching axons to almost every part of the brain, injecting tiny amounts of their special juice.

Then there is dopamine. It is made by neurons whose cell bodies are in a few central regions of the brain. One such is the 'substantia nigra' which also sends out axons to distant regions, in particular to an area below the great cerebral hemispheres called the striatum which is concerned with computing the muscle actions required for complex voluntary movements. Patients suffering from Parkinson's disease find it difficult to initiate actions. The disease appears to be due to inadequate production of dopamine by neurons of the substantia nigra: symptoms are relieved by treatment with L-dopa, an immediate precursor in the biochemical manufacture of dopamine[30].

Here we are close to one aspect of consciousness: conscious control. But control *of* the consciousness, the control of feelings, is close by too. Feelings may become literally crazy if monoamine transmitter systems are interfered with. Amphetamines for example, artificially boost dopamine and produce strange pleasures, and hallucinations and delusions like the symptoms of schizophrenia. Likewise LSD appears to mimic serotonin, to which it is chemically related, and the hallucinogen mescaline is a close chemical relative of dopamine . . .[31].

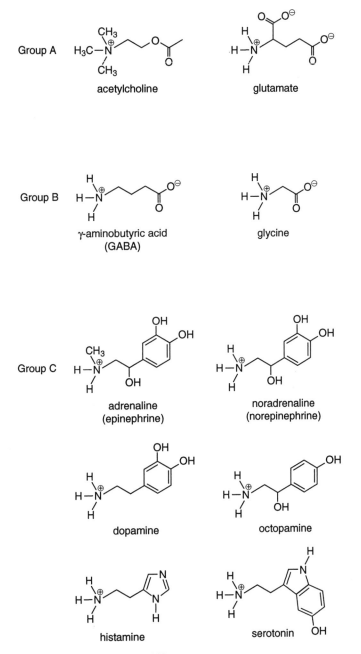

Figure 3.13. For caption see p. 120.

Group D

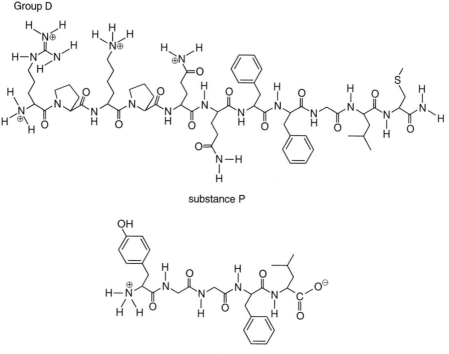

substance P

met-enkephalin

Figure 3.13. Examples from four groups of neurotransmitters and neuromodulators.
Group A – Usually associated with fast excitatory synapses.
Group B – Usually associated with fast inhibitory synapses.
Group C – Monoamines.
Group D – Neuropeptides.

Representatives of a fourth group, this time of putative neuro-transmitters, are shown in figure 3.13D. These are peptides: that is, short stretches of protein chain. The neuropeptides often mediate rather broad and slow-acting effects, again often associated with conscious states, with pleasures, pains, hunger, thirst, sexual arousal, and so on. Morphine, although not a peptide, is of a shape to mimic the enkephal-ins and endorphins and binds to receptors for these neuropeptides in the brain and spinal cord within general regions known to be concerned with pain and emotions[32].

One neuropeptide (substance P) appears to be a more or less conven-tional transmitter, but others seem rather to modulate the effects of non-peptide neurotransmitters to help to relay more complicated advice to receiving cells than 'yes' or 'no'. One idea is that there are sometimes different types of vesicles in axon terminals, some of which contain only a non-peptide neurotransmitter while others have also one or more kinds of neuropeptides in them. Then, according to the general level of stimulation, one or both kinds of package are released leading to sharply different consequences[33]. It seems likely that these usually include wider (paracrine) effects on nearby cells[34].

There are about fifty known or suspected neuropeptide messengers in the brain, although this estimate is likely to go up. That there should be so many fits with a paracrine role: if signals are broadcast at all then they have to be more specific themselves to avoid confusion.

Recalling the idea that a ligand that fits well with a protein should be regarded as joining in the secondary–tertiary structure of the protein (page 74), we might suppose that the often quite large neuropeptides would be particularly adept as ligands – that is, able to work even at very low concentrations and easily bringing about substantial changes in the shapes of their receptor proteins.

Like monoamine neurotransmitters, neuropeptides are often found in other parts of the body acting as paracrine signals or hormones, although again there is no necessary relationship between what these molecules do in the brain and what they do elsewhere[28].

Yet the brain and the hormonal system of the rest of the body are tightly interconnected. The master endocrine gland, the pituitary, is situated just below the brain and part of it, the posterior pituitary, is indeed an extension of part of the brain: the hypothalamus. This is a central brain region especially in touch with both the neuronal and endocrine control systems. For example, the production of the hormone thyroxine starts at least two steps back in the brain, with the hypothalamus producing a neuropeptide which in turn acts on the anterior pituitary which then produces another peptide which then travels in the bloodstream to the thyroid gland in the neck which then produce thyroxine, which *then* controls diverse cellular functions relating to growth and energy metabolism ... This very indirect action by the nervous system allows the signals to be amplified: at each stage a few molecules cause many more molecules to be produced to trigger the next stage. On the other hand some hormone-producing cells remote from the brain are under direct nervous control through being 'half neurons' which receive nerve impulses, but instead of being induced to produce neurotransmitters produce hormones instead.

All this helps to reinforce one of the main themes of this chapter, that the nervous system really only had one 'new idea' – long-distance telegraphy – over and above the style of chemical communication on which the rest of the biochemical control machinery is based, and where allosteric proteins are time and again the critical agents. The more we look, the more of a piece it all seems.

But then what of consciousness? Is this a control system at all? If not, why is it there? We have been unable to avoid brushing with it over the last page or two. Clearly our consciousness has something to do with chemistry. Even if those neurosubstances which seem so close to it are only switches, what can they be switching if not the activities of molecules? If the rest of the story of the evolution of forms of intelligence is anything to go by, we might expect the element of conscious control to be in there too, among the molecules, the cells, the long-range cable communications between cells . . ., economically using some of the same mechanisms – and adding another new idea. What could it be in physical terms? The basic molecules and cell design have hardly changed through evolution, although their uses have changed in subtle ways as new forms of behavioural control have emerged one from another and blended and cooperated with each other at each stage. Chemical, neuronal, conscious, there are these three forms of control to be discerned. The first two were the subject of this chapter. They are clearly molecular, and we can see quite well how one could have evolved from the other. If the third form seems to us to be disjointed I doubt that Nature has such an opinion. Casting back to chapter 1, we might suspect rather that our present failure to understand in molecular terms the conscious element of conscious intelligence comes mainly from our not understanding molecular matter – and that our main mistake here has been to believe too much in our toy models.

Notes

[1] We have already touched on categories of biological control: in gene replication (G → G – hereditary control), in gene expression (G → P – developmental control). The third category is in coping with the environment: 'P → E control' we might call it. Serebriakoff (1987) sees evolution as a form of intelligence in Nature. I prefer to be somewhat more restrained and use intelligence only in relation to P → E control.

[2] The ability of cells to recognise and stick to each other is crucial in

embryological development, in repair processes, or in the immune response (where foreigners are recognised, but elaborately killed rather than embraced). For a review of carbohydrates in cell recognition see Sharon & Liss (1993).

[3] Warren (1990) provides a lead-in. For a more detailed discussion see Rothman (1994).

[4] The difference is that GDP and GTP have the guanine base rather than adenine (see figure 2.1 for structures).

[5] Bourne, Sanders & McCormick (1991) review a whole class of proteins which are 'switched on' by GTP and off again when it hydrolyses to GDP.

[6] Baars (1988), p. 85.

[7] Barres (1991).

[8] Morell & Norton (1980).

[9] Kimelberg & Norenberg (1989).

[10] Dani, Chernjavsky & Smith (1992).

[11] The brain uses about 20% of the *ca.* 100 watts the body needs for 'ticking over'; Iversen (1979).

[12] Wurtman (1982).

[13] Bunge, M. B. (1986); Hollenbeck (1990); Okabe & Hirokawa (1990).

[14] Allen, R. D. (1987).

[15] As in most cells the potential difference across the neuron's membrane represents an enormous potential *gradient* because the membrane is so thin: about 100 000 volts per centimetre. This is about three times as much as will cause a spark to pass through air. It is not surprising that membrane proteins may 'notice' changes in membrane potential.

[16] The pumping of the Na^+ is the most important bit since the measure of permeability of the cell membrane to K^+ would bring K^+ in anyway to compensate for the positive charges going out with the Na^+: but there will be a small component due to a dynamic effect since equilibration takes time. So the driving force available for use is mainly in the difference in the Na^+ concentrations outside and inside the cell. If you made a big hole in the membrane the first effect would be for Na^+ to RUSH in, with at first only a small (if any) tendency for K^+ to go out. Soon K^+ would be rushing (out) too, but as a secondary effect to compensate for the positive charge being brought in by the Na^+. Opening a specific Na^+ channel thus 'excites' a neurone, while opening a K^+ channel has an 'inhibitory' effect.

[17] Shepherd (1988), p. 97.

[18] *Ibid*, p. 119.

[19] Llinas (1982). Ca^{2+} is a particularly effective signal within cells because like

sodium its concentration is actively kept very much lower there than in the surrounding fluids. For a more recent review of synaptic vesicle control processes, see Greengard *et al.* (1993).

[20] Some hormone-secreting cells are similarly 'half neurons'.

[21] Shepherd (1988), pp. 138ff.

[22] Tank & Hopfield (1987); Psaltis *et al.* (1990).

[23] *Scientific American* articles on neurophysiological aspects of memory: see Mishkin & Appenzeller (1987); Alkon (1989); Kandel & Hawkins (1992); Goldman–Rakic (1992).

[24] Collingridge & Bliss (1987); Gustafsson & Wigström (1988); Morris, Kandel & Squire (1988); Kalil (1989); Silva *et al.* (1992 a, b); Madison (1992).

[25] Alberts *et al* (1989), p. 1099.

[26] Hebb (1949); Milner (1993).

[27] Stevens (1990); Artola, Bröcher & Singer (1990).

[28] It may be that the blood – brain barrier allows the same signals to be used for different purposes in the brain and in the rest of the body, rather as the same word can have different meanings in different countries.

[29] Bradford (1987), p. 560.

[30] See Iversen (1992) for a lead into research on dopamine receptors in the brain.

[31] Aghajanian & Rasmussen (1987); Snyder (1984); Cooper, Bloom & Roth (1987).

[32] Iverson (1979).

[33] Shepherd (1988), p. 170; Hokfelt, Johansson & Goldstein (1984).

[34] Alberts *et al.* (1989), p. 1095.

4

Places in the brain

From a few houses on the river through a village and then a town the great city evolved. One street, several streets, a market square, a church: then new needs and opportunities: workshops, factories, more houses, more streets, shops, bars, banks, and a railway station, with roads and lanes between: more needs and opportunities leading to successive developments, factories, parks, spreading suburbs coming to surround the older parts of city, with their hypermarkets, swimming pools, tennis courts . . . Favourite cities often seem to have evolved like this without too much in the way of master plans, through modifying and adding; conservative at the centre with most of the new developments at the edges, becoming established in their turn . . .

Such a pattern of growth is called organic, with good reason. It is more or less the way organisms evolve. In spite of its amazing inventiveness the process of evolution through natural selection has been quite as amazingly conservative. There are design ideas that have persisted for millions, even billions of years. The 'old city' parts of our biochemistry, such as the general systems for making protein molecules, were already there in a common ancestor from which all the forms of life that we now find on the Earth evolved. These systems must themselves have evolved, but long before: by the time of the common ancestor these central systems – even some of the most intricate details of their working – were so well established that they could not change. No doubt by this time too much had come to depend upon them[1].

There were to be many biochemical innovations, of course, but these would have been peripheral when they first appeared: they would have been small modifications going with subtle changes of function. A typical example would be a protein already doing one thing being used also in a makeshift way for something else, and then gradually splitting off to add a new piece of protein machinery through successive changes in amino acid sequence that would alter the composition and folding of the new protein and improve the new function . . .

A similar story of novelty grounded in conservatism has been true at higher levels, in the eukaryotic cell for example with its subtle but similar systems in all higher forms of life: from yeast to yucca to yak, and then again in the large-scale morphology of animals.

Two simplifying construction plans for animals appeared early on. One was to have a body made up of similar segments joined together ('segmentation'); the other was to have the whole thing similar right and left ('bilateral symmetry'). These features seem to have appeared in some primitive worm, to be inherited by most animals: insects, fish, reptiles, birds, mammals . . .[2]

The brain is conservative at the deep biochemical level like everything else, and at the cellular level too. As I remarked in the last chapter, the neuron is a standard eukaryotic cell with some exaggerations and really only one new idea. The evolution of the large-scale structure of the brain has again been fundamentally conservative, proceeding through modifications and additions. There is an old city, old places in the brain, which are vital. They were not superseded but modified, old and new often collaborating or working in parallel[3].

Since mammals appeared the most vigorous developments have been going on in one part of the suburbs so that our Greater Brain, the great hemispheres of the **cerebrum** occupy most of the skull (figure 4.1). The cerebral cortex, more usually referred to simply as the **cortex**, is the convoluted outer shell of the hemispheres. As one might expect of a recent suburban sprawl, the newest part of the cortex – the **neocortex** – is in some ways less critically made than the deeper structures which it now largely conceals. For example there are significant differences in details of the folds of a cortex, between individuals and between the two hemispheres of an individual.

These biggest and newest places in the brain are also in an important sense less vital. Damage to these areas may be devastating, even fatal if extensive: but not always by any means. Damaged areas can often have their functions taken over by nearby areas[4], and surgeons have found that there is indeed no single part of the the neocortex whose destruction is always fatal, or even necessary for the continuation of consciousness[5]. Most astonishingly there have been cases recorded of people who have been born with hardly any neocortex at all and are yet still able to survive and function more or less[6]. It seems indeed that a small baby does all

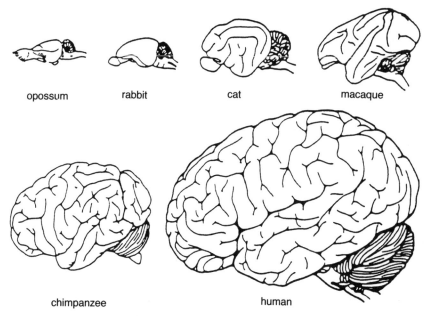

opossum   rabbit   cat   macaque

chimpanzee   human

Figure 4.1. Brains of mammals drawn to the same scale.
From Eccles, J. C. *Evolution of the Brain*, after J. Jansen. © 1989 Routledge.

that touching baby stuff – kicking, sucking, gurgling, mewling and puking – without seriously engaging her neocortex[7].

In relation to its smallest working parts the brain is enormous beyond belief. Recall that even a single eukaryotic cell is a 'city' in itself. But taking the cell as a unit, comparable say to one person, with the (*ca.* 10^{11}) neurons as the key workers and the (*ca.* 10^{12}) glial cells as providing support services, then the population of the great city that we have been imagining would be some hundred to a thousand times greater than the entire population of the Earth.

And what a place it is! Even at the anatomical levels visible to the naked eye there are hundreds of locations distinctive enough to have been assigned long Latin names by neuroanatomists down the ages (usually names that mean 'the little hill further up' or 'the bit that looks like an almond' – things like that). I refer the interested reader to an excellent Atlas[8]. We will be hardly more than tourists set on getting a feel for some of the main districts, centres and highways; and perhaps noting some names of important places. So you need not be too intense about the map-reading (unless like me you just like maps).

The five-part central nervous system

If evolution through natural selection operates by modifying what is already there under the immediate pressures of immediate needs, there is another set of constraints set by the processes of development through which the brain of every individual is made, as the whole individual is made, from one cell and some dry-looking DNA instructions. These are acted on in an appropriate order at appropriate stages and in appropriate places during the incredible unfoldings of embryological and later development. So if there was some feature that selective evolutionary forces might, as it were, have 'wanted' to modify to improve the efficiency of an organism then it must have done so, if at all, in such a way as not to unhinge the overall process of development.

It is perhaps no surprise, then, that development too is conservative: there is a similar grand plan of development to be found in the brains of all animals that have evolved from that enterprising worm (or whatever it was). Like the brains of all vertebrates – sardines, snakes, swallows . . . – your brain started as a swelling at the front end of a rudimentary spinal cord which then divided into three parts later to become a hindbrain, midbrain and forebrain. Simplifying and formalising:

The forebrain then further subdivided to give five main districts of the Central Nervous System:

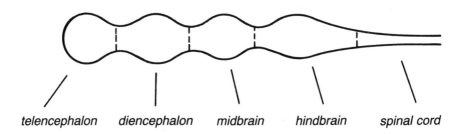

telencephalon   diencephalon   midbrain   hindbrain   spinal cord

Figure 4.2 is a cartoon for brains of mammals.

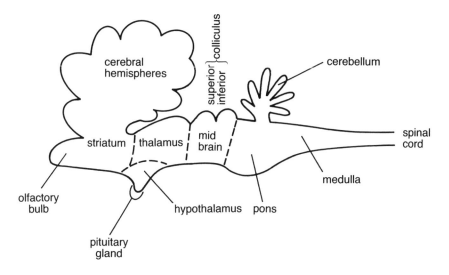

Figure 4.2. Sketch map of districts in a mammal's brain.

Spinal cord   Like the vertebral column within which it lies, the spinal cord is bilaterally symmetrical, and 'segmented' too in the repeating pattern of nerve connections to it. A typical cross-section of the spinal cord might look something like this:

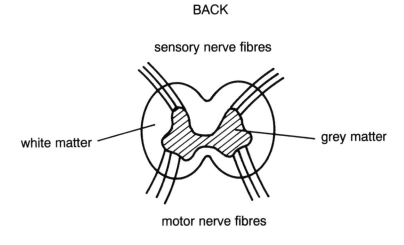

The cord is a huge bundle of myelinated axons, showing up as white matter, with a grey matter core rich in cell bodies and their dendrites. If we might be inclined to dismiss the white matter as mere 'wiring', the grey matter at least is more intricate computing equipment – 'processors' somewhat analogous to computer chips.

The spinal cord could as well have been described as part of the brain. The cord's computing abilities are illustrated by simple reflexes such as the burnt finger reaction: if you accidently touch a hot plate your hand will have jerked away from it before the brain would have had time to get involved, long before you felt any pain for example. The familiar knee-jerk reaction is another case: the forced stretching of a tendon caused by the Doctor's little hammer is sensed by the spinal computer, through changes in impulse trains coming to it through sensory nerve fibres. The computer then generates new signals to be sent out along motor nerves to arrange for compensating muscular contractions ... All of which is quite useless in this case, of course, but it illustrates the working of a computer system that normally keeps us from falling over.

Indeed the lower levels of the control of walking are mainly done at spinal computer level[9]. We still have the habit of waving our arms in sync. as we walk, as if our arms too were legs; but a more vivid illustration of the spinal computer at work is to be found in the legendary talents of the hen which has just had its head cut off and which can run (three times is it?) round the farmyard. Of course higher levels of control, such as whether to bother running round a farmyard, are brain-directed, at least when the brain is there and the animal is not asleep.

Hindbrain, midbrain, diencephalon Moving our attention head-ward into the skull we find that the cord widens out and becomes much more complicated, forming an ancient and vital part of the brain, the **brain stem**. This consists of all the more central parts of the hindbrain (the **medulla**) and the midbrain (see figures 4.2–4.4).

The segmented arrangement is now less obvious. There are still paired nerves, but not so neatly arranged as in the spinal cord. Ten of the twelve pairs of **cranial nerves** are connected to the brain stem. Mostly these have to do with sensory and motor functions nearby: hearing, control of face and eye muscles and so on, but not all. For example the tenth nerves, the great pair of vagus (wanderer) nerves, have numerous sensory and

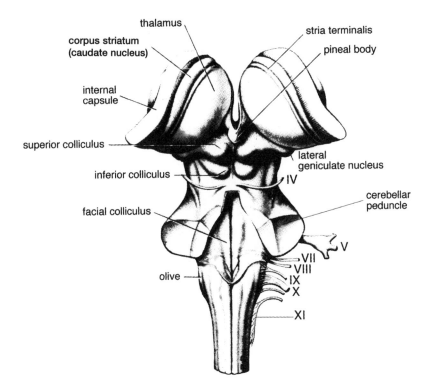

Figure 4.3. Brain stem and diencephalon viewed from behind.
From Noback *et al.*, *The Human Nervous System*, 4th ed., © Williams & Wilkins 1991.

motor branches going all the way back down into the body, to the viscera, the heart and other organs to help keep control here – and keep us alive.

Figure 4.3 shows the brain stem and diencephalon from behind as it would appear with overlaying structures removed. On the under side (figure 4.4) is the **pons**, a bridge-like swelling which acts among other things as a kind of junction box.

One of the structures removed from figure 4.3 is the **cerebellum**. It is attached to the back of the brain stem opposite the pons (see figures 4.2 and 4.5). Its main purpose is higher-order processing of motor functions: which is to say that if you know how to ride a bicycle, or eat a plate of spaghetti (or indeed both at once), most of your specific unconscious expertise will be set up, somehow, in your cerebellum.

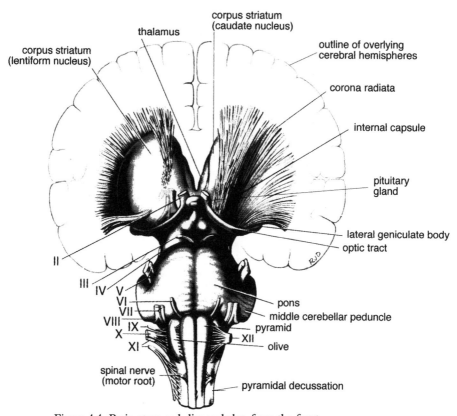

Figure 4.4. Brain stem and diencephalon from the front.
From Noback *et al.*, The Human Nervous System, 4th ed., © Williams &
Wilkins 1991.

The pairing of the cranial nerves provides an example of an approximate bilateral symmetry of the brain which is retained almost everywhere.
Most brain parts are paired like this, although they are often talked about
in the singular: as one may talk about 'the eye' without implying that
there is only one. Those structures that are centrally placed such as the
pineal body (see figure 4.3) are still symmetrical in themselves with similar
right and left sides.

You can already see from the pictures what a complex structure the
brain stem is. Much more complexity is revealed on further dissection,
more still on microscopic examination.

Among some of the smaller brain stem places are concentrations of cell
bodies such as the substantia nigra and the locus ceruleus referred to in

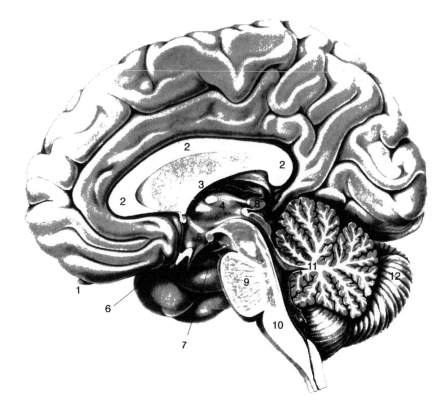

Figure 4.5. View of the right half of a bisected human brain.
 1 Olfactory bulb
 2 Corpus callosum
 3 Fornix
 4 Thalamus
 5 Hypothalamus
 6 Optic chiasma
 7 Oculomotor nerve
 8 Pineal body
 9 Pons
10 Medulla oblongata
11 Vermis of the cerebellum
12 Right hemisphere of cerebellum
From Nieuwenhuys *et al.* (1988).

the last chapter, but there are dozens and dozens of other grey matter 'loci' or 'nuclei'. The central core of the brain stem is continuous with part of the central grey matter of the spinal cord, but more swollen and more diffuse. In this region there are cells of different shapes and sizes with their dendrites arranged in bundles to form a kind of network known as the **reticular formation**. Together with local nuclei and other structures, to which it is richly connected, the reticular formation constitutes a kind of central sensor and activator.

Individual reticular formation cells have been found to respond to all kinds of sensory stimulation[10]. Nauta & Feirtag described them as having 'their dendrites – their cellular hands – spread across several millimetres, hoping, it seems, to catch any kind of message'[11].

Signals go out too. Branching axons arising from reticular cells and those of nearby nuclei go to all parts of the central nervous system, to the cerebral hemispheres, to the spinal cord – everywhere. Especially well connected are brain stem neurons which use serotonin as neurotransmitter, and have highly branched axons 'comprising the most extensive neural network yet described'[12]. You may recall that serotonin is one of those monoamine neurotransmitters allied to drugs which powerfully affect states of consciousness and have a somewhat diffuse (paracrine) mode of action. The reticular formation, it seems, is the core of a system for alerting (or subduing) the central nervous system as a whole: controlling levels of arousal, including general conscious arousal, and possibly also more specific control of conscious attention.

Returning to figure 4.3, the upper part is a mass of lumps and hillocks constituting what can be seen of the midbrain and diencephalon from this view. The midbrain is relatively small. The part visible in the picture consists mainly of four hillocks: the **inferior** and **superior colliculi** and their connections. The inferior colliculus is concerned with processing signals from the ear. The superior colliculus is more concerned with the visual system, with processing signals and controlling eye movements. But you can take it that they do many other things too: like regions of a city, specialisations of regions of the brain are seldom sharp.

Parts of the **thalamus** which can be seen near the top of the picture are also auditory and visual processors: here the medial and lateral geniculate bodies, respectively. By now we are in the diencephalon, which is dominated by the thalamus and the small but critical hypothalamus below it (and so not visible in this picture, but see figure 4.5). The fist-like thalamus is about the most central of all structures in the human brain.

It is virtually surrounded by the cerebral hemispheres and is well connected to them, as it is to the brain stem reticular formation. Like the reticular formation the functions of the thalamus seem to be closely associated with phenomena of consciousness – with sensory awareness.

Telencephalon   Further forward still we reach the telencephalon with those giant cerebral hemispheres dominating everything. The final stop here is the pair of olfactory bulbs, which in man are relatively tiny. They are situated immediately above a thin area of bone in the cavity of the nose and through which pass short nerve fibres from olfactory sensor cells lining that part of the nose.

Big maps of the city

Figure 4.5 is a picture of a human brain as it would be seen if sliced along the central plane from front to back. Notice that the ballooning cerebrum and cerebellum have been accommodated by an approximately 90° change from the direction of the spinal axis, which takes place at about the midbrain–diencephalon level.

Figure 4.6 is of another cut, this one from side to side made along the plane indicated by the arrows in figure 4.5. Here we are looking from the front, so we get another view of parts of the brain stem and cerebellum and we can see their relationship to the cerebral hemispheres. We can see something too of what is inside the hemispheres. There are a number of holes (ventricles) filled with fluid, reminding us that the brain and spinal cord develop from a simple tube. But like elsewhere in the central nervous system most of the space is filled with nervous tissue: white matter ('wiring') and grey matter ('processors').

Where grey matter is on the outside

In contrast to the spinal cord the grey matter in the cerebral hemispheres is on the *outside*: in the cortex, that is. The cortex is a continuous sheet of cells from 2 to 3 mm thick on average, and for the most part made up of six sublayers which have in them a variety of types of neurons (figure 4.7). Some of these, such as the 'chandelier' and 'basket cells', make local connections, while **pyramidal cells** have long axons making

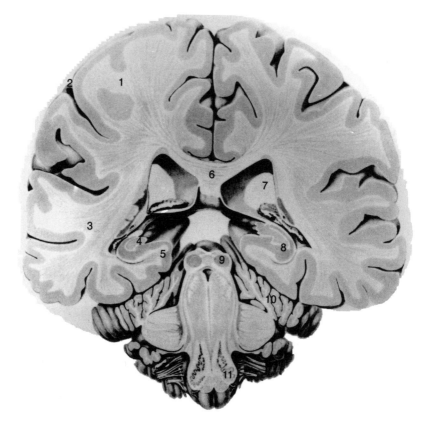

Figure 4.6. Section of human brain viewed from the front.
1 Parietal lobe
2 Postcentral sulcus
3 Temporal lobe
4 Dentate gyrus
5 Parahippocampal gyrus
6 Corpus callosum
7 Lateral ventricle
8 Hippocampus
9 Inferior colliculus
10 Cerebellar hemisphere
11 Olive From Nieuwenhuys *et al.* (1988).

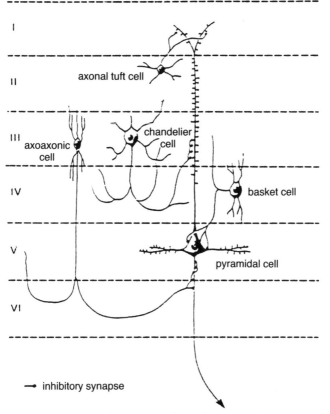

I

II

axonal tuft cell

III
axoaxonic
cell

chandelier
cell

IV   basket cell

V   pyramidal cell

VI

→ inhibitory synapse

Figure 4.7. Some cortex cell types and wiring. See also p. 101. From Noback
et al., *The Human Nervous System*, 4th ed., © Williams & Wilkins 1991.

more distant connections and thus contributing to the underlying white
matter. Pyramidal cells that have their cell bodies in the more upper layers
of the cortex (layers two and three) connect to other parts of cortex itself
while those lower down (in layers five and six) send their axons to places
outside the cortex altogether.

The folds and convolutions of the cerebral hemispheres became more
elaborate in our line of mammalian evolution (see figure 4.1 on page 127).
This can be seen as having been a way of increasing the relative amount of
'processor' as against 'wiring', while keeping to the 'grey matter outside'
rule. There would have been plenty of other ways of increasing the relative
amounts of grey matter, so perhaps we should be saying rather that the convolutions are a sign that it must be an especially good idea to have the cerebral processors arrayed in a continuous thin sheet as they are. The rule
seems to be important. The brain stem is not organised like that, it is more
like the spinal cord. On the other hand the cerebellum is – but with much
tighter convolutions and less white matter as a result . . .

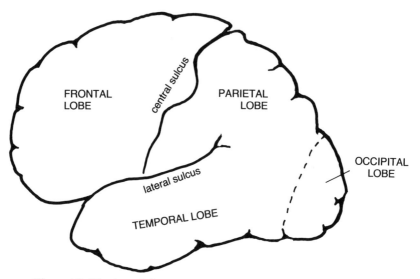

Figure 4.8. Districts of the cortex.

Neocortical places

The main anatomical divisions of the cortex into **frontal, parietal, occipital** and **temporal lobes** are indicated in figure 4.8 together with two of the major dividing valleys. (In describing the cerebral convolutions a valley is usually called a **sulcus**, a ridge a **gyrus**.) The ballooning of the cortex in mammalian evolution was such that its more primitive parts are relatively small and concealed in such views of the brain. What we see is neocortex, the new extensions.

The six-layered neuronal fabric is general in the neocortex, but there are subtle differences in texture – in thickness, in details of how many of different types of cell are present, and so on – which early in this century allowed K. Brodmann to make more detailed maps (figure 4.9).

Primary processors   Nineteenth-century phrenologists would probe an individual's character by feeling for bumps in his head which were supposed to correspond to such things as having a bad temper, a good sense of direction, and so on. It never worked out. But a ghost of the idea remains in Brodmann's areas. Some do indeed correspond to mental functions. For example, we have a bump for seeing: the back parts of the pair of occipital lobes known as the visual cortex. Damage

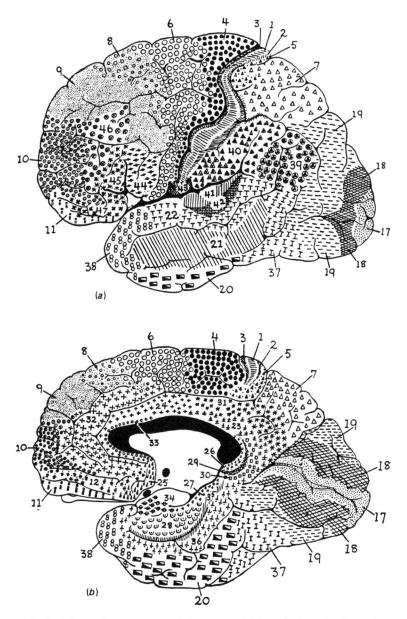

Figure 4.9. Brodmann's areas of the cortex, (a) lateral view of left hemisphere, (b) medial view of right hemisphere (i.e. as seen with brain cut down the middle).
From Brodmann (1914).

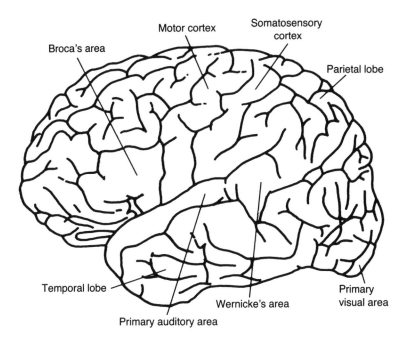

Figure 4.10. Some functional areas of the cortex.

to these areas can lead to blindness, even if there is nothing wrong with the eyes.

Primary cortical areas are concerned directly with a particular function. The primary visual and primary auditory areas are shown in figure 4.10. Just to the rear of the central sulcus in both hemispheres, and arching over into the cleft between them, is another primary sensory area: the **somatosensory cortex**. (This too is indicated in figure 4.10 and corresponds to Brodmann areas 3, 1 and 2, shown in figure 4.9.) Sensations from different parts of the body are 'mapped' onto the somatosensory strip of cortex on the opposite side of the brain, as is clear, for example, from the effects of damage to particular parts of it.

Voluntary movements of our bodies are mediated through corresponding areas of the brain that are just *forward* of the central sulcus, on the frontal lobe side. Again we know this, among other things, from the (paralysing) effects of damage to these areas. This is the **primary motor cortex** (Brodmann area 4 in figure 4.9). Again the effects are 'contralateral': the motor strip on the left side of the brain is concerned with moving the right side of the body and *vice versa*. Again there is a 'mapping'. For example, control of the muscles of the (right) leg is mediated through an area around the top point of the (left) strip. Movement of the hand is controlled through a relatively large region a bit lower down, while the tongue and lips also have large motor areas near the base of the strip. Those parts of our bodies which require intricate control seem to have more extensive computing facilities available to them.

Higher-level processing

As you can see from figure 4.10 the primary motor and sensory areas make up a considerable fraction of the neocortex (about a quarter); and there are other areas near to them whose functions can be designated if not quite so sharply. In front of the primary motor cortex, for example, (Brodmann's area 6) is the premotor cortex, which appears to be concerned with formulating complex actions; while regions adjacent to the primary visual cortex, have directly to do with higher-level analysis of visual information. But there are still large areas that are not at all clearly designated. These are vaguely called 'association areas'. Presumably they are to do with still higher levels of analysis and synthesis, with thinking of one sort or another, with recognising situations, planning actions and so on – with more remote aspects of what must go on between analysis of sensory inputs and formulation of motor outputs ... Even here, though, not all is dark.

While there is probably no unique part of the brain concerned with such high-level analyses as wondering whether to have cheese for supper, there are some places in the brain, away from the primary areas, that have been identified as sites of high-level computing. For example, there is an area (on the underside of the temporal lobes) that can be said to be our bump for recognising faces[13]. That there should be such a specialisation, and so much brain space given over to it, is perhaps not so surprising when you consider how important face recognition is for us, and how amazingly good at it we are. Then again there are fairly clear areas dedicated to what is perhaps our greatest skill as humans: speaking, and understanding speech.

Broca's place, and Wernicke's

The left and right hemispheres do not look exactly the same and they do not have exactly corresponding functions in everything. It has been known for a long time that damage to the left side of the brain is not only likely to affect movement and sensation on the right side of the body, but is also likely to affect speech in a way that similar damage to the right brain (usually) will not. Most of us speak from our left hemispheres.

Two areas have been more specifically located (see again figure 4.10). One of these is 'Broca's area'. It lies close to the lower part of the motor cortex, that part which mediates movement of the face, tongue, jaw and throat. The other is 'Wernicke's area' situated further back in the temporal and parietal lobes closer to the lower part of the somatosensory cortex. Damage to either of these areas produces distinctive speech difficulties. Patients with Broca area damage have trouble with grammar: they may know what they want to say but have trouble getting the words out and in putting them in proper grammatical sequence. Patients with damage to the Wernicke area have trouble with meaning, with formulating what they want to say: their speech may be grammatically correct but nonsensical.

It appears then that Wernicke's area is the more 'strategic', higher-level processor, concerned with meaning as such; while Broca's is more like an auxiliary motor area, a wonderful kind of word processor that has been primed with phrases and, knowing the rules of grammar, is adept at string-ing words together to *express* a meaning which has been given to it. This it can do because it has under *its* command the nearby motor cortex through which it can activate and integrate the complex muscular activities of face, throat, tongue etc, which are required for speech. To borrow Serebriakoff's analogy of the brain as like a commercial organisation[14], we might say that Wernicke's area is at some high level of middle management, while Broca's office is nearer the shop floor in touch with the skilled and knowledgeable foremen of the motor cortex who know how to organise the teams of work-ers – the muscles – through which finally we express our thoughts in the wonderful fluency of physical speech . . .

Is this too simple? Yes, of course it is.

The cerebral white matter

However these amazing processors work, we can at least see plenty of wires between them. There are bundles of fibres in each hemisphere con-necting the frontal, parietal, temporal and occipital lobes. For example some long fibres carry signals between the Wernicke and Broca areas. There are also connections from the primary auditory to Wernicke's area,

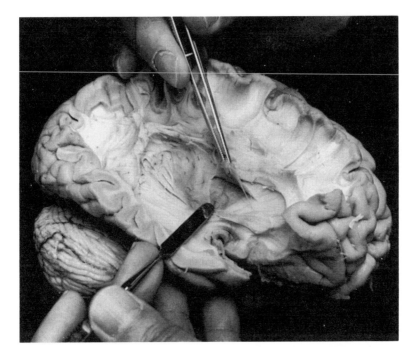

Figure 4.11. Picture from a student's human brain anatomy handbook showing 'technique for fine dissection of the white matter of the hemisphere using
a small spatula and forceps'.
From *The Human Brain in Dissection*, D. G. Montemurro & J. E. Bruni,
© 1988 Oxford University Press.

critical for understanding speech, and to there from the primary visual
cortex, likely to be important in reading . . .

But to cut a long story short there are fibres (axons that is) leading
from everywhere to everywhere in the cortex. At least that is the overall
impression on opening up the cerebral hemispheres and looking inside
(figure 4.11). They are chock full of white matter, of mainly myelinated
axons organised into ribbons (lemnisci) and bundles (fasciculi) running in
many directions (see figure 4.12). Short U-shaped fibres connect adjacent
gyri close to the surface. The longer ones are deeper inside.

The most massive bundle of all is the **corpus callosum**, which connects the two hemispheres. The full thickness and width of this immense
band of wires can be seen in the bisected brain shown in figure 4.5, while
the section in figure 4.6 shows how the individual fibres in it fan out

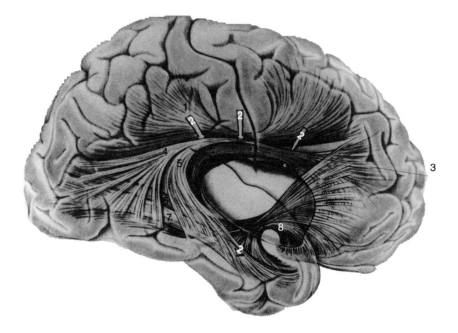

Figure 4.12. Atlas picture of long bundles of fibres in the right cerebral
hemisphere.
1 Superior occipitofrontal fasciculus
2 Site of corona radiata (see figure 4.4)
3, 4, 5 Superior longitudinal fasciculus
6 Inferior occipitofrontal fasciculus
7 Inferior longitudinal fasciculus
8 Uncinate fasciculus
From Nieuwenhuys *et al.* (1985).

within the two hemispheres to make connections between the grey matter
on both sides. Among other things the corpus callosum allows equivalent
grey matter processors on both sides to be directly connected up – for the
left hand to know what the right hand is doing, as it were . . .

In addition to these corticocortical connections, in which in general axons
are running in both directions conveying signals each way, there are groups

of 'projection fibres', some carrying signals to, and others from, parts of the brain outside the cortex. Prominent here is the 'corona radiata', a fan of fibres converging to become the so-called 'internal capsule' and connecting the cortex with central structures. (See figures 4.3 and 4.4.) Among these are connections to and from the thalamus (that central group of cell masses referred to earlier and including 'sensory relay stations').

The **basal ganglia**, which include the **corpus striatum**, is another set of central structures (see again figures 4.3 and 4.4) which is well connected with the cortex. As commented on in the previous chapter, the corpus striatum has to do with the control of body movements.

We will be picking up several of these topics again in the next chapter, and indeed much later when we come to discuss theories of consciousness. In the meantime let us leave the neocortex with this brief tourist glimpse and ride into what seems to be a current centre of the city where some old places and some ancient places abut.

The limbic system

Old cortex

In the previous chapter I referred to the **hippocampus** as being a region of the brain particularly to do with laying down memories. We know this from effects of brain damage and particularly from one case in which the hippocampal regions had been removed surgically to control epilepsy. Patients with severe damage to the hippocampus are left with earlier memories intact but are unable to remember recent events for more than a few minutes.

You will see roughly where the hippocampus is from the brain section in figure 4.6. It is a paired structure, part of the inner curled edges of the temporal lobes on both sides. From its position one might have supposed that this was a new extension. In fact it is one of the oldest regions of the cortex. It is a major part of what is called the archaecortex, characterised, among other things, by having a different cell organisation from neocortex and a distribution of grey and white matter rather more like that of the brain stem, with grey matter masses lying within white matter.

A highly simplified diagram of a shark's brain is shown on the left of figure 4.13. This is somewhat like the idealised mammalian brain sketched in figure 4.2 on page 129 except that the cortex is less obvious and consists

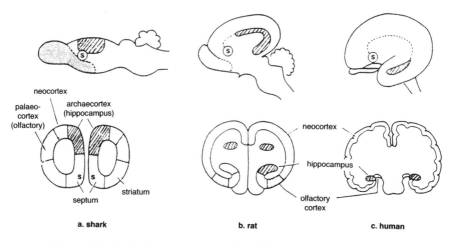

Figure 4.13. Evolutionary migration of the hippocampus.
Top sketches are side views, bottom ones are cross-sections.
From Neurobiology, G. M. Shepherd, © 1988 Oxford University Press.

largely of hippocampus in what seems to be the wrong place. In the shark's brain the hippocampus is close to a central structure – the **septum** – whose equivalent can be recognised in our brains. It appears that in our line of evolution the enormous growth of the neocortex had the effect of separating the hippocampus from the septum, and septal regions, to which it is, however, still connected through nerve fibres in a large bundle. This is the **fornix** (indicated by the dotted line in the top right picture) and which thus still records, as it were, an episode of evolutionary history.

Then there is the **amygdala**, so called because it looks like an almond, or rather two almonds, since again there is one on each side. But really the amygdala is a complex structure. It constitutes the other major part of the archaecortex. These masses of grey matter are also situated within the white matter of the inside wall of the temporal lobes, close to but somewhat further forward than the hippocampus.

The fifth lobe   The structures that we have just been talking about all lie below the corpus callosum, the band of fibres connecting the hemispheres. Looking at the lower right sketch in figure 4.13, or, better, the section in figure 4.6 (on page 136), you will see that there is another hidden edge to the cortex, this one deep inside the cleft between the hemispheres, and this time seen *above* the corpus callosum. Looking at

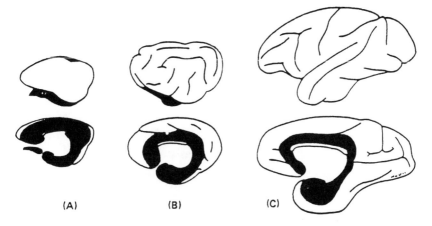

Figure 4.14. Lateral views and medial sections of the brains of rabbit (A),
cat (B) and monkey (C).
From MacLean (1954). © Pitman Publishing.

the section in figure 4.5 on page 133 you will see again, from another
direction, how this edge of the cortex actually curves round the front and
rear portions of the corpus callosum. The strip of cortex nearest the edge
(Brodmann's areas 23 and 24 in figure 4.9b on page 139) is called the
cingulate gyrus.

These edges of the cortex above and below the corpus callosum constitute an overlapping 'fifth lobe'. This includes the cingulate gyrus (which
is part parietal, part frontal), and those inner temporal lobe edges where
the hippocampus and amygdala are located. This fifth lobe is called the
limbic lobe (the latin *limbus* means 'hem' or 'border'). All of it is old:
see figure 4.14, and note relative constancy of size.

Now we are ready to have a look at the **limbic system**: what we might
call 'downtown brain'. Like most city centres it is densely built, seems a
bit of a clutter, is a hive of activity (although to what purpose is not
always clear), is well connected internally and to outlying parts, and has
no definite boundary. (A city will usually have many such overlapping
'centres' when you come to think of it. Like a 'centre of commerce' or
'a centre of culture' there are some places which one can agree should be
included, others with more partial or ambiguous rôles.)

Figure 4.15 is a view of the limbic area showing connections between
its components and with the nearby olfactory bulb. Such Atlas pictures
are formalised. For example the **mammillary body** is shown as a separ-

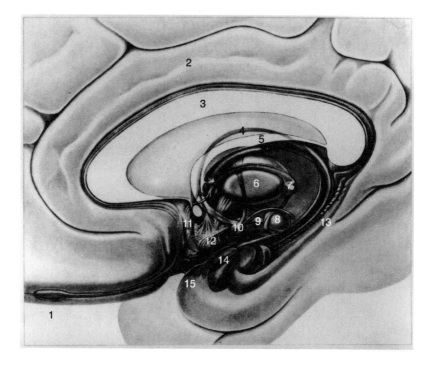

Figure 4.15. Some famous places in 'downtown brain'.

1 Olfactory bulb	9 Medial forebrain bundle
2 Cingulate gyrus	10 Mammillary body
3 Corpus callosum	11 Septum
4 Stria terminalis	12 Fibres from amygdala
5 Fornix	13 Dentate gyrus
6 Thalamus	14 Amygdala
7 Habenula	15 Prepiriform cortex
8 Red nucleus	

From Nieuwenhuys *et al.* (1988).

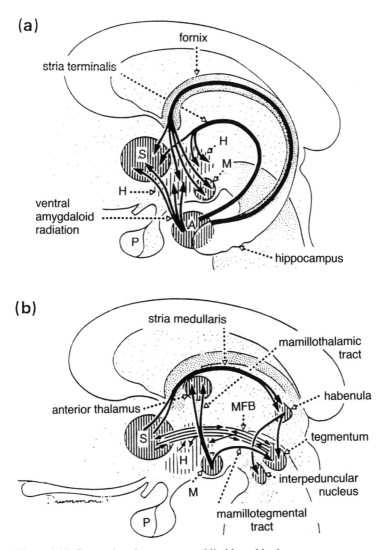

Figure 4.16. Connections between central limbic and brain stem components. (a) An oblique cut, (b) vertical, nearly mid–plane as in figure 4.5. H, hypo-thalamus; S, septum; M, mammillary body; A, amygdala; P, pituitary; MFB, medial forebrain bundle.

From McGeer et al. (1978).

ated ball, but is in fact a pair of swellings on the underside of the hypothalamus. Figure 4.16a is still more formalised and simplified, but shows
the directions of some of the neuronal connections. For example, the
fornix is the main output pathway from the hippocampus, which is to
say that it consists largely of axons whose cell bodies are in the hippocampus. Outputs from the amygdala are also emphasised here, as well as
inputs to the septum, and the hypothalamus and its mammillary body.
Figure 4.16b concentrates on other connections, for example to a part of
the thalamus and to cell masses in the brain stem. Figure 4.17, still more

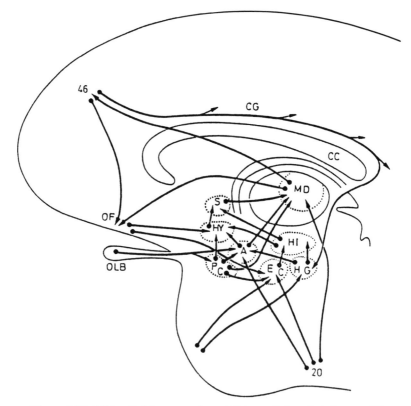

Figure 4.17. Wider limbic connections. MD, mediodorsal thalamus; OF,
orbital surface of the prefrontal cortex; HI, hippocampus; S, septum; CC,
corpus callosum; EC, entorhinal cortex; A, amygdala; CG, cingulate gyrus;
OLB, olfactory bulb; PC, piriform cortex; HG, hippocampal gyrus; HY,
hypothalamus; 46 and 20 are Brodmann areas.
From Eccles, J. C. *Evolution of the Brain*, © 1989 Routledge.

schematic, indicates how another part of the thalamus is tied into the central circuitry. It also shows connections with the cortex. Some of these are routed via the cingulate gyrus; others are direct connections to outlying districts in the frontal and temporal lobes.

There is by no means general agreement as to what the limbic system should include, or indeed whether it is a useful idea at all[15]. Part cortex (the limbic lobe) part diencephalon (areas of the thalamus and hypothalamus), part brain stem, perhaps the main justification for bringing together such diverse components and regarding them as constituting a system is that in the brain they *are* together, they are brought together by the way in which the brain develops and they are strongly connected.

In 1937 James Papez had suggested that a cyclic pathway of connections – from the mammillary body of the hypothalamus to part of the thalamus, from there to the cingulate gyrus of the cortex, then to the hippocampus and back to the mammillary body – was an integrating circuitry through which *emotions* could have their effects. The details have changed and the Papez circuit now seems too simple[16]. But the idea that somehow it is in 'downtown brain' that emotions are regulated has some good evidence in support, as we shall see in the next chapter.

Notes

[1] Evolutionary innovations need not always be peripheral in the literal sense. But Darwin's broad principle remains that further modifications through evolution seem to be easiest in those parts of an organism's structure that have most recently been modified (*Origin of Species*, chapter 5).

[2] Sarnat & Netsky (1981) support the nemertine worm hypothesis. A case of the early worm making the bird perhaps?

[3] Sarnat and Netsky (1981) stress the common structural organisation of all vertebrate brains with nevertheless different developments, and different associations and uses of parts, in different lines.

[4] Pons *et al* (1991); Calford (1991) on cortical re-wiring following damage. Aoki and Siekevitz (1988) describe how in the developing cortex wiring patterns are very significantly affected by experience.

[5] See quotation from Penfield (1966, p. 234) in the next chapter (on page 174).

[6] Thatcher & John (1977), p. 123; Livingston (1967).

[7] This is guesswork, but babies with no neocortex are able to do these things (reference 6).

8 Nieuwenhuys, Voogd & van Huijzen (1988).

9 Shepherd (1988) Chapter 20.

10 Thatcher & John (1977), p. 84.

11 Nauta & Feirtag (1979).

12 Nieuwenhuys, Voogd & van Huijzen (1988), p. 202.

13 Geschwind (1979), pp. 158, 164.

14 Serebriakoff (1987), p. 103.

15 For example, one distinguished neuroanatomist has recommended that 'the use of the terms 'limbic lobe" and 'limbic system" should be abandoned' (Brodal, 1981, p. 690).

16 Shepherd (1988), p. 575.

5

Correlates of consciousness

'I am sorry Mr Lippincot: you *say* you have an appalling toothache, but as no one has yet come up with a satisfactory *definition* of such subjective experiences I cannot take your statement seriously: there is nothing in there that I can see is wrong . . .' What would you make of a dentist with that sort of attitude?

I have found that when I bring up the question of consciousness in a scientific context people are apt to make a great meal out of the difficulties of defining it – often with the intention of stopping what they see as a fruitless conversation ('if you can't even say what you are talking about, well . . .'). But surely these people must be playing some sort of intellectual game. They must know what consciousness is: what you lose under anaesthetic or when deeply asleep; what you regain more or less gradually as you wake up . . .

Indeed it is difficult to find a crisp definition of consciousness, as it is difficult to find one for, say, life. If by *life* you mean life in all its detailed richness then this cannot be encompassed in a crisp definition. Yet (now) life can be understood as a product of evolution through natural selection. That provides us with a general definition, but of a kind that only became possible, because it could only make sense, after Lamarck, Darwin, Wallace and others had discovered evolution and started the lines that led to our current understanding of it.

Some such general definition of consciousness will come (at least I think so): but only after we have a similarly deep understanding of the connections between toothache and physics; between conscious experiences and the motions of molecules, or whatever it turns out to be that is critical. But all this is not to say that the phenomena of consciousness must meanwhile be regarded as outside science any more than the phenomena of life were, before Lamarck *et al*. A general definition of consciousness will be a culmination not a starting point. In the meantime, like poor Mr Lippincot, we all know well enough what conscious phenomena are. They are all of them feelings of one sort or another[1].

Consider our feelings

We may say of a mood that we are feeling bad tempered or elated or depressed ... We often describe an emotion too as a feeling: of fear, sympathy, desire, anger, determination or whatever. Indeed we do not have to be particularly emotional. We use the word 'feeling' for the direct sensory experiences of touch. The word 'sensation' is more usual when talking about other senses – say when describing the experience of a colour or a taste – but a sensation is a kind of feeling too.

Words like 'feeling' are indeed often used instead of words like 'thought', as in 'It is my feeling that ...' or 'I now feel satisfied with the argument'. Conscious thought *includes* feelings. Intellectual feelings we might call them, subtle pleasures, satisfactions, irritations, frustrations ... Some of these – feelings of dismay, of recognition, of conviction and so on – we can give names to. Others, like the feelings engendered by listening to music, may be more difficult to describe; yet all such feelings are part and parcel of conscious thought. It seems to me that it is precisely the element of feeling in conscious thought which makes it conscious. At the end of this chapter I will return to the general notion that *feeling*, broadly understood, is the essential quality of consciousness[2].

While on words, let me say what I mean by *mind*. I take it that mental activity includes both conscious and unconscious processes, that mind has a broader meaning than consciousness. I nearly go along with Minsky's 'Minds are simply what brains do'[3] – except that I would remove the deadly word 'simply' with its implication that there is nothing more to be said, and that we actually *know* what brains do.

In particular it is not good enough just to say that feelings 'are to be identified with brain processes'. As it happens, I think they are: but there are both deep and more immediate kinds of question which have to be faced. The deep questions amount to 'How on Earth could this be so?', I will leave these till the following chapters. The more immediate kind, which we come to now, are difficult enough: 'With what brain processes are feelings to be identified?'. What goes on in the brain when we are conscious in different ways?

Ways of finding out

A start was made on investigating physical correlates of consciousness long ago with the first person who saw stars when hit on the back of the head, or got drunk. Now we have much more detailed information, on effects of neurotransmitter-like drugs for example. There are also voluminous data based on effects of brain damage resulting from accidents, strokes, tumours or surgical procedures.

The discovery of 'brain waves', oscillating electrical potentials recorded by electrodes attached to the outside of the head (EEG[4]) provided an early way of assessing brain activity during waking and sleeping. More recently other such techniques have been developed. For example the brain has mechanisms for increasing the blood supply in places where it is most active. A PET[5] scan machine can detect tiny amounts of tracer substances injected into the blood stream and come up with an image of the brain showing where the blood supply is greatest. With such a machine one can almost watch someone thinking: one can see which regions become active with different kinds of mental activity. For example, the Wernicke and Broca areas 'light up' on the left side of the brain when someone starts to speak, while frontal areas especially are among those which become active while an action is being planned.

Techniques such as EEG and PET provide global information on the collective activities of groups of many millions of neurons. In stark contrast to this, electrodes have been developed which are so fine that their tips can be inserted into single cells so that the firings of individual neurons in some brain location can be monitored. These techniques are invasive, but not very: they require operations under anaesthetic for tiny electrodes and their guide tubes to be inserted. It is possible to see how an individual neuron reacts when an animal is looking at an object moving sideways, or seeing the colour blue, or planning an action . . .

The most direct sources of information on states of consciousness have come from locally anaesthetised patients who, while undergoing brain surgery for some other reason, have heroically agreed to take part in experiments of the 'what does it feel like when I stimulate this bit' kind.

Emotion

In chapter 3 we discussed the role of the hypothalamus as an intermediary between the brain and chemical control systems of the body. The hypothalamus can detect directly changes in body temperature and some changes in blood chemistry, and is at least indirectly in touch with every organ in the body. Largely through its connection with the master endocrine gland, the pituitary, it can in turn exert generalised control on the activities of organs outside the brain, especially in relation to emotions. Feelings such as fear, anger, lust . . . set our endocrine glands going, in preparation for appropriate actions. But the hypothalamus has also a more intricate rôle in emotion: in emotional responses, in organising the muscular activities required for executing 'appropriate actions'. Rather as a hen with no brain at all can run, using its spinal computer, so animals with no forebrain (cortex plus thalamus), but with the hypothalamus intact, may exhibit all the outward signs of angry attack ('sham rage') against real or imaginary adversaries[6].

Other parts of the limbic area have been associated with contrasting moods and feelings. The septum, for example, can be said to be a 'pleasure centre'. Mild electrical stimulation through small electrodes inserted into the brain in this region has repeatedly been found to give rise to pleasurable feelings, often with sexual overtones. Stimulation of the amygdala, on the other hand, tends to produce nasty feelings, although results here are less clear-cut: it seems to depend among other things on exactly which part of this complex structure is stimulated[7].

There was the case studied by R. G. Heath[8] of an epileptic who had periods of impulsive behaviour that could not be controlled by the usual kinds of treatment. This patient had electrodes inserted through his skull with their active tips located at a variety of different places in the brain. He was wired up to a set of buttons so that he could stimulate different parts of his own brain and report on what he felt. At the same time a record was kept of how often the different buttons were pressed. Some results from these experiments are shown in the table 5.1. Notice that sites at or near the central limbic area were the most effective, although in this case the hippocampus rather than the amygdala was the strongest 'aversion centre'. Notice too how little effect there was on stimulating neocortical regions.

Interestingly, the button most frequently pressed was one which you might have said was 'aversive' in that it produced feelings of anger and frustration. The patient said of pressing this button that it created a half-formed memory which he was unable to grasp. 'The frequent self-stimulations were an endeavour to bring this elusive memory into clear focus.' Enough said.

This is one of many indications that (limbic) emotional circuits and memory circuits are closely tied together[9]. (Recall the role of the hippocampus in the laying down of memories: page 145.) Perhaps this is why traumatic experiences are not easily forgotten. Then again

Table 5.1. *Data from studies of electrical self-stimulation of the brain in man*

Region stimulated	times/hour (average)	Subjective response
L. centromed. thalamus	489	Partial memory recall: anger & frustration
R. posterior septum	395	'Feel great'; sexual thoughts; elimination of 'bad' thoughts
L. caudate (fig. 4.4)	373	Cool taste; 'like it OK'
Tegmentum (fig. 4.16)	280	'Drunk feeling'; 'happy button'; elimination of 'bad' thoughts
Anterior amygdala	258	Indifferent feeling; somewhat pleasant, but feeling not intense
Posterior amygdala	224	Moderately rewarding; increase of current requested
R. hippocampus	2	Strongly aversive: 'feel sick all over'
L. paraolfactory	0.4	Moderately aversive
R. parietal cortex	0.5	
R. frontal cortex	0	No significant effect
R. occipital cortex	0	
R. temporal cortex	0	

Source: Heath (1963).

although our repository of stored memories is part of our unconscious, memories of the kind which we can recall[10] are, like our emotions, essentially to do with consciousness. To recall something is to become conscious of it, and we best remember things – perhaps only remember things in a recallable way[11] – which we consciously noticed at the time. We have indeed another kind of memory, 'habit memory', memory of acquired skills which we cannot explicitly recall and in which consciousness hardly plays a part. Interestingly, this kind does not appear to require the limbic circuitry[12].

Is the limbic system the seat of emotion and mood consciousness? The evidence goes no further than to suggest that limbic circuits may have to be active for emotions and moods to be felt or for recallable memories to be laid down. *Where* emotions are felt (if that means anything) or where memories are laid down is another matter . . .

Knowing and doing

We would like to know which parts of the brain have to be working for us to experience colours, tastes, sounds, and so on, and more generally to become consciously aware of what is going on around us. And then we would like to know what has to happen in the brain when we consciously act. As we shall see these questions are complicated by the fact that only part of our awareness, and only some of our actions, are conscious. Yet it is clear that much of the machinery is common to unconscious and conscious forms of knowing and doing: for each the sense organs are the sources of information and the muscles the means of action; and at least much of the circuitry between is common too.

Circuits of perception

Figure 5.1 is a wiring diagram showing some of the routes though which signals go from sense organs to the brain. Note the central position of the thalamus as a processor or relay station for sensory signals on their way to the neocortex; and notice too how different parts of the thalamus, specific nuclei, make two-way connections with specific areas of cortex.

Consider a commonplace action: you take and eat a chocolate from a box – and all your senses come into play. Signals set up in your eyes go for further processing to the lateral geniculate nuclei of the thalamus and then on to the primary visual cortex. Visual signals are also going to the superior colliculi from which connections are made to the 'alerting' system of the reticular formation, to areas that control eye movements, as well as to another pair of nuclei of the thalamus on its way to another area of cortex near to the primary visual area . . .

Meanwhile sounds, perhaps of rustling paper, are converted in the ear to signals that first travel to a nucleus in the medulla, then through the inferior colliculus to the *medial* geniculate nucleus of the thalamus and thence to a quite different part of the cortex, in the temporal lobe.

The smooth coolness of the chocolate is registered first in the fingers from which signals travel via the thalamus to the somatosensory strip of parietal cortex. Then yet other parts of the cortex are due to become active. Signals from taste buds in the pharynx and tongue go via their own processing stations in the medulla and thalamus to the gustatory cortex[13].

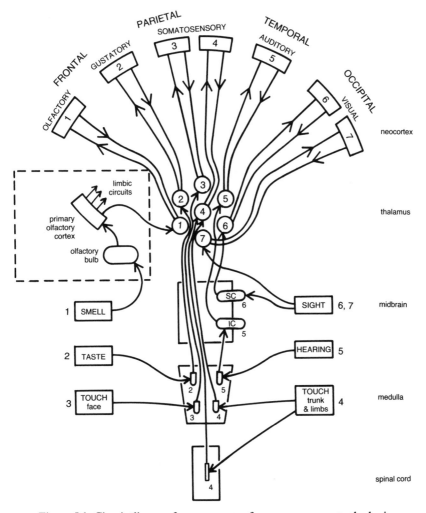

Figure 5.1. Circuit diagram for some routes from sense organs to the brain. SC, superior colliculus; IC, inferior colliculus. Small circles represent nuclei of the thalamus as follows: 1, medial dorsal; 2, medial ventral; 3, ventral posterior medial; 4, ventral posterior lateral; 5, medial geniculate; 6, pulvinar; 7, lateral geniculate.

Even if you had not noticed the slight chocolatey smell before, now that you have got the chocolate in your mouth its aromas begin strongly to influence olfactory receptors in your nose, and soon another thalamic nucleus will come into play and another neocortical area.

Here, though, the circuitry is rather different. It starts with a direct connection to the old cortex of the olfactory bulbs. These are joined to the limbic area by their stalks (see figure 4.15 on page 148) from where signals go to many places – including the thalamus and then on to frontal neocortex in an attempt, it might seem, to appear conventional after all.

Among countless things not represented in figure 5.1 is a whole sensory system of muscle tension detectors which keep the central nervous system informed, for example about where your limbs are. These were helping you to maintain the appropriate pressures to hold the chocolate without squashing it, and now that you have it in your mouth they are helping to tell you whether you have chosen a soft or hard centre, and no doubt contributing to your appreciation of the quality of chewiness to add to the taste and the aroma, and to your sense of overall enjoyment or otherwise.

Unless perhaps you are a connoisseur of chocolates you would hardly have been aware of most of the various sensations as separate. In general we seem less interested in analysis than in synthesis, in an Overall Impression (was it nice to eat?) and with Big Decisions (should I have another?).

Even if we are paying attention to details our conscious perceptions, even more our Big Decisions, seem ludicrously simple compared with all the processing that is going on in our brains at about the same time (and remember the molecular fuss involved in even one firing of one neuron . . .). Let us keep with analysis for the time being and consider now in a little more detail the best known of the sensory computing systems: vision.

Divisions of vision   A dark box with its iris diaphragm and lens near the front forming moving, upside-down images of the surroundings on its retina at the back: the eye has obvious resemblances to a camera. The retina, even, is a film. It is about a tenth of a millimetre thick, and transparent through most of its thickness with a backing of light-sensitive rod and cone cells (figure 5.2). This film, though, is most unlike a photographic film. It is connected to the brain – rather, it is *part* of the brain, and it thinks, in its way. The signals that our two retinae send through the optic nerves and on by their main routing via the lateral geniculate

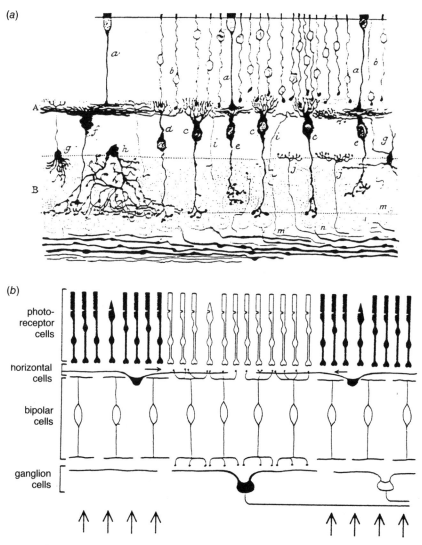

(a)

(b)

photo-
receptor
cells

horizontal
cells

bipolar
cells

ganglion
cells

Figure 5.2. (a) Semi-schematic drawing by Ramón y Cajal of neurons in a mammalian retina based on microscope observations using the Golgi staining technique, which picks out and stains completely only a few cells (cf. figure 3.7). (b) A more formal diagram of this computer. The central network of cells are joined both vertically and horizontally. These, as well as the mass of fibres from the output or ganglion cells, all lie *in front* of the light-sensitive input cells, the rods and cones.

Part (a) from Ramón y Cajal (1909–11/1972); (b) from Masland. The functional architecture of the retina. Copyright © (1986) by Scientific American, Inc. All rights reserved.

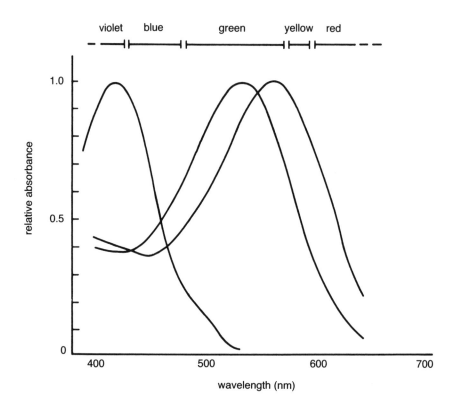

Figure 5.3. Absorption of light by three kinds of human cone pigments.
From Mollon (1989), *Journal of Experimental Biology* **146**. © The Company
of Biologists Limited.

nuclei of the thalamus (figure 5.3) have been processed and re-processed
by the time they reach the primary visual cortex.

The optic nerve has about a million fibres in it, not nearly enough for
each of more than 100 million rods and cones in a retina to have a direct
through line to the rest of the brain. The fibres that make up the optic
nerve are the axons of less numerous classes of neurons at the front of the
retinal film, called ganglion cells, separated from the rods and cones by a
rich computer network of small and richly varied neurons[14].

The rods and cones respond simply to light. They do not in any sense
'see'. Even the cones have no knowledge of colour although they are the
primary instruments of colour perception. There are three kinds of cones
with different sensitivities to photons of different wavelengths. They are

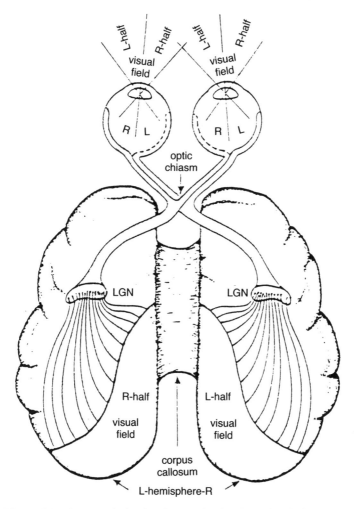

Figure 5.4. Diagram of visual pathways showing how signals from the left and right halves of the visual field go from each eye, via the lateral geniculate nuclei of the thalamus (LGN), to the right and left visual cortex, respectively.

From Popper & Eccles (1977).

often said to respond to red, green and blue light, but this is a loose way of talking. They cannot individually discriminate colours. Each kind responds to a wide band of wavelengths (which peak at about 560, 530 and 420 nm) and these sensitivity bands overlap strongly (figure 5.3)[15]. A 'red' cone, for example, would be unable to distinguish a weak red light from a stronger stimulus that was off its peak (say in the yellow or green region of the spectrum). To recognise a colour our eye–brain has to *calculate*, to compare the signals from several adjacent cones of the different types. Computations of this sort are essential to all forms of perception and several kinds of them have already started in the 0.1 mm of retinal brain that lies between the cones and the layer of ganglion cells. In fact it is a subclass of rather small ganglion cells which are part of a relatively slow but high-resolution computing system which deals, among other things, with colour.

Another subclass of (larger) ganglion cells have little interest in colour. They are the output neurons of another computing system which again works by comparing inputs from the light-sensitive cells: both the rods and the cones this time. This second system is less sharp-sighted because it pools inputs from somewhat wider patches of retina, but it is faster and tuned especially to detect tonal contrasts and rapidly changing intensities, the kind of information required for the perception of edges and movement.

The partly processed signals are then sent along the optic nerves from each eye and reach a junction box, the optic chiasma, where the fibres are re-organised. As you can see in figure 5.4 those from the right-hand side of *each* retina go to the right lateral geniculate nucleus of the thalamus (LGN for short) which in turn is connected to the right primary visual cortex: likewise those fibres coming from the left halves of the retinae inform the left LGN and cortex. The rule that the left side of the cortex deals with the right side of the body is not consistently adhered to in the neck and face, but in an important sense the eyes keep to it, because the lens inverts the retinal image. What you *see* to the left is processed by your right visual cortex and *vice versa*.

Figure 5.5 shows some of the more detailed circuitry. The computations which had started in the retina are taken further in the LGN. This has a six-layered sandwich structure. The top four layers to which the smaller ganglion cells of the retinae are connected are described as parvocellular (they too have smaller cells). The bottom two (magnocellular) layers receive their inputs from the larger retinal ganglion cells. The two main computing streams (named the parvo and magno pathways) are now more distinctly separated.

Another kind of separation is maintained also, since the inputs from corresponding parts of the two eyes arrive at different layers of the sand-

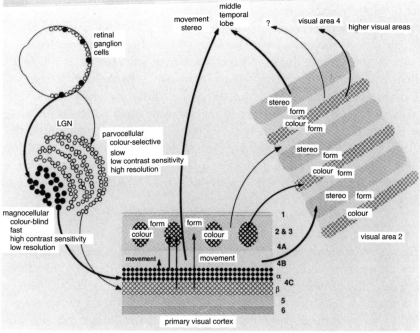

Figure 5.5. Diagram showing how different parts of the brain deal with different aspects of vision (see text).
Reprinted with permission from Livingstone & Hubel, *Science* **240**: 740–9.
© 1988 American Association for the Advancement of Science.

wich. For example the left side of the retina from the left eye connects with layer two (magno) and layers three & five (parvo) of the left LGN; while the left side of the retina of the right eye connects with cells in layer one (magno) and layers four & and six (parvo) of the same LGN.

All six layers retain a spatial correspondence with the retinae: points that are close together on the retina connect with points that are close together within each of the layers. Furthermore all six of these 'maps' lie in exact register on top of each other.

The LGN on each side is connected to its primary visual cortex (Brodmann area 17, p. 139) by a great 'radiation' or fan of fibres within the cerebral white matter (figure 5.4). Magno and parvo fibres arrive at separate lower levels within the thickness of the grey matter sheet of the primary visual cortex (figure 5.5). Their signals are further and separately processed between there and the upper levels of the sheet. Indeed a subdivision of the parvo system now becomes evident: there are clusters of cells, 'blobs', located dominantly within the upper cortical layers and which specialise more particularly in colour. From these upper layers signals pass to the second visual area nearby, in Brodmann area 18.

Recall that each of the LGNs receives signals from both eyes but keeps them in separate layers. This separation of signals from the different eyes is maintained in the primary cortex, but in different areas rather than different layers. Any small area of the primary visual cortex is found to be connected to a part of the retina of one eye, but move over a little and all the connections may suddenly change to a corresponding part of the other eye. In fact the whole surface of the primary visual cortex has a pattern of interdigitating 'left' and 'right' narrow stripey zones, which can be made visible with suitable techniques[16].

There is a somewhat similar transformation from layering to zoning between the first and second visual areas, this time in the way in which the magno and both of the parvo computing pathways are kept separate in a rather more complex system of zones of three different kinds 'thick stripes', 'thin stripes' and 'interstripes' (see again figure 5.5).

Figure 5.6 serves to summarise and extend the progress of the magno and parvo computing pathways which you will see do not end in visual area 2 but extend eventually to areas in the temporal and parietal lobes. And it goes on: studies of monkey brains have indicated that there are numerous distinct cortical areas (at a recent count upward of twenty[17]) *each* of which contains a representation or 'map' of the retinal image.

Discussing this splitting and divergence of the visual computing pathways, Margaret Livingstone and David Hubel[18] comment that 'The response properties of cells at levels beyond area 2 suggest that the segregation of functions begun at the earliest levels is perpetuated at the highest levels so far studied. Indeed the segregation seems to become more and more pronounced at each successive level, so that subdivisions that are interdigitated in visual areas 1 and 2 become segregated into entirely separate areas at still higher levels'.

To have different subsystems computing different aspects of vision is understandable enough. The analysis of forms, colours, movement, etc. are different tasks which you might expect would call for specialised cell types and circuitry. And we can understand too why different levels of analysis might also call for specialised equipment and be carried out in different places. What is not at all clear is how, or whether, the computing streams finally come together to give an integrated 'picture'. The retinal Humpty Dumpty is in pieces it seems. Where are the King's horses?

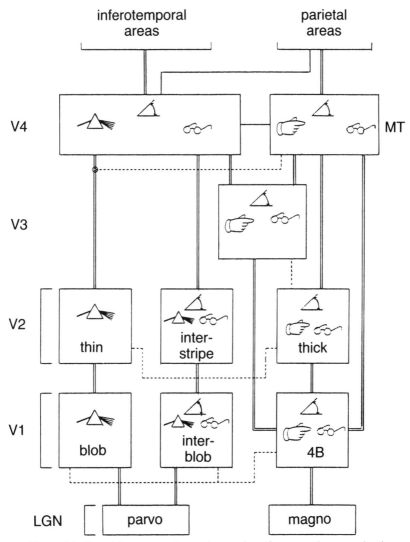

Figure 5.6. Pictorial representation and extension of parvo and magno visual pathways showing places with many cells responding selectively to colour (prisms), orientation (angle), direction (hand) or binocular disparity (depth cues – spectacles). Compare figure 5.5 and text. V1–V4, visual cortex areas; MT, middle temporal lobe; 4B, one of the more central layers of V1; LGN, lateral geniculate nucleus.

From DeYoe & Van Essen (1987).

The lower temporal lobe has seemed a plausible *place* for putting Humpty together. Mishkin & Appenzeller, noting that individual neurons here would react to a number of kinds of visual stimuli, have suggested that this may be where the main streams of visual information about an object finally converge[19]. There is other evidence that temporal regions are concerned with higher functions to do with recognition and interpretation, for example 'the bump for recognising faces' referred to in the last chapter. Wilder Penfield called one temporal area the interpretive cortex[20]. He had found that electrical stimulation here of locally anaesthetised patients often produced a sudden 'interpretation' of a present experience: of seeming familiar, or strange, or of things coming nearer or receding and so on.

So there must be something in the idea that there are 'higher centres' in the cortex (recall also the Broca and Wernicke speech areas), yet Hubel has his doubts as to whether the visual computing pathways ever really converge on any – or would have to: 'we sometimes wonder if it is necessary to suppose that they get together at all. Could they not just be parallel and independent and not have any final common pathway?'[21]

Output

Rather as the primary visual cortex is not a final destination, but a fairly early stage in the processing of visual information, so the motor strip has turned out to be a fairly *late* stage in the processing of signals required to move appropriate muscles.

Asking 'Where in the neocortex do sensory inputs end up?' we got the answer 'all over the place'. Well, it is *from* all over the place, it seems, that signals for action originate; in particular from all over the place in the neocortex.

So let us start from there. Figure 5.7 is another wiring diagram along the lines of figure 5.1, this time showing something of the output circuitry of the brain. At the top we have again a symbolic neocortex. From there is a fan of downward arrows to indicate that the neocortex as a whole informs the striatum. (Recall that this structure lies at the base of the neocortex. It is close to and somewhat above the thalamus.) Receiving signals from all parts of the neocortex, the position of the striatum for motor control has some analogy to that of the thalamus in sensory perception: the thalamus sends signals to all parts of the neocortex. But the connections between thalamus and cortex are much more strongly back

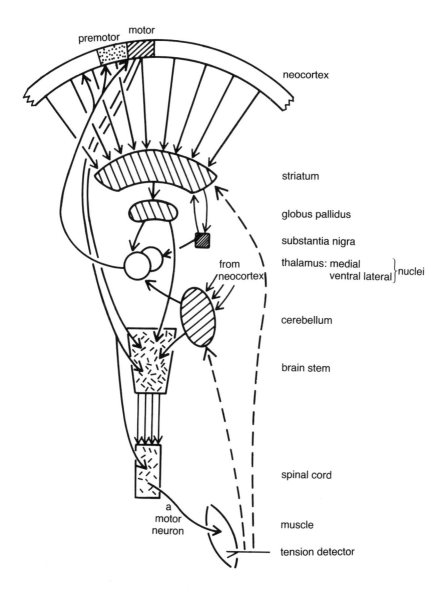

premotor motor

neocortex

striatum

globus pallidus

substantia nigra

thalamus: medial
ventral lateral ⎱nuclei

from
neocortex

cerebellum

brain stem

spinal cord

a
motor
neuron

muscle

tension detector

Figure 5.7. Some routes from thought to action (see text).

and forth between specific parts of each, while the striatum receives signals from the cortex but funnels most of its output through a smaller companion structure, the globus pallidus[22]. From here signals pass to the lateral ventral nucleus of the thalamus (just in case you were beginning to think that it was all going to be too simple). This nucleus also has inputs from muscle tension detectors and from that great repository of unconsciously learned high level skills, the cerebellum. Other signals go straight to the reticular formation . . .

Now from the lateral ventral nucleus signals go to the motor cortex and other frontal lobe areas. One of these, the premotor cortex, is an area just in front of the motor strip and has been found to be one of the first places to become notably active during the *planning* stage of a movement.

John Kalaska and Donald Crammond found that it took about 0.07 seconds after the presentation of a 'reaching target' to a macaques monkey for cells in this region to begin to respond[23]. About 0.04 seconds later the first primary motor cells are responding too, and there follows a build up of activity in both these populations of cells until, big moment, the arm starts to move to grasp the banana (or whatever). This happens about 0.3 seconds after the initial presentation by which time about 85% of the cells in each region are as active as they are going to be.

As indicated in figure 5.7, there is another somewhat parallel control circuit from the cortex generally through the cerebellum rather than 'the basal ganglia' (striatum, globus pallidus and substantia nigra).

A small proportion of the masses of axons emerging from the motor strip are directly connected to final output neurons, **motor neurons** in the spinal cord. (We have a mere 3 million or so of these, with their cell bodies in the spinal cord, medulla and midbrain, and they are the only neurons in direct axon contact with muscles which may be arm's length or more away.) But most of the fibres from the primary motor cortex connect with motor neurons only indirectly, *via* brain stem and spinal cord nuclei, as indicated in figure 5.7.

Also indicated in the picture are the muscle tension detectors which keep earlier stages in the system informed about what is actually happening so that readjustments can be made: there are upward connections to the cerebellum and striatum. The cortex is apparently involved in such feedback too. In the reaching experiments just referred to the appropriate region of the primary somatosensory ('body sensing') strip of cortex comes into play about 0.04 seconds after cells in the corresponding region of the adjacent motor strip.

There are a dozen or more cortical regions known to become active in different parts of the brain in preparation for what we might consider to be a simple action such as reaching out. These regions have specialised functions up to a point: *more* cells in a particular area may respond in a particular way. For example one group may respond particularly when an arm is to be moved to the left, another where the intention is to push something away rather than grasp it; but in each case similarly responding cells may be found, if more sparsely, elsewhere.

To Hubel's question of whether sensory pathways ever have to come together there is a corresponding question here. Are the sources of action ever together, or are they too somehow 'parallel and independent'?

Decentralised control

Highly devolved control systems are certainly feasible. Rodney Brooks has a laboratory at MIT for making and studying the behaviour of robot 'insects' which can pick their way over rough ground (on their six legs), will stalk infrared sources such as people, and do other creepy things[24]. Their behaviour calls for several quite sophisticated control systems, but Brooks and his colleagues have found that in many ways the simpler and more independent these are the better. Independent computing streams from sensors to effectors can each 'learn' to optimise their own performance and in doing that the overall performance of the beast. And then further such systems can be added on to improve or extend performance . . . This sort of loose collaboration of competences can indeed give a powerful impression of purposeful action.

Actually *E. coli* is a bit like this if you remember. Why does an *E. coli* avoid noxious substances? Because it has a class of nasty substance receptors in its outer membrane which are connected through a chemical computing stream to effectors: its flagella. One can imagine this as having evolved as a kind of add-on system to begin with. With no *means* of central planning and no forethought the process of natural selection can only hit on new systems in some such piecemeal fashion, and although these may subsequently become more highly integrated any creature can be described to some extent as 'a loose collaboration of competences'. Such a design approach is indeed deeply built in. The genetic theory says that an organism is the result of a collaboration of genes, and although in highly evolved organisms (which are the only ones still around) this collaboration is deeply interwoven there remains a certain independence of gene action. After all genes can be swapped around – *are* swapped around in the process of sexual reproduction. This does not speak of a totally integrated and centralised kind of organisation.

But what of the brain?

The question remains: Are the systems that control our behaviour decentralised? The answer here is likely to be yes and no. *Yes*, because, well, that is what biology is like. Yes again because of the evidence from the visual pathways, motor control systems etc. *No*, because there are at least some higher-level centres, and *no* again from introspection because our two-eyed view of the world appears to us as a single stereoscopic view; because our field of vision has no kind of line down the middle of it; because colour, tone, form, movement are barely perceived as separate; more generally because our multisensory experience of the world has a certain unity if only because it is so much *simpler* than the frantic computing which underlies it.

And our decisions to act seem to have to be simple and single-minded to be effective. These may be more or less 'one bit' (should I/shouldn't I) affairs – again in amazing contrast to the underlying neuronal activity.

We may be being deceived but the conscious part of our mind has all the appearance of a high-level controller concerned with Overall Impressions and Big Decisions.

Two extreme ways of trying to deal with the problem of conscious integration – the 'binding problem' as it is often called – can be labelled as the purely psychological (the conscious mind is essentially of a piece) and the purely physiological (the integration of consciousness comes entirely from the connectedness of neurons). Many have taken an intermediate position. An eminent example here was Sir Charles Sherrington, a founder of the modern practical physiological approach to the mind – brain problem. Sherrington maintained that *some* integration takes place 'in the mind', insisting for example that this must be so in the fusion of images to give one perceived stereoscopic image[25].

Another Nobel prize-winning neurophysiologist, Sir John Eccles, has developed, with Sir Karl Popper, a view of mind and matter as existing in separate but interacting worlds[26]. Yet a third, Roger Sperry, underwent a kind of mid-career conversion to the view that consciousness was after all to be taken into account in explaining behaviour[27]. He has recently summarised his position:

In the revised mind-brain model consciousness becomes an integral working component in brain function, an autonomous phenomenon in its own right, not reducible to electrochemical mechanisms.

He goes on to say that

Although the neuro-electro-chemical mechanisms sustain and help determine any given course of action, the choice of action is determined largely at higher levels by conscious mental events[28].

Gestalt physiology

The centres will not hold   Doubts about the adequacy of 'higher centres' to explain conscious integration were touched on in the previous section. Yes, there are 'association areas' in the cortex and within them more specialised centres, but we cannot go on and on saying that there must be a centre for every association the brain is evidently capable of. There would not be enough brain space. For example Broca's place seems in some sense to contain the rules of grammar, and might even have centres within it for implementing different such rules. But, whatever it is, Broca's place is not just a gigantic phrase book with a separate location for every conceivable sentence. Broca's area must be a generalised processor, and this must be true for all 'association centres'. At higher levels of integration, where permutations of possibilities become astronomical, what is called for are increasingly general processors. And these can hardly be small places – 'centres' – when one considers the variety of inputs with which they must be able to deal. For what seems to be the highest level of all, correlating with 'conscious integration', should we not expect to find just one *big* place? Some people think so.

Looking for a big place to think

If physiological integration is what is needed to account for the unity of consciousness then what is needed for *that* is that components are somehow connected, not that they are necessarily close to each other[29]. Recalling all that fantastic mass of wiring which largely constitutes the white matter of the brain, especially in the cerebral hemispheres, and which make connections more or less directly from everywhere to everywhere, there may not seem to be much of a problem. The neurobiologist Gerald Edelman, pointing to this massive connectivity, has suggested that consciousness correlates most closely with 'reentrant signalling', with messages passing to and fro and in looping circuits between distant components, connecting different maps and representations in different parts of the brain, and in that way maintaining a unity between them[30].

Penfield's quest Wilder Penfield had always been interested in which parts of the brain did what, and in particular with which parts were necessary for consciousness. From his experience as a brain surgeon with literally hundreds of patients he says:

> Consciousness continues, regardless of what area of cerebral cortex is removed. On the other hand consciousness is inevitably lost when the function of the higher brain stem (diencephalon) is interrupted by injury, pressure, disease, or local epileptic discharge[31].

Penfield's experiments on patients under local anaesthesia had nevertheless provided evidence that the cortex was implicated in specific experiences: stimulation of parts of the temporal lobe would often create vivid 'flashbacks' so that a patient would almost feel that he or she were re-experiencing some long-forgotten event. On the other hand again it was clear that under normal conditions the orchestration of consciousness was from below, from the region of the thalamus rather than from adjacent areas of cortex. (A cortical area might have all its adjacent connections severed and yet still function, presumably through its back and forth connections with the thalamus.)

In his 1966 review, quoted above, Penfield goes on to say:

> ... it is clear that within the diencephalon there is a system of nerve fibers and gray matter that communicates directly with the functional units of the two hemispheres. It is on the action of this system that the existence of consciousness depends. By means of it, the action of cortical mechanisms is started and stopped.

However, he warns that

> ... to suggest that such a block of brain exists where consciousness is located, would be to call back Descartes and to offer him a substitute for the pineal gland as the seat of the soul.

Well, I am not so sure about this last bit. I think maybe Penfield *did* discover something rather like the seat of the soul – although a big place, actually most of the brain. Let us hear from two more gestalt physiologists.

The act of perception

Walter Freeman has long wanted to find something else than 'the neuron doctrine' in order to see beyond the earliest stages of sensory processing[32]. As an experimental physiologist he has been studying particularly the sense of smell in rabbits. By using EEG techniques he has been able to sample the simultaneous activities of numerous adjacent populations of neurons in the olfactory bulb. Such studies have led Freeman to the view that only the actions of millions of neurons can possibly correlate with a perception proper and he has been developing, recently with Christine Skarda, a general theory of perception which mixes a gestalt physiology with the modern mathematical theory of chaos[33]: mental states are rather like states of the weather, they are global properties which can change from one sort to another sort in ways that are predictable up to a point but . . .

Here is a passage from Freeman & Skarda:

> Our studies of the behaviour of single neurons in respect to the tens and hundreds of thousands of their neighbours indicates that researchers have been searching for neural 'information' at the wrong level. While the activity of single cells appears to be largely unpredictable and noisy, the mass of cells cooperates to produce a coherent pattern that can be reliably related with a particular stimulus. In studies of the olfactory systems of small mammals the results are unequivocal: the information expressed by neurons that is related with the behaviour of animals exists in the cooperative activity in many millions of neurons and not in the favored few. In the first stage of the system where odor discrimination takes place, the olfactory bulb, there is no evidence that the signalling by the bulb to the rest of the brain is by any small number of neurons unique for each odor. On the contrary, for every discriminable odor *every* neuron in the bulb participates. We conclude that it is incorrect to say that the behavioural information exists in the activity of single neurons: it

cannot be observed there. This information exists in patterns of activity that are distributed concomitantly and continuously over tens and hundreds of millions of neurons.[34]

A critical element of the theory is that perception is not driven by stimuli coming into the brain from sense organs; rather these stimuli modulate, or tend to switch between different chaotic states of an activity which is incessantly going on anyway (the 'ever-fluctuating activity of masses of nerve cells that start talking and never stop'). Nor can most actions be in any sense automatic lever-responses to stimuli: the chaotic element of the intermediate circuitry puts paid to that. Here is another passage from the same paper:

> What experimentalists have failed to note is the essential fact that in the typical experiment it is the animal that is controlling their behav-iours: researchers spend, or should have spent, small fortunes on the care, feeding and housing of their subjects: they tailor the equipment and tasks to the capabilities of the species; familiarise and train them, and then sit waiting for them to deign to stop eating, licking, groom-ing, or just looking around long enough for the experimenter to get in a conditioned stimulus for a controlled trial; all this can go on for weeks. What is lost in all this is the fact that these animals are con-tinually producing behaviours from within by anticipating external stimuli to guide and pace their actions. These behaviors express internally generated activity of the nervous system and are not deter-ministic responses to stimuli.

Being in two minds

There are a few people walking about who have had their corpus callosum cut right through, thus severing the direct connection between the left and right hemispheres of their brain. These operations were first carried out on in the 1960s as a treatment for severe epilepsy[35]. As you might imagine there are side effects of 'splitting the brain' like this, but they seemed surprisingly slight at first. It was a decade before the more interesting and profound effects were noticed – particularly from experiments by Sperry and his students at the California Institute of Technology[36].

In one kind of experiment the subject would be put in front of a screen and asked to look straight ahead. Images of objects were then flashed on the screen either to the right or to the left, but so briefly that there would have been no time for the subject's eyes to swivel round so as to bring the image into central view. In this way the images were presented so that those appearing on the left of the screen would be processed exclusively by the right half of the brain and *vice versa*. If the subject was asked about what he saw he would report accurately about images which had appeared on the right but deny all knowledge of those which had appeared on the left. (I am assuming here that speech centres are in the left cortex as is usually, although not invariably, so.)

Now we might interpret this by saying that only those visual images being processed by the left cortex could be 'converted to words' because that is where the Wernicke and Broca areas are. But there was more to it than this. It was not just a matter of the patient being unable to find a word to describe an image: the patient seemed unaware that there was anything to describe. What was happening to the signals going to the right hemisphere?

Well, the right brain may not be able to speak, but it has other forms of communication available to it. When these were made use of it turned out that the right brain was, after all, aware of what was going on on *its* side of the fence. If for example a patient was given a collection of real objects which she could only feel and was asked to pick out with the left hand the one which corresponded to an image (or a simple written word) appearing to the left of the screen she was able to do so.

Such experiments gave an uncanny impression that there were in some sense *two* people in a split brain, only one of whom could speak. The dumb, left-handed 'right brain person' could evidently read simple words, and turned out indeed to be more adept at some things than its twin: at global understanding and spatial awareness, for example. This person was more of an artist, it seemed, than the rather dominant and logical loud-mouth, the 'left brain person', with whom of course the experimenter found it easier to communicate.

This impression of there being two people was particularly vivid in cases where Castor and Pollux were in conflict: for example in experiments in which the right-hand (obeying *its* signals) would undo the work of the left-hand. Such things would sometimes happen in non-experimental circumstances. Sperry describes one such case:

... the left hand after just helping to tie the belt of the patient's robe, might go ahead on its own to untie the completed knot, whereupon the right hand would have to supervene again to retie it. The patient and his wife used to refer to the 'sinister left hand' that sometimes tried to push the wife away aggressively at the same time that the hemisphere of the right hand was trying to get her to come and help him with something[37].

Are there really two streams of consciousness in such people, as Sperry maintained? For that matter, are all of us perhaps cerebral twins? It has now become a well-known idea that even with our brains intact our left and right hemispheres have distinctly different talents. On the other hand we feel like one person, and in spite of the above example so, usually, do 'split brain' patients.

They get along quite well most of the time. How do they do it? Partly by using other channels outside the brain. Usually the eyes move so that each side can see what the other is seeing, the 'right person' can hear what the 'left person' is saying, and they can communicate by touch ... Then again the corpus callosum, although the most direct, is only one of the internal means of collaboration between Castor and Pollux. Within the brain there are other white matter connections via the thalamus and the brain stem. As might be expected from this, states of wakefulness, emotions and moods seem to be similar for each of the twins. Perhaps we should be saying that only high-level consciousness is split into two streams. Indeed perhaps the distinction between two streams of consciousness in collaboration on the one hand, and a single stream on the other, becomes too fine to have any more meaning than separate streams in a somewhat turbulent river ... Such questions have been well discussed[38].

Having it both ways

Like most people, perhaps, my preference is for a piece of the middle ground. I think that our consciousness is highly but not completely integrated, and that it is more integrated at some times than others. Consciousness seems to be most integrated when we are paying attention: concentrating, as the popular usage so aptly puts it. (Maybe we are inclined to exaggerate the unity of consciousness because as we consider these difficult matters we have to concentrate. . .)

On the other hand, to take a common example, think about driving a car while working the windscreen washer, listening to music on the radio, holding a conversation, *and* eating a chocolate. It may not be good driving, but such is by no means an impossible combination of activities. My impression, for what it is worth, is that in such circumstances (when nothing very taxing is required of us) our consciousness spreads out a bit, that we can indeed be conscious, if only weakly, of more than one thing – and not just by flicking continually between one thing and another, although of course we do that too . . .[39]

Or consider looking at a painting. We might concentrate on the high-light of an apple in the old woman's basket: and we can flick about from one such tiny item to another if we want to. But we can also, without even shifting our eyes, expand our awareness to take in the whole compo-sition. When we do *that* we are surely 'conscious of more than one thing at a time' even if we may not be *so* conscious of individual things. For more complex situations where many senses are in play we can similarly not only shift the camera of our attention but zoom in and zoom out as well[40].

The rôle of consciousness

We have arrived at a picture of the brain as a densely connected network of neurons, a massively parallel processor able to do a million things at once. We can already understand quite a lot of what it does in physiological and molecular terms: and what lies ahead seems daunt-ing rather than deeply mysterious – until, that is, we come to the question of consciousness. Yet even here, as we have seen, we are getting a glimpse of which parts of the brain have to be up and working for conscious experiences to be felt. Then again, even although we do not yet have much understanding of how on Earth it works, we are beginning to see what it is *for* in control system terms: con-sciousness (or if you prefer the conscious aspect of the neural com-puter's activities) seems to act as (or along with) a somewhat indepen-dent low-capacity serial computer.

I stress it *seems* to act like this, but does such a picture make sense at all? Well, yes. Philip Johnson-Laird[41] points out that parallel processors need a supervisory serial system to prevent them from getting bogged down, not knowing what to do next as it were. I am haunted by the vision of that split brain patient endlessly tying and untying the cord of his dressing gown: that is the kind of defect that a parallel processor without supervisory control is prone to. He may not have to do much, but ultimately there should be one boss, in one mind about how to proceed (certainly not in a million minds).

Baars Broadcasting   Bernard Baars has been developing a theory of consciousness based on everyday considerations of what consciousness is for, where and how it operates, how its competences differ from those of unconscious neuronal processors[42]. For all its limited capacity the strong point of consciousness is that it has access to a vast store of data and unconscious computing power – in present multisensory inputs, memories, inbuilt and acquired skills and so on.

Baars suggests that what is required in the brain to make sense of consciousness is some kind of 'global workspace'. As he puts it

> an information exchange that allows specialised unconscious processors in the nervous system to interact with each other . . . analogous to a blackboard in a classroom, or to a television broadcasting station in a human community[43].

Given mechanisms for gaining access to this 'big place', this might account both for the huge variety of possible conscious experiences, and for the relative simplicity of any actual experience at any one instant. Baars gives a simple explanation of why we can only really concentrate on one thing at a time:

> There may be powerful advantages for a global broadcasting ability that allows access from *any* component of the nervous system to *all other* components. A truly global message, if it is to be available to any part of the nervous system, must come only one at a time, because there is only one 'whole system' at any moment to receive the message. Thus vertebrates perhaps evolved a nervous system with two operating modes: a parallel (unconscious) mode and a serial (conscious and limited capacity) mode[44].

The 'whole system' Baars has in mind is similar to Penfield's: a combination of the reticular formation, the thalamus, and fibres between the thalamus and the cortex.

Time and motion

Maybe it is a good idea anyway, but one reason why our computer would *have* to be able to work in 'a parallel mode' is because nerve impulses travel so painfully slowly. A fast myelinated axon can transmit a signal at somewhat over 100 metres a second. This may be ten times as fast as a sprinter, but it is nothing compared with an electronic computer where signal speeds approach that of light – they are about 3 million times as fast.

It takes about 0.03 seconds for you to jerk your finger away from a hot object under spinal reflex: for the heat sensors in your finger to be activated, for the message to pass to the spinal cord and then through one synapse back to arm muscles, and then for the muscles to contract. Reactions which involve the brain, such as putting your foot on the brake in an emergency, take a bit longer as you would expect. But still we do such practised things before we consciously know what we are doing. The monkey reaching for his expected banana took about 0.3 seconds to react, and this is typical. Human subjects faced with a simple if–then decision (e.g. if Y appears on the screen press the left button . . .) took between 0.5 and 0.8 seconds to react appropriately[39].

There are indications that an act which *requires* conscious thought in its execution (as opposed to, say, an absent minded or automatic trained response) takes even longer, perhaps as much as 2 seconds.

There are three time periods to be considered. First we have to become (unconsciously or consciously) aware of what is going on; then we have (unconsciously or consciously) to decide what to do; then we have (unconsciously or consciously) to do it. In the conscious mode each of these stages might take years for some people in some circumstances, but let us consider the fastest possible conscious response. First, how long does it take to become consciously aware of anything?

Libet's experiments It is very difficult to time within fractions of a second just when someone becomes consciously aware of a stimulus. By the time the subject is able to move a muscle to tell you about it the awareness is already some indefinite time in the past. The neurosurgeon Benjamin Libet's approach to this problem was to compare the times at which different stimuli were felt.

Libet and his colleagues performed experiments on (yet more) willing patients undergoing surgery (and who by all accounts seem to have been as fascinated as anyone by the research)[45]. It was known that a continuing stimulation of part of the somatosensory cortex caused a sensation in the corresponding part on the opposite side of the body, say a hand; but Libet found that no sensation would be reported unless the stimulation had been going for some minimum period, generally between 0.2 and 0.5 seconds depending on the intensity of the stimulation. From this it was clear that whatever neural processes were needed to generate the sensation they took at least, say, 0.5 seconds to get their act together. I stress that this was not just a question of it taking time to feel something, like the delayed pain of a stubbed toe: there would be *no* sensation, not even a delayed sensation, unless the stimulation had been kept up for the minimum time. This minimum period could be assessed (in a series of trials with different stimulation periods) simply by asking the subject if he had felt anything or not. The minimum period was then used as a standard against which the times of other subjective sensations were compared: in this case by asking which of two sensations had been felt first.

Suppose a weak train of cortical stimulation known to take 0.5 seconds to be effective was started at time zero: then at 0.2 seconds a single short stimulus was applied to the skin of the hand opposite to that in which the cortical sensations would be felt. In such experiments patients would say that they had felt the skin stimulation *first*. From this it seemed reasonable to conclude that it took 0.3 seconds *or less* for the skin sensation to register. In fact from many such experiments with different timings it appeared that patients' subjective impression of when the skin stimulation had occurred was very close to when it had actually occurred. It seemed to take hardly *any* time for a conscious sensation to be produced by skin stimulation, stimulation through the normal channels, as it were. This, however, is only part of the story.

In earlier experiments the skin stimulation had been applied on the *same* hand as the cortical stimulation was being felt. Under these circumstances the cortical stimulation would often block the skin sensation. There was nothing odd about this: cortical stimulation often interferes with normal function in this sort of way. What seemed very odd indeed was that a cortical train of stimulation could block a skin sensation even although it had only started a few tenths of a second after the skin stimulation had been applied, – and *after* it would normally have been felt.

Libet's own interpretation of this curious effect is, first, that the neuronal activity required for a skin sensation to be felt indeed takes a few tenths of a second, perhaps as much as half a second, during which time it may be blocked; but that, second, the actual sensation is subjectively referred back to the earlier time[45]. More precisely this time is that at which the first neural signals were arriving in the cortex from the stimulated skin. (Their journey via spinal cord and thalamus would take only about 0.01 to 0.02 seconds.)

Is it true, as Libet seems to be saying, that a time sequence in consciousness need not correspond in detail to the march of neuronal events which supposedly underlie it? This would seem to imply a distinct dissociation between consciousness, where one can seemingly jump back in time, and the brain where presumably there is no such licence. Indeed Popper and Eccles use Libet's results in arguing for the idea that mind and matter have distinct domains of existence[46]. But there are less radical interpretations.

For example the philosopher Patricia Churchland has suggested that the effect of a subsequent cortical stimulation might be to erase the memory of a skin stimulation which had actually been felt at the time[47]. Then again the neurophysiologist Ian Glynn has suggested more recently[48] that there may be a substantial 'latent period' an additional half second or so, before the cortical stimulation is felt, and that on this assumption, and that there is a similar latency for the skin sensation too, the relation between the subjective timing of the two events can be maintained without needing to bring in 'retroactive blocking'[49]. This seems a good idea to me, but the question is still being hotly debated[50].

The ping-pong problem   The mathematician Roger Penrose toyed with a similar idea, that perhaps our internal clock runs half a second slow, so that when we perceive *anything* it is always this much after the event[51]. But he rejected this notion – because, among other things, it would be impossible to play ping-pong or carry on an interesting conversation with such time delays in conscious perception.

Indeed it was not only the apparent delays in perception which led Penrose to this rejection. Conscious decisions to act seem to take even longer than perceptions do to register: they take a second or more. EEG experiments by H. H. Kornhuber and others had suggested this[52]. In a typical experiment of this type a subject has electrodes attached to suitable points on the outside of his head and is asked to perform a simple act – say flexing a finger – at will and at any moment he likes. The EEG traces gave a clear indication of specific brain activity preceding the moment at which the action was made, by as much as 1.5 seconds.

I can not help suspecting that such a boring decision might come slower than decisions made in the thick of a game of ping-pong, but, discounting the decision time entirely, even half a second is a long time in ping-pong.

For Penrose the time delays of consciousness make no sense in terms of our usual intuitions about time:

> ... I think that it is possible that a very different conception may be required when we try to place conscious perceptions into a conventionally time-ordered framework[53].

Maybe so. Certainly something spooky is going on between the molecules of the brain and the contents of consciousness, but in this chapter I have been trying to see how far we can go without such seismic changes of view as Penrose is hinting at in this passage, and it seems to me that the ping-pong problem is not enough to demand such a change.

It comes back to the question of how and how much our consciousness plays a part in our moment-by-moment activities. If silicon-based unconscious computers can play chess I do not see why our neural unconscious computer cannot play ping-pong, pretty well all on its own with some guidance, on a timescale of a second or two, from its lazy supervisor (if we can put it that way). Looking at the expressions on the faces of ping-pong players only confirms my suspicion that they are largely 'on automatic pilot' as the saying goes. Of course a player will tell you that her winning stroke was intended and conscious, and it probably was in a sense: *intended* in the sense that it was a rational product of highly intelligent and flexible neural computing, and *conscious* in the sense that the player became quickly alive to what she had done.

As for animated conversations, a sentence usually takes a few seconds to say, and a concise sentence cannot be understood in less since it takes more or less the whole of it to convey the meaning. (For a long-winded sentence we have all too much time anyway.) Then again, in speaking, we do not choose our words consciously, one by one, any more than we understand them that way; nor does any new idea that a sentence may occasionally contain sink in within fractions of a second – at least not in my experience as either teacher or student.

The stuff of consciousness

I said at the start of this chapter that for me the word that comes nearest to the essence of consciousness is *feeling*[1]. Admittedly this word has to be used in a stretched version to include (at least) moods, emotions and sensations, as well as intellectual feelings, both named and unnamed . . . You can be forgiven for wondering if a word as stretched as this is of any use. I think it is because of what it still excludes.

For example it excludes *thought* as essential because there are unconscious forms of thought. Indeed most of the time we operate intuitively, making judgements and arriving at conclusions without quite knowing why. If unexpectedly challenged: 'What makes you say that?' we may respond with something like 'Um well I suppose I was thinking that er . . .' to win some time to uncover the thought processes which had really been going on – or to invent some new ones. Most of us are also familiar with occasions in which the solution to some problem comes to us, fully formed, after a period when we have been consciously thinking about something else. It has become part of my own writing routine to start work before breakfast (before even shaving) so that I can harvest the night's solutions to little problems which I had seen but not quite solved the day before: it then seems to me that I had been putting two and two together while I was asleep.

Some people conclude from this sort of thing that we must have another quasi-consciousness, an 'unconscious mind', that is more than just a collection of neural computers: perhaps a split-off piece of our consciousness of which the Main Consciousness is never aware. But as you will have gathered by now my inclination is to go the other way and to say that most of our intelligence is in our unconscious processors, that is to say in pieces of machinery which are understandable, if not yet fully understood, in terms of – well, molecular biology and computing.

Conscious and unconscious thinking are similar enough in their outputs for it to seem that they are somehow different versions of the same thing, presumably using at least some of the same neural equipment. So are the brain processes behind conscious and unconscious actions (applied thinking if you like): the consciously performed actions of the beginner are a stumbling version of the more unconscious actions of the skilled performer. Conscious and unconscious forms blend into each other: thinking, whether pure or applied, may be *more* or *less* conscious. There is no hard line. A conscious thought is, to put it crudely, an unconscious process plus feeling: sometimes more feeling, sometimes less.

It might sometimes be true to say that the more strongly we feel the more conscious we are. For emotional or sensual experiences we might say this, perhaps in listening to the soupier sorts of romantic music where we get carried away. But intensity is not the real issue for *thought* (or listening to Bach). Here it is not so much the intensity as the intricacy of the involvement of the feelings that makes our thinking more conscious or less conscious.

Consider this: 'As soon as she came into the room she had this horrible feeling that something was wrong: Herbert would never leave his umbrella on the chair like that.' Particularly in a crisis we may feel that something is wrong, and that it is sinister, before we seem to have figured out why or how[54]. Our unconscious brain must have figured it out all on its own and communicated its conclusion as a feeling. This would be an example of unconscious thought *followed* by a (gut) feeling. Now what I am suggesting is that we might regard all conscious thought as similar, except that usually the unconscious brain processes are running concomitantly and in a kind of intricate counterpoint with complex, intellectual feelings changing from moment to moment.

Now think about *awareness*. Awareness feelings – perceptual feelings – come in different sorts. The more immediate ones we describe as sensations (colours, smells and so on). But there are also higher-level sensations or feelings: a sense of movement, a sense of distance, a sense of space, a sense of coherence and so on. These we may call 'interpretive feelings', following Penfield, who found that such feelings would suddenly appear on stimulation of parts of the temporal lobe, what Penfield called the interpretive cortex[55]. At higher levels of interpretation such feelings (recognition, dismay . . .) blend into the intellectual feelings, and perceptual feelings generally can have a certain complexity of structure which puts them closer to the feelings of pure thought than those of emotion or mood.

I know that many people take awareness to be a synonym for consciousness[56], but I do not think this is quite right. As with thought there are both conscious and unconscious forms of awareness. Our normal awareness of what is around us is largely, perhaps mainly, unconscious. You may not be consciously aware of the visible contents of a familiar room, but you are aware alright. Just see what happens if that picture over the mantelpiece (which maybe you have not consciously looked at for years) is missing one morning. Then again we have to be aware of all kinds of detailed things in performing a skilled task such as riding a bicycle but not consciously aware: once we have mastered such a skill we are left with a general feel for it, but our awareness about details, and our detailed actions, become almost entirely unconscious[57].

As discussed at the end of the previous section, *volitions* are not necessarily conscious either. Even conscious intentions to act have preludes of unconscious mental activity, and decisive actions are often taken without conscious intervention. All of this is not to say that volitional feelings – yearnings, desires, urges, itches . . . – are not part of our Greater Control System, that such feelings do not matter, that they can have no physical effects. We will be coming back to all this in the next chapter.

That feelings are sometimes there and sometimes not shows us at once that states of consciousness are not simply to be identified with brain processes. It would only be in some brain processes, or more strictly some aspects of some brain processes that we might one day be able to say 'See the way this is happening in his brain rather than that? Well *this* is the process which is to be identified with what if feels like to be eating one of Aunt Elsie's delicious if slightly underdone pancakes looking out of her bay window on a summer afternoon: *that* is what it feels like to be cycling fast down the hill between Glenkens and Portshee'.

Whatever these Ultimate Correlates turn out to be we know that they must be quite complicated. They must come in many forms: they must in this sense hold quite a lot of information. And yet they are not as complicated, nor are nearly so many things going on at once as there are in the 'wires and switches' bit of the computer which we may think we more or less understand.

The gestalt physiological theories discussed in this chapter seem to be on the right road. Yet the elusive Ultimate Correlate cannot really be anything we understand in terms of current models of molecular biology and computing: the more we can account for the functions of consciousness in these terms the less comprehensible the phenomenon of consciousness becomes, because the less reason there is for ever feeling anything. (If feelings evolved they must be *for* something, as we will be discussing in the next chapter.)

In saying all this I am not trying to say that the forms of consciousness are beyond science, only that the present models of neuroscience are inadequate, that there is more to matter than is represented by them. Neuroscience picked up these models from molecular biology, which got them from chemistry and physics. Somewhere along the line the warning label fell off:

Caution!
These models are based on a theory
which nobody understands

Perhaps the easiest way of emphasising that feeling really is the crux problem is to think about machines that mimic brain functions but are made out of materials other than proteins, lipids, etc. and are designed quite differently. If we can mimic a function in that way then perhaps we understand it. Well, we can make computers that can solve problems, that mimic unconscious thought; we can make burglar alarms that can be unconsciously aware; no doubt Brooks's MIT lab is working on artificial insects that can play ping-pong. But machines that feel?

There are only brains, like that great city of molecules behind your eyes. It can make feelings, you know that. And if we believe it was a product of evolution through natural selection, and that it is a molecular mechanism like everything else in biology, then if we really knew all that molecules can do we should surely be able at least to outline the design of a feeling machine that was made of materials other than 'the molecules of life'[58]. After all, these molecules were not selected in the first place with an eye to their future use as components of conscious mechanisms. They were molecules which some very early microscopic form of life happened to hit on, molecules which were suited to *its* requirements and which then became fixed in to provide the basis of all molecular engineering from then. Few new small molecules were even added to the basic types when it came to making brains – a few modified amino acids as neurotransmitters, a fancy lipid here and there . . .

And then again at the level of the cell the machine that makes our conscious experiences was cobbled together out of only somewhat modified eukaryotic cells. All this does not speak of consciousness as a phenomenon that can only be created in one particular way.

So, yes, it should be possible to make a machine that feels, and almost certainly with other than 'biological' components.

Hands up who knows how.

Notes

[1]   No doubt 'feelings' is not wholly satisfactory as a single word to try to express concisely the contents of conscious experience. James (1890/1983, pp. 185–6) discusses this problem and various terms philosophers have used. Certainly 'thought' hardly covers toothache: 'sensations' are too tied to the senses; 'perceptions' are now known to be complex processes; 'state of consciousness' is too global to cover an itch, and is anyway cumbersome; and so on. James decided on making do with 'feeling' or 'thought'. Descartes, with his 'I think therefore I am', seemed to be

preferring the latter. Humphrey (1992) would say 'I feel therefore I am'. I go along with that. Even intelligent thought can be unconscious and to a large extent similar to computer activity: it is only conscious thought which is the deep puzzle and (I am suggesting) it is precisely the elements of feeling in conscious thought which makes it conscious. That 'purer' feelings like toothache have underlying brain processes is no particular difficulty: one can say that a toothache – the actual pain of it – is part of a more complex phenomenon which, like a thought, has unconscious and conscious elements or aspects, and that it is only the conscious elements or aspects to which the word feeling should be applied. Similarly when one talks of a 'gut feeling' it is only the feeling that is in the consciousness, not all the deep reasons for it. In sum, then, by the word 'feeling' I mean 'an item or element of conscious experience' and I am asserting that conscious experience consists of nothing else than feelings thus broadly defined.

2 Some people talk of 'unconscous feelings' but you will see that my use of terms makes this a straight contradiction.

3 Minsky (1988), p. 287.

4 EEG = Electroencephalogram.

5 PET = Positron emission tomography. This and other similar techniques for 'watching people think' are described by Raichle (1994).

6 Shepherd (1988), p. 572.

7 Eccles (1989), p. 102.

8 Heath (1963), p. 574.

9 See Mishkin & Appenzeller (1987), p. 70, on 'mixing memory and desire'.

10 What Ryle (1949) called 'declarative memory'.

11 See Baars (1988), p. 351, on the debate about whether you have to be conscious to remember in this way.

12 Mishkin & Appenzeller (1987) suggest that the striatum is the critical brain structure.

13 The primary gustatory cortex is situated deep within the lateral sulcus: see Rolls (1989) on taste pathways and other brain places involved.

14 Masland (1986).

15 Mollon (1989). See also Mollon (1992) on variant pigments in man.

16 Constantine–Paton & Law (1982) on maps and stripes in the brain.

17 Edelman (1989), p. 70.

18 Livingstone & Hubel (1988).

19 Mishkin & Appenzeller (1987).

20 Penfield (1959).

[21] Hubel (1988).

[22] Hoover & Strick (1993); Graybiel *et al.* (1994).

[23] Kalaska & Crammond (1992).

[24] Wallich (1991).

[25] Sherrington (1940), chapter 9.

[26] Popper & Eccles (1977); Eccles (1987).

[27] Sperry (1975, 1976, 1983).

[28] Sperry (1987).

[29] The philosopher Lockwood (1989) comments that it is arguably 'a kind of superstition to think that substantial spatial separation is inconsistent with phenomenal unity'.

[30] Edelman (1989), chapters 4 and 7.

[31] Penfield (1966).

[32] Freeman (1975, 1991).

[33] Gleick (1988).

[34] Freeman & Skarda (1991).

[35] Gregory (1987).

[36] Sperry (1966); Gazzaniga (1967); Gregory (1987).

[37] Sperry (1966), p. 304.

[38] For example by Nagel (1979), chapter 11; MacKay (1987); Lockwood (1989), chapter 6.

[39] See Pashler (1993): apparently it is not in perceiving or doing, but in thinking, that there is the bottle-neck preventing us from doing and acting on more than one thing at a time.

[40] McCrone (1990) discusses awareness in terms of foreground or background awareness, or focal and peripheral: pp. 138ff. and 225.

[41] Johnson-Laird (1983, chapter 16; 1987).

[42] Baars (1988).

[43] *ibid*, p. 74.

[44] *ibid*, p. 350.

[45] Libet *et al.* (1979).

[46] Popper & Eccles (1977).

[47] Churchland (1981).

[48] Glynn (1990).

[49] Churchland (1981) pointed out that much depends on an assumption that the minimum time needed for continuous cortical stimulation to be able generate a sensation is the actual time at which the sensation would be

felt. It might be longer, as Libet *et al.* (1979) had made clear, although there was no positive evidence that it was longer (Libet, 1991).

[50] Libet (1991); Glynn (1991).

[51] Penrose (1989), pp. 439–47, discusses time delays of consciousness.

[52] Deecke, Grötzinger & Kornhuber (1976).

[53] Penrose (1989), p. 443.

[54] Anthony Trollope makes a similar point: 'But yet her mind was intent on the letter, and she had already augered ill from the handwriting and even from the word of the address. Had Lady Lufton intended to be propitious, she would have directed her letter to Miss Robarts, without the Christian name; so at least argued Lucy, – quite unconsciously, as one does argue in such matters. One forms half the conclusions of one's life without any distinct knowledge that the premises have even passed through one's mind.' *Framley Parsonage*, chapter 35.

[55] Penfield (1959, 1966).

[56] Some go further and say that *self*-awareness is the essence of consciousness. Humphrey (1983, 1987) goes further still and says that the purpose of *that* is that we can thus understand the behaviour of others. This may very well be part of the explanation for the biological success of consciousness, and why perhaps in man it is developed particularly (supposing it is). But it is not the use, it is the nature of consciousness that fascinates me. How does it connect with physics and chemistry, how do feelings connect?

[57] Subliminal perception, 'perception without awareness', is a well-established phenomenon. It strongly suggests that 'the brain processes underlying conscious experience differ from those that mediate between incoming signals and outgoing responses' (Dixon, 1987).

[58] People often say that you could never know if a machine had feelings, but when they say this they are usually assuming that feelings do not actually *do* anything. If they do (and I will be arguing in the next chapter that they must), if feelings can have physical effects, and we understand how; and if we have designed and made our machine so that it will only work if it has feelings as part of its mode of operation, then of course we would know if the feelings had not after all switched on. Other problems there would be: What exactly were the feelings like? (Even here, though, we might have a good idea if we knew in detail how feelings were made by brains.) Much more serious would be ethical problems. But of course the point being made in the text is that we have no deep understanding about how feelings are made.

6

Dreaming aware

Even before that critical point when the eyes actually open for the first time each day there are figments of consciousness, little puddles and pools of it, images and thoughts flittering about (Mr Henderson is in the sitting room wearing purple galoshes . . .); changing slowly from dreaming asleep to dreaming awake, still mainly aimless wonderings, but beginning to connect up now with reality; going from dreaming awake to dreaming aware.

Do we then wake up? No, no, when we are 'dreaming aware' we are well awake. When we start to do things, rolling over to look at the clock, getting up to open the curtains and see what the weather is like, we indeed move on to higher levels of wakefulness. But it is all still dreaming aware. Our waking thoughts make more sense than our crazy fragmented dreaming thoughts; and no doubt perceptions, the feel of the curtains, the look of the sky, are still better connected with reality. But the process of waking shows us each morning that there are no sharp distinctions to be made between dreams and other forms of our conscious being.

Dreams are evidently manufactured. (I have not met Mr Henderson for twenty years, and I have never seen a pair of purple galoshes.) Yet for all their higher-level absurdities our dreams are usually manufactured out of sensible enough parts including those 'elements of consciousness', feelings and sensations.

But then feelings and sensations must somehow be manufactured too, and not only in dreams. There is no more reason to believe that the sensation of purple is 'out there' especially attached to purple objects than that any other such elements of conscious experience are thus simply 'out there', whether in dreaming or imagining, or remembering – or perceiving.

Arguments for the indirectness of our experience of the world go back at least to Plato. What we now know of the events that lead to perception seems to clinch the matter. All our sense organs generate trains of action potentials travelling to the brain along the vast numbers of axons in sensory nerves, arriving in the brain city whose entire population is in incessant chatter[1]. Those signals that come in along the nerves from the eyes produce visual sensations, from the ears aural sensations, from the tongue, tastes and tactile sensations . . . They are the same sorts of trains of impulses in each case. The difference is in where they arrive and in what the brain is then induced to do. It seems inescapable: the brain manufactures the feelings and sensations of the structured inner world of our consciousness. It makes the smell of onions, it makes the blueness of a sky, it makes a sense of space, of wonder, of recognition, of enthusiasm . . .

Now should we say that our sleeping dreams are half-baked imaginings? Not quite, we can more or less control *imaginings*: but our dreams are thrust upon us. Dreams are more akin to hallucinations. They are half-baked perceptions. A dreaming brain is, I think, practising parts of its main activity of building a perceptual world.

A model in the head

To say all this is nearly but not quite to say that we dream up the external world. To be 'dreaming aware' is to be connecting up conscious experiences with the structure of our surroundings – and at several levels. At a basic level we can say that objects of the same perceived colour[2] probably have something in common in the external world, in the way they interact with light. At higher levels there are no doubt more detailed correspondences between the complex orderings of feelings and the existence of Things in the mysterious world out there. In our waking life our feelings are organised, it seems, in ways that correspond to aspects of the organisation of the 'real' world: there is an abstract structure which corresponds.

So our inner perceptual world can be thought of as a kind of representation or model, similar to the models used in science (see the final section of chapter 1). A scientific model is a kind of hypothesis, and Richard Gregory has suggested that there is a close analogy between our actual moment by moment perceptions and scientific hypotheses; that we are all the time forming such hypotheses in order to make sense of what we see[3]. The idea gains vivid support from ambiguous images such as a skeletal cube which, as you stare at it, switches about between seeming to have one orientation or another. It very much looks as if we have in our brains hypothesis-generating mechanisms which keep on putting up suggestions – 'what about this way? OK then, what about that?' – with also a choosing mechanism, which in the case of ambiguous images can never quite come to a clear decision. The mechanisms for putting up the hypotheses are evidently unconscious, and the choosing mechanisms seem to be too, or at least mainly, since it is usually difficult or impossible consciously to determine which of two interpretations of an ambiguous image to fix on.

Another well known example in support of the perceptual hypothesis idea is the curious behaviour of the moon when it is low down in the sky. It looks bigger than usual. This seems to be because the unconscious brain has figured out that anything near the horizon is probably far away and so will look smaller than it really is, and so needs a bit of perceptual magnification to compensate . . . Well, that does not work for the moon, which is not an ordinary object. We have no means of getting a proper sense of its distance. Again we are helpless; we know that it is absurd but our consciously perceived moon just is bigger when near the horizon. Notice that it is quite a high-level hypothesis that generates the moon illusion: it is based on considerable knowledge of the way the world (usually) is.

It seems clear that particular perceptual hypotheses cannot, as it were, be thought up from scratch; there simply would not be time. When a putting-up mechanism says 'How about this?' there must be some limited set of alternatives to choose from, presumably derived from general rules about what is likely. That is to say, not only do we form new superficial hypotheses all the time, but I think there must be underlying layers of increasingly general hypotheses too. It is this whole caboosh which we might say is our perceptual world. Such a coherent set of models would then indeed be remarkably like the corpus of science with its small day-to-day concerns on the one hand ('How is it that these three spots don't match up?') generating particular superficial hypotheses, and the increasingly general ideas on or within which these are formulated.

Sensible hallucination Imagine you have just arrived at a party and are being shown into the main room. Within seconds you feel yourself to be well aware of the general situation: you are in a room full of people – friends, acquaintances, strangers, – tables, chairs, walls, pictures, and so on. Already you are wondering where the drinks are, whom to talk to, whom to try and avoid . . .

Yet how much of all this did you really take in, in those first few seconds of your view from near the door? Not much, yet at once you were in a real room. Of course you largely dreamt it up. You had neither the time nor the opportunity to check out that the room was not some sort of stage set or hoax, that the tall balding man gazing out the window was not made of wire and papier mâché, that . . .

Usually, 99.99% of what we see does not have to be double checked. Normally we need only a few critical cues to activate appropriate parts of our inner model. It seems that since birth we have been building up a set of expectations which is more than a mere catalogue of remembered instances: we have been building upon a basic perceptual model which we inherited.

Suppose that instead of going to that party you had decided that it would be more interesting to take part in an experiment in which you were deprived of sensory cues, floating in a dark silent tepid tank of water . . . You would then most likely have started to hallucinate wildly[4]. As it was you went to the party and hallucinated *sensibly*. We do it all the time. We *make* our perceptions from moment to moment, keeping them on the rails by having our eyes and/or other perceptual channels open, or at least ajar[5].

Craik's model   It was Kenneth Craik who in the early 1940s first introduced the idea that the brain might contain a model of the world. By this he meant 'a physical working model which works in the same way as the process it parallels'[6]. It was the heyday of the analogue computer and Craik thought of the brain as being like an analogue computer which represents aspects of reality in the form of, say, the positions of cog wheels or a pattern of voltages.

Craik's idea was that effective thinking has three steps to it:

(1) 'translation' of external processes into symbols
(2) arriving at other symbols by a process of reasoning, and
(3) 're-translation' of the symbols into external processes.

Any control device which converts some aspect of reality into coded signals which are then manipulated before having their effects can be said to be in the model-building business. *E. coli.*, for example, converts information about the presence of its foods, and of substances harmful to it, into chemical signals. It has an inner world of phosphorylations, methylations and so on through which it decides what to do (chapter 3). Perhaps we superciliously see this as a cutting down of reality to a very small inner representation indeed, but I would guess that an articulate *E. coli sapiens* would say that its representation was closer to reality than ours.

If a Craik model might be said to consist of, say, voltage patterns and *E. coli*'s of modifications to signal proteins, of patterns in *what* should we say that our inner model consists?

A large part of the answer will be similar to *E. coli*'s, because apart from anything else our treasury of stored memories very much looks as if it consists of diffuse patterns of chemical modifications to neurons (chapter 3). But there is also what we might call the working part of our model: the particular thoughts going on now, the things being remembered now, the things being perceived. Again, much of all this is to be explained in neuroelectrochemical terms (see most of the last chapter), but the explanations in these terms stop short at feelings. Craik's model has no place for feelings, nor does there seem to be any need for them to explain *E. coli*. So how and why did feelings ever come out of brains? How and why do we ever wake up? What is it to be consciously aware of something – to perceive something?

Let us regress a little

Francis Crick was once trying to explain why it is so hard to understand how we can ever perceive anything at all[7]. His listener could see no particular difficulty because she could imagine something like a little television set in her head. Crick then enquired: 'So who is looking at it?' – at which point, it seems, there was a general falling of scales from the eyes.

Crick was making a crucial point, yet perhaps his listener should have stuck to her guns. She had a good analogy as far as it went. The brain *is* a bit like a television set in that it uses incoming signals actively to make something quite different. And the domain of consciousness can be thought of as something like a 'big screen', as Baars and others have suggested. Of course there are all sorts of ways in which the brain is not in the least like a television set, and the analogy is admittedly misleading when it suggests that consciousness is a passive sort of 'picture', implying a viewer and conjuring up those dreadful visions of endless nested beings looking at pictures of pictures of pictures . . . But actually the alternatives 'model' or 'representation' are not much better than 'picture', since we might ask in a suitably Johnsonian tone of voice: 'Who, pray, is examining the model?' or 'Who cares about a representation?'

So we have to admit that our perceptual reconstructions of reality are in important respects *unlike* television pictures, maps, or the models of science, for all that they are similar in other respects. Yes, all of these things have features corresponding to reality through which decisions about future actions can be made, but ordinary pictures, maps, and the models of science are made to be looked at, thought about, played with: they are not *made* to do anything on their own.

The kind of model Kenneth Craik was thinking about has no place for consciousness, as I said, but at least it is active, so perhaps it can help us all the same. More precisely, a Craik model is part of a control system which is wired up to other parts which take appropriate action. An example of such a model can be found in a robot aeroplane such as a Cruise Missile which has in it a kind of map of the territory over which it is flying. It keeps on course by continually comparing what it 'sees' with its sensors with what it 'knows' from its map, and automatically makes suitable adjustments to its motors and control surfaces. *E. coli* has different interests and techniques but its control mechanisms are similar: you might say that it has knowledge of molecular good and evil built into the protein receptors in its outer membrane.

There is nothing to be feared from a regress so long as it is not infinite. At one time it seemed to some that in the fundamental control processes of life there was an infinite regress: to make one enzyme you would surely need many *more* enzymes . . . at least so it was said[8]. If enzymes were self-replicating this would formally eliminate the regress at its root, but there were no signs of this and it was difficult to see how such things as enzymes would be able to replicate.

We know now that there is a finite regress. The information in proteins derives from information in RNA molecules, which in turn acquire it from DNA molecules. This does not go on for ever because DNA molecules replicate.

It might seem a roundabout way to go but really it is very sensible. It separates two different kinds of functions. Protein can, as it were, concentrate on doing all the things that it is good at: making clever mechanisms for molecular sensing, catalysis, locomotion, etc., without having to be designed *also* to be a replicable kind of molecule as DNA is.

In a finite regress what is going on at each level changes until finally the regress is short-circuited in some way or another. *E. coli*'s perception of substances in its surroundings is like this. The causal train: external substances → binding to the outside of a membrane protein → activation of the catalytic part inside → modification of signal molecules → binding of signal molecules to flagellar motors . . . does not go on and on for ever because the motors at last *do* something. Similar although much more elaborate trains of cause and effect presumably underly our unconscious perceptions and resulting unconscious actions.

But what about conscious perception? As we saw in the last chapter there are different kinds of 'representations' of reality on the way to it; starting with neuronal signals and circuitry, all that kind of stuff, coming eventually to consciousness – another kind of stuff altogether.

Introspectively our consciousness is not just a kind of passive 'picture', anyway not when it has been properly switched on and we are up and doing. The 'picture' is only part of it, as the Cruise Missile's map is only part of *its* higher-level control system. Our consciousness has a certain unity and yet at the same time it has passive and active aspects to it: perception and volition. Anyway that is what it seems 'from the inside', and it is what is needed finally to short-circuit a regress at the level of consciousness. Consciousness must *do* something. Feelings must have effects.

Evolutionary considerations lead to this conclusion too, as William James was one of the first to realise.

James and the efficacy of consciousness

I have no doubt at all that when I go along to the shop to buy the Sunday papers my walking actions are almost all to be explained in standard neuroelectrochemical terms; but if all my actions are to be explained like this so that consciousness can always be left out of any objective discussion of how I behave then my consciousness has no actual rôle in controlling my behaviour and hence, seemingly, no biological rôle at all. This might sound OK: maybe it just is the case and I should accept it. Maybe we are all of us 'conscious automata'. A number of nineteenth-century think-ers thought so[9].

James savages the automaton theory in Chapter 5 of his great book *The Principles of Psychology* (1890). In the following passage he starts respect-fully enough, but then begins to show his hand:

> If neural action is as complicated as mind; and if in the sympathetic
> system and lower spinal cord we see what, so far as we know, is

unconscious neural action executing deeds that to all outward intent may be called intelligent; what is there to hinder us from supposing that even where we know consciousness to be there, the still more complicated neural action which we believe to be its inseparable companion is alone and of itself the real agent of whatever intelligent deeds may appear? 'As actions of a certain degree of complexity are brought about by mere mechanism, why may not actions a of a still greater degree of complexity be the result of a more refined mechanism?' The conception of reflex action is surely one of the best conquests of physiological theory; why not be radical with it? Why not say that just as the spinal cord is a machine with few reflexes, so the hemispheres are a machine with many, and that that is all the difference? The principle of continuity would press us to accept this view.

But what on this view could be the function of the consciousness itself? *Mechanical* function it would have none. The sense-organs would awaken the brain cells; these would awaken each other in a rational and orderly sequence, until the time for action came; and then the last brain-vibration would discharge downwards into the motor tracts. But this would be a quite autonomous chain of occurrences, and whatever mind went with it would be there only as an 'epiphenomenon', an inert spectator, a sort of 'foam, aura, or melody' as Mr Hodgson says, whose opposition or whose furtherance would be alike powerless over the occurrences themselves[10].

James relates how as a medical student in 1869 he had started to write an essay 'showing how almost everyone who speculated about brain-processes, illicitly interpolated into his account of them links derived from the entirely heterogeneous universe of Feeling' – but had then perceived that really the evidence was in their favour[11]. It was probably three or four years later[12] that he realised that Darwin's theory, far from imposing a purely 'mechanical' explanation on mind, provided the most powerful support yet for the efficacy of consciousness.

If God made us as a special act of creation then it might be possible to suppose that He wired us up so that we would be rewarded or punished in a way that was appropriate to our actions, even if this could have no physical consequences. But if it was natural selection that was the engineer then there must be consequences to feelings; they must have actual physical effects or there is no reason to expect that the means to produce them would have evolved.

Now I suppose one might say that feelings never had to evolve, because they are normal concomitants of many, perhaps all, physical processes (brain processes being a special class only because we happen to have access to them). So perhaps no special mechanisms had to evolve to produce feelings. But this would still not explain why feelings are appropriately produced. It would not explain why pleasures on the whole go with acts that promote our survival and pains with the opposite. Only natural selection could have contrived *that*, and if natural selection contrived anything there must have been a functional reason for it. There could be no such reason unless feelings can have physical effects. Let me try to underline this critical point with a parable.

My refrigerator and I   As I hear my refrigerator humming happily in the kitchen I wonder whether maybe it *is* happy on this spring morning. Well, actually no. But let us have a look at the idea that my fridge has sensations associated with its activities: that if we were to say, 'listen, the fridge has switched off its motor because the bimetallic strip in the thermostat has bent over far enough now to disconnect the circuit to the motor', we may indeed be giving a perfectly correct and causally adequate description of what is happening, but that we are only getting an *external* view of events. There is also perhaps an internal version: an account from the refrigerator's point of view. It too has a cause-and-effect logic, but this time based on sensations and volitions. Like our feelings, which (some say) are identical to the patterns of action potentials, etc., which govern our actions, the fridge too has feelings identical to states of *its* control machinery. It had a sense of relief when it threw that switch: the prior fridge-states (including that state of bentness of the bimetallic strip) was realised internally as a feeling of unease, anxiety or pain . . .

I take it that the above speculation is balderdash. Why? Because having seen how a refrigerator works in terms of plumbing and circuitry an emotional description is redundant. In any case it would have been of no consequence whether my poor fridge had felt relieved, irritated, queasy or bored when its motor switched off – the motor would have switched off anyway. I can see that, because I can see how it all works.

Brains are another matter. On the one hand we do not understand completely how brains work in terms of neuronal circuitry. On the other hand we know from our experience of them that pleasures and pains make causal sense. That the conscious part of our mind has distinctive uses and properties, as discussed at length in the previous chapter, suggests that the physical mechanisms underlying it are distinctive too. Unlike my fridge there is not only plumbing and circuitry in our central controller, there is a third system which we are only beginning to get to grips with.

Here is William James again:

> . . . the *distribution* of consciousness shows it to be exactly such as we might expect in an organ added for the sake of steering a nervous system grown too complex to regulate itself. The conclusion that it is useful is, after all this, quite justifiable. But, if it is useful, it must be so through its causal efficaciousness, and the automaton-theory must succumb to the theory of common-sense[13].

Matter *is the queer stuff*

Opposing James's common sense there were those who maintained that the idea that feelings can have physical effects was itself patently absurd. Along these lines Charles Mercier (1888) asks us to imagine the purely conscious *idea* of food causing the actions of eating. He says that this would require that the idea was able to alter molecular arrangements in the brain: say, for the sake of example, by preventing some molecule from decomposing into two smaller molecules. Mercier goes on:

> How is the idea of food to prevent this decomposition? Manifestly it can do so only by increasing the force which binds the molecules together. Good! Try to imagine the idea of a beef-steak binding two molecules together. It is impossible[14].

To which James replies that it is indeed hard enough to imagine but that:

> . . . since Hume's time it has been equally hard to imagine *anything* binding them together. The whole notion of 'binding' is a mystery . . .[15].

Indeed it was. Indeed it is. The modern quantum theory now gives us excellent accounts of chemical binding, but the roots of that theory are, as we touched on in chapter 1, full of paradox. James had seen the root of the trouble not in the nature of mind so much as in the nature of matter.

In trying to connect up psychology with physics and chemistry he could do little more than emphasise just how weak the prevailing matter theory was:

> ... when one asks for a 'reason', one is led so far afield, so far away from popular science and its scholasticism, as to see that even such a fact as the existence or non-existence in the universe of 'the idea of a beef-steak' may not be wholly indifferent to other facts in the same universe, and in particular may have something to do with determining the distance at which two molecules in that universe shall lie apart. If this is so, then common-sense, though the intimate nature of causality and of the connection of things in the universe lies beyond her pitifully bounded horizon, has the root and gist of the truth in her hands when she obstinately holds to it that feelings and ideas are causes[17].

Later in the chapter he comes out with a robust 'of course':

> 'If feelings are causes, of course their effects must be furtherances and checkings of internal cerebral motions . . .[18]

If Mercier (and others to this day) could so confidently assert that feelings cannot affect molecules directly or indirectly, that was, I suspect, because he thought he knew what molecules were: little hard massy immutable atoms, *à la* Newton, joined together with sticks, or something of the sort. James was not so sure: he believed that matter and mind have the the same substratum. If you believe that indeed there is a *Weltstoff* to underlie both matter and feeling then there is no reason to insist anything about how the two might interact except that they might very well do so.

James thought it to be an especially odd consequence of the automaton theory that it implied that feelings, not being able to affect brains, could not even affect each other:

> If, for example good news was the consciousness correlated with the first [nerve] movement, then joy turned out to be the correlate in consciousness of the second. But all the while the items of the nerve series were the only ones in causal continuity; the items of the consciousness series, however inwardly rational their sequence, were simply juxtaposed[19]

Feelings as separately made?   There is evidence that feelings, some feelings at least, are generated by the activity of specific brain circuits.

Recall, for example, the experiments by Heath and by Penfield described in the previous chapter (on pages 156 and 168). Pleasant and unpleasant emotive feelings, as well as interpretive feelings, can evidently be switched on by simple physical means. Then again there are the well-known effects of drugs such as LSD in triggering bizarre perceptual feelings as well as dangerously faulty interpretations of what is possible ('I felt sure I could fly . . .'). As we saw, such chemically induced feelings seem to result from interference in particular sets of brain circuits which use monoamine neurotransmitters[20].

A revealing example of this sort of thing has been discussed recently. It seems likely that there are distinct brain circuits which generate specific feelings of recognition independently of the actual recognition itself. John McCrone relates such feelings to the joyful 'aha!' sensation of seeing the solution to a problem. In some circumstances these feelings can be had independently of any just cause[21].

I still remember vividly an experience of my own some thirty years ago which has ever since made me skeptical about placing too much credence on feelings of conviction that are not backed up by anything else. Going under a general anaesthetic to have a tooth out I remember this whirling galaxy which it was obvious to me represented Knowledge and Understanding of the World, but in a curiously inverse way. As I went under, the whirling mass became smaller and smaller and as it did so I knew that I was understanding more and more about the world: and I could see that when the spiral finally shrank to nothing I would understand Everything – and that this would be precisely the moment at which I would become unconscious. Well, maybe I did understand everything at that moment but I am sorry to say I have forgotten it. I did not know it at the time, but this kind of effect of 'laughing gas' (producing nonsensical feelings of profound insight) is well known[22].

The converse of having an inappropriate feeling is not having an appropriate one. What appears to be an example of this is provided by a rare and bizarre condition known as Capgras's syndrome. The sufferer comes to believe that his family and friends have all been replaced by doubles, people who look the same but, he is convinced, are not. What seems to be happening is that the sufferer can still recognise faces, but that owing to damage of a separate pathway in his brain the normal feeling of familiarity is absent[23].

An orchestral metaphor   The dissociation of a feeling from reality brought about by physical or chemical means makes it clear that feelings, even high-level interpretive feelings, are brain-made. This tends to go against the idea that, say, the consciousness of good news must directly cause the joy that follows – at least in the full sense of one state of consciousness actually making or generating the next. It adds to the drift of the start of this chapter that we are capable of a varied but bounded set of feelings, and that these must be essentially brain-made.

Yet if we might thus say that an evolving state of consciousness is a kind of symphony of feelings played by an orchestra with a large but still limited set of physical instruments, and that much of the actual music they play is also brain-made, that is not quite to say that every nuance must be so controlled or that the timing of when different instruments come in and the sequence of the phrases they like to play is not open to some kind of control from the music itself. It would be a funny sort of music to be self-controlling in this way. We are not allowed a conductor (nor sentient players): we must say that somehow the music *is* the conductor or we are off on a regress with no obvious end.

Self-conducting music is certainly a bit odd, but if nevertheless you will allow me to stretch the metaphor a little further and be more specific we can think of two ways in which the complex of sounds at one moment might influence the sounds that came next. It might be through the music at one moment directly influencing the sounds that came next, because it reverberated and the reverberations then interacted with the subsequent sounds to alter them and then *their* reverberations . . . This would correspond to James's view that states of consciousness can directly influence succeeding states. Alternatively, or in addition, the music at one moment might influence the music at the next by reacting back on the physical instruments to alter the way they were playing, or to switch in different instruments, or different tunes and harmonies, again in a complex changing succession, but which in this case might be literally impossible to predict in detail[24].

The key argument holds

If the unfortunate sufferers from Capgras's syndrome provide one more piece of evidence in favour of the idea that feelings are made by the brain – and so perhaps cast doubt on (but by no means dispose of) James's belief that feelings must be able directly to cause other feelings – they give no succour to 'automatists'. Indeed they give added support to James's key argument that feelings are causes of physical events, causes of behaviour. These patients are seriously disabled by their condition. The 'aha!' of recognition seems to be one more kind of feeling which evidently has a function; and that there appear to be specific brain mechanisms for producing feelings of different sorts[25] adds further weight to this supposition. Natural selection would not make and maintain complex machinery to no purpose.

James's key argument can be split into two parts, in answer to the questions: (1) Why do we have feelings? and (2) Why are the qualities of feelings appropriate?

The answer James gives to (1) is, briefly, because feelings are biologically useful causes. This part of the argument does not by itself deny that we might be conscious automata of more complex kinds than James had been considering. For example, it might be that there are indeed two-way connections between feelings and the brain: that when brain subsystem A makes a feeling, F, then F automatically switches on another subsystem B somewhere else in the brain. Particularly if you think of A and B as distributed systems this might make good sense without the feeling being in any way part of an independent agent (a 'fighter for ends' as James described our conscious being). F, if it operated automatically and independently of other feelings, would simply be a channel of communication. This might very well be biologically useful and so might have evolved through natural selection. We might speculate that, even if we and other higher animals are not such automata, it was through fortuitously discovered effects of this sort that early evolving nervous systems began to incorporate the first elements of what was to become consciousness.

However, in considering the second question of why feelings are appropriate, we are forced to think about their subjective qualities. In particular there are their various forms of niceness or nastiness. Feelings can be effective, it seems, because our conscious being as agent is able to arrange things – ultimately by moving our body – to make the state of itself *nice* rather than *nasty*. (That *is* the way it works, isn't it?) This being so it seems that indeed, along the lines of our earlier discussion, our conscious being breaks a regress, as DNA breaks another, through being (in some weird way) self-controlling.

As we know, many sensations are of themselves pleasant or unpleasant, providing the simplest form of the carrot–stick motivation system. Yet even these are nice and nasty in distinctive ways: our sensory pleasures and pains come in many different forms. Why should this be so? Indeed direct perceptual sensations are often rather neutral, neither particularly nice or nasty. Likewise interpretive feelings may be pleasurable (aha!) or horrid (ugh!) or again rather neutral in themselves.

We might describe as pure perception the unemotional business of creating our moment-by-moment working model of what is going on around us, incorporating neutral feelings at different levels of interpretation. This may proceed some way before we start to think very much about what we are perceiving and decide what to do. It is only then, somewhere between the thinking and the doing, that the carrot–stick motivation system begins to have any point . . .

So I think that to make sense of feelings as a whole, we should indeed say that the general explanation for the existence of the various qualities of our feelings is that they all work as components of (part of) a model-based control system of the kind discussed earlier, the more neutral feelings having more to do with making the working model as such while the more emotive feelings have more to do with the output, active side of the model. Now a point about Craikian models generally is that they have their *own* inner workings, and that these correspond in some way to the workings of the world. Does this mean that feelings should have their own 'inner workings' – that indeed, as James says, feelings should directly influence each other?[26].

In any case our working model is not *only* 'made of feelings': it consists largely of unconscious brain processes. As I remarked in the previous chapter (page 185) even 'conscious thought' is mainly unconscious. But if feelings can be said to be a part of the model we think with, then we should consider the possibility that feelings have their own inner workings too – as in the 'reverberating music' metaphor – that feelings can affect other feelings directly, as well as indirectly via the brain. We will be coming back to this in later chapters.

We will return also to such questions as whether consciousness exists in space and time or whether it is a kind of substance or a kind of process. To spill the beans a little, a conclusion we will reach is that such questions are off the point. Remember the opening theme of this chapter. What if space, time and substance are just dreams, just elements of a inner model? The question then is not what consciousness *really* is, but how to build scientific models for it, to find examples of what consciousness is *like*. We may prefer scientific models which correspond reasonably well to our inherited one, which are framed in terms of three-dimensional space, unidirectional time, enduring substance, and so on, all related to each other in the kind of way we are familiar with. But not all scientific models are like this.

Anyway, that space, time and substance *are* just dreams is the burden of the next chapter.

Notes

1   Freeman (1991).

2   Perceived colour results from high-level calculations which take into account the surroundings (Land, 1977).

3   Gregory (1984), pp. 395–415.

4   Zangwill (1987).

5   We may falsely construct a perception under less extreme conditions, when (say) in a very dim light we mistake a cushion for the cat: perhaps for half a second we actually 'see' the cat . . .

6   Craik (1943).

7   Crick (1979). One of the founders of molecular biology is now set on solving the problem of consciousness. See also Crick & Koch (1992); Crick (1994).

8   Ravin (1977).

9   Should we give credence to the opinions of automata? There were some very distinguished ones, Thomas Henry Huxley among them. See James (1890/1983), p. 134. Glynn (1993) discusses the evolution of consciousness and 'James's unresolved problem'.

10 James (1890/1983), p. 133. James is referring to a work by S. H. Hodgson (1870) *The Theory of Practice*, vol. 1, chapter 3, section 57: Dependence of consciousness on nerve movement.

11 *Ibid.* Footnote on p. 134.

12 Richards (1987), p. 433.

13 James (1890/1983), p. 147.

14 *Ibid.*, p. 139. James is quoting from Charles Mercier's *The Nervous System and the Mind* (1888) p. 8.

15 *Ibid.*, p. 140.

16 The modern equivalents to the nineteenth-century automaton theory are any theories which allow you to ignore consciousness as a causal agent: for example, behaviourism.

17 James (1890/1983), p. 140.

[18] *Ibid.*, p. 141.

[19] *Ibid.*, p. 137.

[20] Chapter 3, page 118. To say that there are brain circuits which have to be active for certain feelings to be produced is not to say that the feelings are to be identified with this activity. The paracrine action of monoamines and neuropeptides gives scope for other things to happen than helping or hindering action potentials. We will discuss in later chapters the idea that consciousness is a physical effect linked to but distinct from the activity of the brain's axon–synapse computer.

[21] McCrone (1990).

[22] This effect of 'laughing gas' was noted more than a hundred years ago by William James (see Russell, (1946), p. 145).

[23] Whitlock (1987).

[24] Here I am thinking particularly of the role that our consciousness seems to play in calling up unconscious specialised processors in the kind of way that Baars (1988) describes, and of the essential unpredictability of many self-controlling processes Gleick (1988).

[25] Dixon (1987); see also chapter 5, Note 57.

[26] Notice that even if feelings were to influence each other directly this would not necessarily banish the conscious automaton – if the feelings not only interacted with the brain like clockwork but also caused each other like clockwork. Even the variety of kinds of feelings might conceivably be interpretable in such terms: I mean that different kinds of feelings might be like cogwheels of different shapes and sizes suited to making different connections. In the end it is only, as far as I can see, that feelings have appropriate qualities of niceness and nastiness that makes any conscious automaton view of higher animals inexplicable in evolutionary terms.

7

Space, time and substance

Space

A trapeze artist or a car driver must judge speeds and distances accurately to stay alive: not by making conscious numerical calculations, from which they can decide, say, that now is the moment to jump or now there is room to overtake, but by 'seeing' it, *feeling* it. The experienced car driver sees such things as clearly as she sees the road ahead or the clouds in the sky ... They are all part of her immediate perceptual world, her dreamt-up world, her reckoning device.

So secure is our space sense that we often construct models that convert non-spatial quantities into spatial ones. Familiar examples are graphs, histograms, pie charts. A chunky pie chart of the kind you see in the newspapers following budget day may let us see what the Chancellor has been up to more vividly than columns of figures. Such models directly represent the actual in the context of the possible.

Suppose we are drawing a graph of the water level in a reservoir over the years. We draw a vertical axis representing water levels and make a time line as the horizontal axis. In doing this we have created an abstract space, in this case a two-dimensional one. We have represented a set of possibilities as a blank area of graph paper. We are ready to insert actualities in the form of points corresponding to reservoir levels at different times.

Three-dimensional abstract spaces, able to deal with three variables, are also familiar. These may take the form of perspective drawings with three axes at right angles to each other representing, say, the time, the water level and the size of the trout population of a reservoir. A point placed within the volume of such a diagram would represent both the water level and the trout population at a given time. There are also more sophisticated kinds, but these examples are enough to illustrate that an abstract space is *an orderly representation of possibilities* to be distinguished from points or figures within it which may be used to represent actualities.

Now if you were to ask me what the difference is between spaces we invent using graph paper, etc., and the space in our heads which we suppose represents 'real space', I would say not very much. Both are inventions – except that our inner sense of space was invented in our ancestors through the processes of evolution: our feeling for space is as brain-made as our sensations of colour, of smell, or of anything else.

Consider: we can only visualise up to three (two-way) directions at right angles to each other – e.g. north–south, east–west, up–down – yet there is nothing in mathematics to correspond to this limitation.

Move a point in one direction over a short distance leaving a track, and you get a little straight line. The track of such a line moved in another direction at right angles over the same distance will give you an area: a square. A similar track of a square in a third direction at right angles is a cube. Similarly again the track of a cube in a fourth direction at right angles is a '4-hypercube' – and so on and on up to hypercubes of as many dimensions as you like. The series from point (zero dimensions) to line (one dimension) to square (two dimensions) to cube (three dimensions) ... stops there in our visual imagination, but can easily be continued in our conceptual, mathematical imagination. A 7-hypercube of edge 5 cm, for example, would have a volume (well, hypervolume) of $5^7 = 78\ 125$ cm^7. You might like to figure out how may edges and faces a 7-D hypercube has: for example, by thinking how the edges and faces multiply as you track successively in different directions [see note 1 for the answer]. We can do all that and more, yet we cannot get beyond dimension 3 in our spatial imagination any more than we can imagine a fourth primary colour. The immediate reason seems clear in each case: our brains are not made for it.

Let us pursue the colour example a little to illustrate an analogy – that colour is three-dimensional – but also to illustrate a contrast, that in the case of colour this threeness does not correspond to anything outside ourselves.

One can apparently produce any colour that any human has ever experienced with lamps of three carefully chosen primary colours, a red one, a blue one and a green one, together with a means of adjusting their individual intensities and a screen to mix their light. Colour films and television make use of this principle. The threeness here is not itself a Deep Truth of Nature but apparently arises from our eyes having only three kinds of colour receptors that are sensitive to different (although overlapping) parts of the spectrum, as discussed in chapter 5. Had we had fifteen kinds of receptors (and a brain to go with them) with each receptor assigned to different parts of the spectrum, we might be living in a richer perceptual world – although with much more expensive colour television.

So sensations of colour only *correspond*, and only more or less, to different photon energies. We can believe, perhaps, that photons are out there in the real world, but not, I think, in anything corresponding to the threeness of our colour perception. That seems to be incidental: our eye–brain might have been made otherwise.

What, then, of our sense of space? To be an effective reckoning device, it must correspond to something 'out there', and in this case a corresponding threeness seems to be out there too. Our threefold representation of space, that is, corresponds to *something* that has three similar variables to it. But to call this something *real space* seems to beg the question: I was going to say fog the issue, but the danger is rather that the issue may then seem too clear – exactly because our sense of space is so vivid to us and we would dearly like to give it a literal objective status.

So what is this something 'out there'? Well, it is a set of possibilities. An odd sort of reality you might say, but I think we should give it that status. It is a reality comparable, say, to the *possible* water levels for a reservoir, or to take an example from chemistry the vacant orbitals in an atom (page 41). At the risk of begging the question anyway we might go on to say that this *something* is a set of possible relations between objects of moderate size, our sense of space being our inner representation of this (objective) set of possibilities.

Why spatial possibilities should apparently be restricted to three dimensions *is*, it seems, a Truth of Nature. Not only can we not imagine, but it seems we cannot *have* seven-dimensional objects of moderate size. If we could, we should know it: for one thing, chemistry would be even more complicated than it is. It seems to be the case that the world, at least the world of slow-moving objects bigger than electrons and smaller than galaxies, is three-variable in some important sense, and that our brains evolved to deal with this.

Indeed the world is full of possibilities that we are aware of without having that kind of synoptic awareness that our space sense gives us. Through our space sense we become directly aware of absences, of possibilities unfulfilled, which impress themselves on us as a vivid kind of reality. It is amusing to speculate that other animals may perceive things very differently from us. (Thomas Nagel does this in a highly recommended essay 'What is it like to be a bat'[2].) I suspect that most other mammals have a much more orderly set of sensations than even wine experts have when they sniff. Perhaps a dog's are organised like our space sensations in distinct dimensions, or anyway so as to give an immediate awareness of absences. Maybe dogs get a 'synolfactic smell' rather than a 'synoptic view' of a place, to make them aware of spaces among smells. We might go into a room in a new house and say 'what a lovely lot of space': but our dog may be synolfactorily perceiving great possibilities for its being smelly in different ways.

The case of the many-dimensional cube may have helped to give some insight into the 'inventedness' of our sense of space. Other parts of mathematics can help similarly. Descartes introduced analytical geometry, which converts spatial ideas into algebra. If you open a modern advanced geometry text you will be lucky to find any pictures at all. Likewise my computer manipulates what we might be inclined to call spatial ideas using binary symbols without making any drawings. I do not know what a Cruise Missile's map is really like, but I would guess it is similar – anyway I doubt very much whether it is of the crinkly unfolding sort . . . When my computer is showing me what an object will look like from different angles it only makes the lines, areas, etc. at the last minute on its screen because it wants to be friendly and it knows my limitations. We humans like to think in pictures, at least many of us do; but when you consider that in so many contexts this is an aid to thought rather than a necessity, it is surely naïve to suppose that what we perceive as space is out there in anything much like the way we perceive it.

Traditionally, spatial aspects of things such as sizes and shapes were said to be among their primary qualities, qualities of the objects themselves, whereas colours or smells were examples of secondary qualities: in the mind.

Bishop Berkeley (1685–1753) refused to see any such distinction and put everything in the mind, going so far as to deny the very existence of matter[3]. We do not have to go quite as far as that to agree with Berkeley in his removal of the distinction between primary and secondary qualities by saying that they are all representations, they are all conversions of reality into readily thinkable forms. Immanuel Kant (1724–1804) took such an intermediate view. He saw space and time as 'pure forms of perception' to be distinguished from 'things in themselves'[4]

Kant considered different ways in which statements or judgments about the world might be true. Some judgments come from observations and they tell us something new which we could not otherwise have known for sure. Yes, the sun rose again this morning and the cornflakes had run out, but such events are not certain beforehand. Other judgments can be made without having to look at the world because they are logically necessary, they simply could not be otherwise: as two and two must equal four once you have defined your terms.

But Kant insisted that there was a third class of judgment, that there are judgments which are necessarily true and yet which are not *logically* necessary. The nature of space provided a prime example, its threeness for a start. Such is neither logically necessary in the sense of being any kind of tautology or theorem, nor, Kant said, was it a matter of incidental observation: it *was* a necessity although not a logical one. Space *had* to be like that. The discovery in the nineteenth century of alternative geometries to Euclid's has led to the rather frequent opinion that Kant was being too mysterious, that the question of which geometry our Universe conforms to is a matter of simple fact to be established by observation.

Maybe so, but there are three kinds of judgment that can be made all the same. Roughly speaking these are between facts and lies; between sense and nonsense; between the imaginable and the unimaginable. Put like this the third category no longer has the kind of necessity that Kant gave it. It is a necessity of the perceptual imagination perhaps, but this does not mean that it is even a necessity of thought: we can think in other ways about a world which has turned out not always to be imaginable. We can use mathematics. We can construct imaginable models: that is to say, if we can't imagine reality we can at least try to imagine a construction which is systematically *like* it.

We may say, then, that space is best understood as primarily a form of the mind which we are stuck with because of the way our brains evolved[5]. In that case we may hope, but should not expect, our space dream to correspond beyond the experiences of our distant ancestors to the ordering of 'things in themselves'.

Time

Time seems to most of us to be a deeper mystery than space, perhaps because the defects of our time dream are nearer the surface. Many of the difficulties are well known. You do not need the theory of relativity to be perplexed, as St Augustine was some sixteen centuries ago, by the curious status of The Present. It alone exists: the past is no longer and the future is not yet. So, St Augustine said, the present must contain the past as memories and the future as expectations. You can't put it much better than that[6]. Yet how long does this overburdened present last? It seems to have no duration itself, otherwise *it* would have a past part and a future part . . . It seems to have no thickness. Can it then be said to exist?

Then again it is often claimed that *really* we live in a four-dimensional world of space and time with past to future as one of the directions in it and with everything that has happened or will happen all laid out to be traversed. Then the present is where we happen to be on our journey through the Landscape of Events. But if you ask where it is it exactly 'we happen to be', or rather *when?*, you are likely to get the answer 'now' or 'the present', which seems to take us back to square one. (And incidentally how fast are we going – at one second per second?) And then we might ask why, if everything is laid out pat, should events bother, as someone once put it 'to go through the formality of taking place'? Perhaps they don't: another suggestion has been that perhaps our consciousness provides a kind of searchlight sweeping through the landscape of Reality picking out one scene after another in succession . . . Mmm.

As I said, such perplexities are well known. Nevertheless 'space' and 'time' are often uttered in the same breath and there indeed seems to be something similar about them[7]. Following Newton they seem to represent a kind of dual stage or setting within which objects are and events happen, defining the ways in which objects *can* be arranged and events *can* happen. But neither space nor time has the kind of objective status that Newton believed they each had. This is not because space and time are merely to do with possibilities (as I said, possibilities can be real enough), but because they fall into the category of representations: they are representations of possibilities and *that* puts them firmly into our heads.

If there had been any doubt about the problematic character of objective or 'real' space and time it should have been removed by Einstein's 1905 special theory of relativity which inexorably connects space with time in an unimaginable way, showing that what we have in our heads (which like the big moon on the horizon we cannot really do anything about) is just wrong: that is to say part of our perceptual model which does not match up.

In particular our head models of space and time do not match up with reality when dealing with objects moving at very high speeds (much, much higher than anything our ancestors ever had to deal with). All objects moving in relation to each other do not quite share the same time, but this only becomes obvious when relative speeds are very large. A favourite story runs something like this.

You imagine that your 20-year-old twin had set off on a journey by rocket to a distant star, and was due to return 60 years later. The time has passed. Now aged 80 you are waiting for the return capsule to splash down. You are wondering if Darren is going to look as old as you feel sometimes, whether perhaps his rheumatics have been playing him up ... Your reveries are disturbed. The capsule has arrived safely and out pops a sprightly 25 year old looking much as you did all those years ago. Greeting you warmly, but mistaking you for his grandparent, he remarks that the journey had been much shorter than he had expected ...

Science fiction? Yes of course. No one has actually done *that* experiment. But we know for sure that objects do indeed 'age' more slowly, for example clocks tick more slowly and unstable particles last for longer, if they are moving at high speeds[8].

So what is time? It must be a representation of possibilities, or to put it the other way round a representation of some general restriction on the way things can happen. It is the way we perceive *some* sort of 'rule of engagement'. That our time sense is part of a representation rather than of reality itself is suggested by the fact that sometimes it works but other times not. The twin paradox is a case in point: here our inner sense of what should be does not guide us to the right answer. On the other hand the idea of travelling backwards in time both seems impossible to us and (most people would say) *is*[9].

There is another kind of story to make this point. Suppose you *could* go back in time and pick your mother from her cot and bounce her once on your knee saying '*Isn't* she a pretty baby' (and then return promptly to Now). The chances are that this would sufficiently affect her developing patterns of neuronal connections (and thus alter in an increasingly unpredictable way the subsequent course of her life) as to to have a bearing on the question of which of billions of sperms eventually fertilised which egg ... Almost certainly, it seems, you would prevent your own existence[9].

So it seems that it really *is* impossible to meddle with history; that there really is *some* sort of rule of engagement here about how events can be ordered in the world. But to say that therefore time has an objective status is not to speak clearly. As with space it depends on what we mean. If we mean by time that which we experience, then it is not objective, it is just one of our dreams. If we mean that there exists a set of possible ways for things to happen of which one slightly flakey mode of representation is with our time feeling, then this is OK. It might be OK too to say that it is *as if* events are arranged (say) on a one-way street down which we all travel willy nilly; or to represent time as a line in a graph or a symbol in an equation ... But all such ways of describing time can only have *as if* status.

Can an *as if* statement be an objective truth? I do not know, but I do not see what more we can hope for in discovering the world. In any case all the statements of science are like this, as we discussed in chapter 1.

If I have read it correctly the latest news is that St Augustine was right. The past does not exist, although it can be inferred from traces in the present. Nor does the future exist except as 'expectations' in the present – probabilities – about what may happen next. As with the weather, what will happen is never completely predictable even in the short term and soon enough becomes unpredictable over the longer term. If relativity gives us an image of a 4-dimensional Landscape of Reality, quantum theory together with the theory of chaos has left us with a quite opposite picture of a world in which at every fraction of a second, as previous 'expectations' are not all quite realised, the new 'expectations' are modi-fied – and so on and on in an endless adventure with no predictable outcome.

As for that wafer-thin Present, it becomes slightly less perplexing when we have put time into our heads. Then we can decide for ourselves how long the present lasts. It is only a dream anyway[10].

Substance

Bertrand Russell (1872–1970) was the main advocate this century of the general view which we are more or less following here that mind and matter are neither of them 'the stuff of the world' but represent different ways of organising a more fundamental 'stuff'[11]. According to Russell (1927) it is *events* of some sort, not substances, which are fundamental. There are events which when arranged one way constitute matter, and when arranged another way constitute mind – and in the brain there should be events which are both. An item of perception would be for Russell an example of an event which is a part of mind and at the same time of (brain) matter.

Russell came to his denial of substance as the ultimate reality mainly from relativity, which shows us that space and time are inseparable. There is only space–time, and when you come to think about it an item in space–time must be, strictly speaking, an event. At base there are no objects made of Substances which endure By Their Very Nature, but clusters of events which hang together more or less. The discovery of the interconvertibility of matter and energy; the realisation now that the Universe evolves – that nothing lasts for ever – can all be taken in support of Russell's view. So could the emerging quantum theory of matter of which Russell was fully aware. For example, as discussed in chapter 1, while states of electrons in atoms can be likened to standing wave forms, say in a piano string, there is nothing in the atom to correspond to the string itself.

We do not have to deny the existence of an external world with matter in it provided we are careful with the word 'matter' and do not suppose that we know by direct insight what it is. It is related to the idea of *substance*. But substance is in our heads. It is another of those dreams we have, an inherited part of the model we think with.

Naturally in trying to imagine matter on a very small scale we go ahead and think of it as substance and even have an audacity (which must make poor Kolbe turn in his grave) to expect that, say, huge balls of matter joined together with great big wobbly springs *must* be a good analogy for matter on a scale that our fishy, reptilian and mammalian ancestors never had to think about. The audacity paid off amazingly well, as we saw. It was a piece of luck for molecular biology that *usually* the dream of substance only begins seriously to dissolve at levels below that of the molecule.

Perhaps it was not such good luck for the mind–body problem.

Energy and light

Nor exactly is energy the stuff of the world, in spite of $E = mc^2$.

Energy is a more 'scientific' idea than substance, a deliberate construction, a concept rather than part of our natural way of thinking. In the first place energy was a construction from vivid dreams of motion and force. Energy, we sometimes say, is what a cricket ball has when flying through the air. But then more mysteriously we may perhaps go on to say that it is what a book has more of when on the table than on the floor, or a clock spring has more of when wound up. To say that objects in high places or wound-up clock springs have 'potential energy' sounds a bit artificial. ('Hey, it's either energy or it's not: what's this *potential*,' I can hear an innocent voice crying.) And then if we go on and say that the energy of a book on the table is a kind of *substance*, well, that is really weird – which is to say, at odds with our dream. Yet there are times when the substance dream can be pressed into service to give us an understanding of energy. For example when we are talking about how there is a loss of mass when bigger atoms are built up from small ones (page 29) we may think of this in terms of substance having been lost in the form of radiation: photons pouring out.

But then the photon is just one of the latest comfortable substancy things through which we try to imagine the spooky world of physics. It is, if you like, a replacement for an earlier imagined substance, the aether, within which light was said to be an undulation. The aether was a sensible enough idea: if light really is like waves in water then surely there should be something to correspond to the water. But then it turned out that the aether seemed to have no independent existence: like phlogiston and caloric before it, the aether was just a thought.

If we like we can think of photons as being like bullets: they are countable, come in different sizes, seem to fly through space and hit things to some effect . . . But this analogy too soon falters. Remember how photons behave when passing through a pair of slits (page 35)? (Try fitting that into your dreams.) Or consider this: if your twin had travelled faster he would have aged less. Well, photons travel faster still and at precisely the speed at which they do not age at all. In this sense they do not exist 'in time'. (Try fitting *that* into your dreams.)

Remember too that the whole idea of the Universe consisting of discrete objects in time and space had become an evident approximation as soon as it was realised that objects can act on each other at a distance, when the idea of fields of force began to emerge. That was already spooky, never mind the two–slit experiment.

And it has got worse. Experiments carried out over the past few years have further eroded any confidence we might have had in a Universe of objects with definite localities. There is an optical device called a down-converter which can take a photon fired into it to make two new ones (each of half the energy), shooting them off in opposite directions (in bullet language) to different places. Yet however far they travel from each other – metres, light years – they remain 'as one': what happens to happen to one of them can simultaneously have a 'consequence' for the other[12].

In talking about the two photons produced by a single event in a down-converter it is difficult not to say that (for example) this one went over here and that one went over there having moved through space and taken a bit of time to do it. We use that kind of language to order what is going on in our heads and tell each other about it. Don't blame photons if they do not need ideas like 'place', 'trajectory', 'space', 'time' to keep their books straight. Their being *is* orderly, we know that. There are definitely restrictions on what can happen. But their rules are not, as it were, formulated in the way that our ancestors ordered the world in their heads to make sense of it. Anyway photons are not objects. Between being produced somewhere and absorbed somewhere else there is literally no saying what happens to them[13].

Yesterday I used my switch card in a shop and £10 moved from my bank account to the shop's account. I do not know how it happened, but clearly there was something well-ordered going on. What I am pretty sure did *not* happen was that ten pound coins flew through space between the banks. (*Do* photons fly through space?)

If photons are not objects, neither are electrons. You can do a 'two-slit' experiment with them too, and with neutrons, protons, *atoms* even[14]. We should not say that any of these things are really particles, little bits of *substance*. It is just that as we come to bigger and bigger things – through small molecules, big molecules and crystals, and then to matter on a large scale, that dreams of substance fit better and better. Substance is not 'that out of which matter is made' but a dream to which matter begins to approximate on a large enough scale.

The atom of happening

If the velocity of light represents one rather unexpected upper limit on how things can happen – how fast they can go – there is that other rule of engagement which we came across (page 32) in which Planck's constant places a lower limit: not on how slow things can go but on how little can happen. You cannot have less *action* than 6.63×10^{-34} – measured in joules times seconds, energy times time. If events are the stuff of the world then here are their atoms: all the same size[15].

Recall that the energy of a photon is constrained by the relationship:

$$E = h\nu$$

where ν is the frequency of the light, thought of as wave motion (say the number of times per second the wave crests pass a given point). Notice that we seem to be able to have a photon of any energy we like, provided we accept the frequency that the above equation will then insist on. Likewise the frequency is on a smooth sliding scale: you can have any frequency you like. But these sliding scales are linked in an unexpected way. Putting the equation another way, the ratio E/ν is fixed and always the same: h. So it is not energy which is 'the sandy stuff', it is energy divided by frequency[16]. A funny sort of sand.

All this was part of Planck's bomb, dating from the start of this century. By the 1920s the mystery had deepened and with it the significance of h.

The principle of indeterminacy   One of the most intriguing 'rules of engagement' in the whole of physics was discovered by Werner Heisenberg (1901–1976) around 1927. It is another of these principles which tell us that our intuitive models are wrong. In the first place it showed that some things that might have seemed possible were not.

A stream of electrons travels from the back of a television tube to the screen to make the picture. Electrons like these seem like no-nonsense little particles moving through space, and we might reasonably expect to be able to find out *precisely* the location, speed and direction of motion of a particular electron at any instant – its position and momentum – as we can do pretty well for planets or cricket balls. Perhaps we could simply shine a light in the direction of an electron and look – or rather, since we are on such a tiny scale, bounce a single photon off it and use instruments to see what had happened to the photon: we could try to find out in what direction and with what energy the photon had emerged from its encounter and use this information to deduce where the electron must have been and with what momentum it must have been moving.

Well, to cut a long story short, it turns out that although experiments like this have often been done nobody has ever devised *any* way of determining both the position and the momentum of an electron at the same time with anything like the accuracy which would be needed to follow it in the kind of way in which we can follow cricket balls.

Many thought experiments – and actual experiments – were carried out using different ideas of how to pin down positions and momenta of very small particles but it soon became clear that there were more than practical snags in the way. Like the continued failure of plausible designs for perpetual motion machines, there was a deeper significance in these failures. Heisenberg expressed it more or less like this. If we make a measurement on *any* object and manage to determine its momentum, p_x, (its component of momentum in a certain direction) with a level of uncertainty which we will call 'the p_x-uncertainty' we cannot at the same time know the position, x, of the object (in this x-direction): we cannot minimise the 'x-uncertainty' indefinitely because

> *the p_x-uncertainty times the x-uncertainty*
> *can never be less than about h.*

This is the best we can do; and for cricket balls it would be superb if we could get anywhere near such precision (because *h* is so tiny). But for more *h*-sized things like electrons it is hopeless: they simply cannot be properly located, measured, followed through space . . .

Again we have the magic *h*. Again it is in the combination of two things that the restriction lies. There is nothing in principle to stop us knowing the momentum as exactly as we like provided we abandon all hope of having the foggiest idea of where the electron is. Similarly we may have reasonably precise knowledge of position at the cost of having proportionately less ability to know the momentum.

Heisenberg's dictum is generally known as 'the uncertainty principle' but 'the principle of indeterminacy' is a better term. It is not that *really* there is a precise momentum-plus-place for tiny objects which because of this infernal principle we are prevented from finding out. Nor has it to do with technical incompetence. There is nothing to find out. It is just wrong-headed of us to suppose that what we conceive of as a tiny object *could* simultaneously have a precise momentum and place.

Now although this principle may seem to be bad news for us, restricting what we can know in terms of our usual ways of talking, it is OK for the photons, electrons, etc.[17]. It is a positively liberating principle for them, allowing them to do all sorts of secret things which are highly counter-intuitive. But I will leave these mysteries till the next chapter.

Large-scale quantum effects

With *h* so incredibly small we might have expected the bizarre 'quantum world' to be safely separate from our everyday world of space, time and substance. To be sure, we do not have to wrestle with quantum theory when playing cricket. And, as I said, even in chemistry we can imagine most of the time that atoms and molecules are objects. If the ways in which atoms stick together to make molecules can only be understood ultimately in terms of quantum theory we can get along very well with higher-level rules: carbon atoms can make four bonds with atoms around them, there are weaker forces operating between molecules – etc., etc., etc. That sort of level of chemistry has been good enough for molecular biology to have provided a profound understanding of the nature of life. At higher levels of biology, going from molecules to cells and multicellular life, there seems hardly more need to mention h than in playing cricket. In all that stuff about how nerve cells work, how they communicate, how they can compute, we seem to be able to leave the ultimate nature of the ground substance further and further behind, using neat little diagrams to show connections between neurons and groups of neurons in different brain places . . . The brain itself being such an enormously bigger thing than h then *surely*, you might say, we are quite safe from worries about the principle of indeterminacy, or about the unmentionable behaviour of photons between their departures and arrivals . . .

Let us not be so sure. In a number of places the quantum world invades the larger-scale world of common sense in ways that might make even the man on the Clapham omnibus blink. As it happened it was a large-scale effect which opened the whole box in the first place: Planck's 'provisional' attempt to make sense of the colours of hot glowing objects. And there are plenty of other examples, the two–slit experiment for one. But you have to know quite a lot to be surprised by examples like these, as you do indeed for many quantum phenomena which are so familiar that they make nobody blink any more. I started this book with one of them: the conduction of electricity through wires.

We can send messages through telephone wires many thousands of times further than shouting distance. Even more extraordinary, we can send power – enough power to run a town – through a few dozen groups of aluminium wires suspended by insulators from pylons . . . How can such enormous flows of electrons be *directed* so far, so narrowly, so simply? To channel this energy the electricity industry depends as much on there being good insulators – materials that are wonderfully bad at conducting electricity – as on there being good conductors like copper or aluminium.

There are some amazing contrasts. Think of a grain of sand one tenth of a millimetre across: compare this to our galaxy which is about ten thousand light years (about 10^{17} kilometres) across. It would take then about 10^{24} of the grains of sand touching in a line to stretch across the galaxy. Well, 10^{24} is about the number of times copper is better at conducting electricity than pure quartz glass.

How can the electrons in glass be *so* immobile? The arrangement of the atoms in glass is somewhat higgledy piggledy but as with the more orderly arrangement of the same atoms in a quartz crystal the atoms in glass are pretty well close-packed: they fill the space. More precisely, the nuclei of the atoms – the oxygen nuclei with eight positive charges and silicons with fourteen – occupy only about a million million millionths of the space. The rest is the domain of the electrons, enough of them to neutralise the positive charges of the nuclei. With these electrons thousands of times lighter than the nuclei, and with so much room, how can they be so firmly held in place?

'Attraction between opposite charges' can only be part of it. If that alone could stop the electrons in glass from flowing it would stop them in copper too: copper also consists of an array of positive nuclei with neutralising electrons in between. And then the wave – particle ambiguity of electrons hardly seems to help. How can an electron be 'held in place' when it does not even seem to *have* a definite place?

If in some respects the 'quantum world' may seem hazy and vague (because of the silly questions our dreams impel us to ask about it) in other respects it could hardly be more definite. It has its own hard and fast rules. We came across a key rule in chapter 1: Pauli's exclusion principle. No two electrons can be in exactly the same *state* in an atom (an idea which only very roughly corresponds to our dream-rule that you cannot have two things in the same place at the same time). You may not quite know where they are but you know that they are 'in' certain orbitals. Well, the critical electrons in glass are all 'in' covalent bonds – in molecular orbitals between atoms – and they are stuck there, abiding by hard quantum rules.

As for metals, they too consist of positive nuclei with electrons in between. And again most of the electrons are firmly tied in atomic orbitals. But this time there are also outer electrons which are not in atomic orbitals or molecular orbitals but are citizens of the whole piece of metal . . .[18].

The quality of spin

The electron was first conceived of as the unit of electric charge; then as a proper little particle with a distinctive mass as well. Later on it turned out to have a spin. These are its three essential attributes, but there is more to be said about them. The charge is negative and never other than the unit charge. The mass is about 1/1836th that of the proton and never other than that (more strictly this is the 'rest mass' since the mass of anything increases noticeably when it is moving relative to us at very high speeds).

To get some idea of what the electron's spin *is* we can start by naïvely thinking of an electron as being, after all, a tiny sphere. Such a thing could be set spinning, creating in effect electric currents going round and round in circles; these currents should produce a magnetic field *à la* Faraday. Well, good news for naïve realists: an electron *is* a tiny magnet.

The bad news is, first, that the spin of an electron is, as I said, an *essential* attribute. There is no such thing as an electron that does not have a spin. This is a bit of a surprise if we are still trying to imagine the electron as a sphere. Then second, the electron has *a* spin, only one, only one 'rotation speed'. This might sound like the Earth's rotation except that for the Earth its speed is only incidentally once in 24 hours: it might be otherwise (it was and will be). Spin is not an essential attribute of the Earth, still less its actual spin speed. But for the electron there are no options and no gradations in amount. 'Amount of spin' comes in quanta (of course h comes into it[19]) and the electron has one of them as surely as it has one charge. No more, no less.

Spin is conventionally measured in multiples of $\frac{1}{2}$ so that allowed spins for elementary particles are 0, $\frac{1}{2}$, 1, $1\frac{1}{2}$ etc., although $\frac{1}{2}$ and 1 are the most usual. For example electrons, protons and neutrons are spin-$\frac{1}{2}$ particles. Photons are spin-1.

If mass, charge and spin size are unchangeable attributes of electrons, other attributes can be said to be optional or incidental, to do with where or how an electron happens to be. For example the electrons in atoms can be in different distinct states, and may sometimes jump from one state to another, throwing out or absorbing a photon to make up for the change in energy involved.

Now the electron has one such freedom with regard to its spin. A spin may not be able to change its size but it can be in different *directions*. The electrons in an atom will some of them be spinning in one direction with the rest of them going the other way; electrons in atoms are often represented as little arrows pointing either up or down[20].

Now let us get back to Pauli's exclusion principle. Remember that *two* electrons are allowed to occupy each of the standing wave modes, 1s, 2s, $2p_x$, $2p_y$, $2p_z$, etc., as illustrated in figure 1.8. This is not an infringement of the exclusion principle: two are allowed, but only if their spins are opposite, one up and one down, so that they are not in exactly the same state[21].

Fermions and bosons

Spin shows up at its most mysterious in yet another rule, a rule about a rule: the exclusion principle applies sharply to fundamental particles which are spin-$\frac{1}{2}$ (or spin-$1\frac{1}{2}$, spin-$2\frac{1}{2}$ etc) and not at all to the others (spin-0, spin-1, spin-2 etc). The first class are called **fermions,** the second class **bosons.** If fermions are fastidious in shunning the company of their exact peers (like Groucho Marx, who did not want to join the sort of club that would have *him* as a member), bosons are quite the opposite: when two or three are gathered together, why then more want to join in. And the more that are already gathered together the greater is the tendency.

Lasers I described in chapter 1 how ordinary light is 'incoherent'. It is not a single wave train because it is produced as the result of separate sudden transitions between quantum states. For example, many of the atoms of hot sodium vapour in a street lamp have had their outer electrons 'excited' into normally vacant higher-energy (3p) orbitals. When they jump back down to the normal (3s) state they emit a quantum of energy of a particular frequency determined by the difference in energy between the two states, producing that rather boring yellow light. But each high-energy sodium atom chooses, as it were, its own time to emit a photon: you can find out the odds of its happening for a sodium atom over a given period, but not exactly when any particular one will go.

Such 'spontaneous' emission of photons leads to incoherent light; but there is another way in which an excited atom may give up its excess energy, through what is called the 'stimulated' emission of a photon: an atom may be persuaded to give up its photon instantly by another photon of the same frequency in the vicinity. When this happens the new photon is precisely in phase, in exactly the same energy state as its stimulator. (Recall that photons are bosons: there are no Pauli restrictions here.)

A laser lamp makes use of this effect. Here a 'working substance' (such as neon gas) is intensely activated (for example by a beam of ordinary light) so that virtually all the atoms of it are 'pumped' into a particular high-energy state. Imagine one of these atoms dropping back spontaneously to its lower level and emitting a photon; but suppose, too, that this photon is prevented from escaping too easily because there are reflecting mirrors at opposite ends of the tube holding the working substance. So the photon zooms back and forth between the mirrors, giving it a chance to stimulate the production of more photons from the excited atoms in the tube. These new photons all join in, stimulating the production of yet more of them . . . Soon (very soon) – bang! – all the excited atoms have given up their photons and not much later these have found their way out of the tube through a little hole craftily placed in one of the mirrors. An intense pulse of laser light emerges, all their waves in unison . . .

Laser action depends especially on three things:

1. Pumping: atoms in a working substance are excited to a high energy state.
2. Photons are bosons: ones of the same energy 'want to get together' into a single quantum state and can do this through stimulated emission.
3. The more photons that are already in such a state the easier it is for others to join in.

The third point is reminiscent of a condensation process such as the formation of droplets of water (or ice) in the atmosphere. Here there is a similar bandwagon effect. The atmosphere may be overloaded with water but not actually form clouds. Quite a number of water molecules must be gathered together (usually on a particle of dust) before a droplet is big enough to be stable and able to grow with increasing ease by attracting more molecules from the atmosphere around it.

Well, water molecules are held together by 'ordinary' secondary forces. However, you can see that what happens in the build up to a laser pulse is also a let's-all-join-in phenomenon, a kind of condensation: related to what is called a Bose or Bose–Einstein condensation[22].

Superfluidity Helium gas condenses (in the ordinary sense) if cooled down to 4.21 on Kelvin's absolute scale of temperature. It becomes a liquid. But then at 2.17 K it quite suddenly loses all viscosity. This is odd to say the least (I mean, most liquids – engine oils for example – become more viscous when they get colder). Nobody fully understands what is going on but the effects can be very odd indeed. For example it becomes impossible to contain liquid helium in an open vessel: it simply runs up the sides and flows over. It will even squeeze out through crevices so fine that they would be normally be gas-tight: a screw-top bottle would be a useless container.

What seems clear is that the superfluidity of liquid helium is indeed a 'macroquantum effect' – a gross invasion from the quantum world – and that something like a Bose–Einstein condensation is responsible. Atoms of the common helium isotope, ^{4}He, consist of a nucleus with two (spin-$\frac{1}{2}$) protons paired up, and two (spin-$\frac{1}{2}$) neutrons also paired up, around which there are two paired up electrons. All the spins cancel and it seems that because the whole atom is thus spin-0 it behaves like a boson duly undergoing a Bose condensation at low enough temperatures. Now the viscosity of a liquid arises from molecules getting in each other's way being forced into different ways of moving. At normal temperatures there are large numbers of energy states ('motion states') that the molecules can be in, so many that it is of little consequence that there are only a finite number of them. But as the temperature drops towards absolute zero, more and more of the molecules are found in one particular state, the lowest possible energy state. Then as the temperature continues to drop the bandwagon effect sets in. Vast numbers of molecules are now in exactly the same quantum state, moving 'as one'[23].

The other isotope of helium, ^{3}He, has only one neutron in its nucleus and so its net spin is a half – not at all like a boson. ^{3}He becomes a liquid at 3.19 K, a similar temperature to ^{4}He, but this isotope does not become superfluid until the temperature drops all the way down to around 0.003 K. That ^{3}He becomes superfluid at all rather spoils the simple boson story: the idea is that here, at these incredibly low temperatures, the ^{3}He atoms form weakly interacting pairs and it is *these* that behave like bosons[24]. This may sound like a cooked-up idea, but pairs of fermions behaving like bosons has long been a basis for the explanation of another similar large-scale quantum effect which we will now look at briefly.

Superconductivity   Many ordinary metals loose all electrical resistance when cooled to low enough temperatures. It happens in lead, for example, at 7.2 K. A (smallish) current set up in a lead ring will continue to flow round and round for ever. That kind of perpetual motion we only expect to find on the scale of atoms and below (as with electrons blithely 'spinning' for ever). But here there are huge numbers of electrons – maybe 10^{24} or more – escaping the effect of haphazard collisions which will usually slow them down.

The main part of the standard explanation here is that although electrons are fermions, pairs of them with opposite spins will behave like bosons. The pairing force is very weak for the mobile electrons in metals, easily disrupted by normal thermal motions. But at low enough temperatures the electrons are able to pair up. Eventually there comes a point at which the pairs undergo a kind of Bose condensation, they crowd into exactly the same state and move as one, in the kind of perpetual way normally found only in tiny 'quantum objects': the superconducting electrons constitute a 'quantum object' writ large[25].

What has all this to do with the mind? Well, in the first place there are people who think that consciousness actually *is* a macroquantum effect of some sort. (And I will be trying to persuade you later on that this is by no means a daft idea.) In the second place, if we are looking for a theory of consciousness, quantum or otherwise, it is as well to have in mind what a scientific theory is supposed to do and what it is not supposed to do – and quantum theory is a very interesting example of a scientific theory. This was a thread laid down at the end of chapter 1 and picked up again in this chapter. A theory is not *of* reality exactly. A theory is a model or analogy or representation of reality in terms that we can calculate or think about. A scientific theory is only about what reality is *like*. We will continue for a bit on this tack.

Notes

[1] A 7-D hypercube has 448 edges and 672 faces. You never know when you might need this information.

[2] Nagel (1979), chapter 12.

[3] Berkeley (1710/1713/1988); Russell (1946), chapter 16.

[4] Körner (1955), esp. chapter 1; Russell (1946), chapter 20.

[5] Herbert Spencer (1855) was of this view. Richards (1987, p. 287) remarks that: 'Spencer had demonstrated, in his evolutionary-Kantian fashion, how the forms of space, time, motion and force had been derived from experience and had then solidified into heritable categories of thought . . .'. Bohm (1980, chapter 1) took a similar line: that such categories of thought are 'in a certain sense . . . a kind of theory'. Then again Lockwood (1989, p. 297); 'I regard belief in an objective, external material world, of things that occupy space and persist through time, as having the status, essentially, of a *theory*'.

[6] In St Augustine's *Confessions*; see Russell (1946, pp. 373–4).

[7] Kant's view of time was that, again, it is a form of the mind.

[8] So far has relativity become part of the common sense of modern physics that now it would be baffling beyond belief if your twin had *not* emerged younger than you.

[9] But see Deutsch & Lockwood (1994): a 'many worlds' view (see pp. 264–6 here) may provide a let-out.

[10] See James (1890/1983, pp. 573 ff) on the idea that 'the sensible present has duration' – the 'specious present'; also Lockwood (1989, chapter 15).

[11] Russell used the term 'neutral monism' to characterise his general view, which he said was 'suggested in Mach's *Analysis of Sensations*, developed in William James's *Essays in Radical Empiricism*, and advocated by John Dewey, as well as by Professor R. B. Perry and other American realists' (Russell, 1927, chapter 27). On this view reality is neither matter (Materialism) nor mind (Idealism) nor both (Dualism) but lies at a deeper level from which both matter and mind are derived. Double Aspect theories are similar (Priest, 1991, chapter 6).

[12] Cussedly, this is not in a way that would allow you to pass messages faster than light (Barrow, 1990, 147–8). This is just as well, come to think of it, or you might be able to shout back to your mother 'Who's a pretty baby' with all the trouble that could cause, because messages going faster than light would go backwards in time. For accounts of experiments demonstrating 'non-local' effects see Shimony (1988); Horne, Shimony & Zelinger (1990); Horgan (1992).

[13] The same can be said of electrons. Herbert (1985, p. 168) in discussing John Wheeler's view of quantum reality remarks: 'Electrons certainly exist – with the same mass and charge whether you look or not – but it is a mistake to imagine them in particular locations or travelling in a particular direction unless you happen to actually see one doing so.'

[14] Foot (1992).

[15] Physicists try to quantify everything. 'The amount of action' is to be seen as a product of energy and time: if something happens more slowly than before there is more action even if the total energy involved is the same . . . Well, if they say so.

[16] That is to say energy times time.

[17] Herbert (1985), p. 110.

[18] This is not the whole story of course. See for example Animalu (1977).

[19] The unit is $\hbar/2$, where $\hbar = h/2\pi$.

[20] Conventionally, the direction of a spinning object can be defined by a straight arrow lying along its spin axis (such as the axis of the Earth) and pointing in such a direction that looking along that direction you would

see the object spinning clockwise. The Earth's arrow, for example, points from south to north.

[21] Since electrons are little magnets it is perhaps not surprising that they pair up like this when close together – a pair of bar magnets would do likewise – but it turns out this is not nearly a strong enough force to account for Pauli's prohibition: see Feynman, Leighton & Sands (1965), p. 4.14.

[22] It is *like* a Bose condensation (see Sewell, 1986, p. 201).

[23] Tilley & Tilley (1986); Feynman, Leighton & Sands (1965), p. 4.12. See Donnelly (1988) on the creation of macroscopic quantum mechanical objects – in the form of vortices in liquid helium.

[24] Tilley & Tilley (1986), p. 28 and chapter 9.

[25] Tilley & Tilley (1986); Feynman, Leighton & Sands (1965), p. 21.7.

8

Making theories

I start with a tale of a Victorian physicist who became an enthusiastic follower of Faraday. He liked analogies and used them in trying to account for electric and magnetic effects. But not for him mere lines of force traversing space. This man filled up space with vortices, idler wheels, all sorts of things. To give you a flavour of his thinking, here he is in the middle of describing what he seems to imagine is the stuff of a magnetic field:

> I conceived the rotating matter to be the substance of certain cells, divided from each other by cell walls composed of particles which are very small compared with the cells, and that it is by the motions of these particles, and their tangential action on the substance in the cells, that the rotation is communicated from one cell to another[1].

(It goes on like this for pages.)

He is not going to get anywhere with such extravagant nonsense, you might say. (Am I giving you this as an example of a *senseless* theory?) Banish such thoughts. *He* was Clerk Maxwell.

Maxwell's imaginings were part of his method. Indeed it was precisely through these elaborate ideas that he arrived at his famous equations of the electromagnetic field, as austere as could be, what Einstein described as the greatest development in physics since Newton[2].

Here is another quote from Maxwell to help us see what he was up to:

> The conception of a particle having its motion connected with that of a vortex by perfect rolling contact may appear somewhat awkward. I do not bring it forward as a mode of connection existing in nature, or even as that which I would willingly assent to as an electrical hypothesis. It is, however, a mode of connection which is mechanically conceivable, and easily investigated, and it serves to bring out the actual mechanical connections between the known electro-

magnetic phenomena; so that I venture to say that any one who understands the provisional and temporary character of this hypothesis, will find himself rather helped than hindered by it in his search after the true interpretation of the phenomena[3].

Indeed, Maxwell believed that theory should seek to simplify and he saw in mathematical forms the most compact means of expression: but a proper scientific theory is never a piece of pure mathematics, and never only about fitting the immediate facts or predicting immediate consequences[4]. By the use of analogies, what Maxwell called 'physical hypotheses', one may 'obtain more extended views of the connections of the subject'[5]. In terms of the three neo-Kantian forms of understanding touched on in the previous chapter, one might say that all three should be represented in any theory which has any hope of extending our horizons. A useful theory should fit the facts. It should be logical. It should engage the imagination.

Engage the imagination? Is this not inviting the kind of 'naïve realism' (believing one's dreams) that it was most of the purpose of the last chapter to explode?

I was not arguing against *using* our dreams. Not to do so would be to shut down most of our brain power and leave a calculator. What I have been arguing against, on and off since chapter 1, is *belief*; believing that any of our perceptual dreams, any of our equations, any of our models, can ever have more than 'as if' status, can ever be more than analogies.

Separating imagination from belief

They should be imaginable, but whether 'physical hypotheses' are believable or not is of no consequence. Faraday had seen it indeed as a positive advantage for analogies to be *unbelievable*[6]. To separate imagination from belief is the critical attitude. It is what makes the Faraday–Maxwell programme so modern. How they would have liked quantum theory.

The fact is that even fantastic analogies often work and can extend our theoretical horizons. Although many of the more practically minded physicists will tell you that quantum theory is simply a system of equations which comes up with the right answers (so far *always*, so forget the mysteries they may say), there have been others throughout this century who have adopted the Faraday–Maxwell attitude to great effect. de Broglie was one, with his extension of the fantastic idea that light is both particle and wave at the same time: his extension of this idea to *any* particle. As we saw, this was to provide one of the keys to our present understanding of chemistry. I think we will arrive at an agreed coherent theory of consciousness in a somewhat similar way – anyway, it will *seem* crazy, which brings me to my next example.

Another lesson in model building

In one of the most fruitful pieces of extravagance in more recent quantum theory, Richard Feynman (1918–1988) used a combination of the naïve and the unbelievable, rather as did de Broglie.

Remember the two-slit experiment and the awful dilemma about which slit the photon went through and the *awful* conclusion that it must have gone through both without dividing in two – that it took both paths at once? Well, Feynman extended *this* absurdity. Even a photon going innocently from A to B in empty space (whatever that is) does not just go one or two ways. It goes *every* way, every way available to it. Figure 8.1 shows a few of them.

If we were to think of water flowing in a similar maze of channels between A and B then it would become easier and easier the more channels there were, but possible light paths either help or hinder. Recall the classical interpretation of the two-slit experiment (figure 1.7 on page 34 yet again): if the lengths of two paths are exactly the same or if they differ by the tiny amount equal to the wavelength of the light (about 0.000 75 mm for red light, about 0.000 45 mm for blue); or if the paths differ by an exact multiple of the wavelength, then the light rays will arrive exactly 'in phase' at their destination and reinforce each other's effect, producing a bigger combined wave, one with twice the amplitude. But if the path lengths differ by just half a wavelength (or $1\frac{1}{2}$, $2\frac{1}{2}$, $3\frac{1}{2}$, etc.) then the light rays will be exactly out of phase and cancel their effect completely: zero amplitude. In between there are partial reinforcements or cancellations, so the possibilities for two interfering wave trains of the same amplitude will range between zero and twice the original amplitude.

net wave would be twice the original and can be represented by laying arrows end to end:

Exactly in phase:

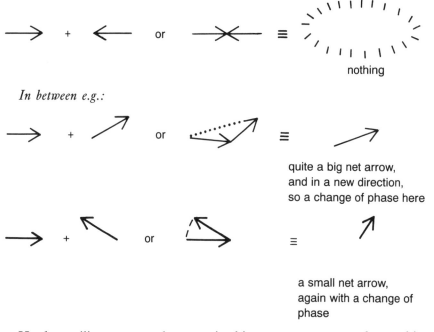

But we can drop the notion of wave from the discussion and just talk about 'amplitudes' and 'phases', calculating them by adding little arrows together. In the above case although the amplitude is doubled the phase is unchanged since the big arrow is still pointing the same way.

Other possibilities can be similarly represented:

Exactly out of phase:

In between e.g.:

Head-to-tailing many such arrows in this way can represent the combination of as many different paths as you like. For example if you were to lay *all* the arrows on the right hand side of figure 8.2 head to tail in the manner described above, then the size of your net arrow, drawn from the tail of the first to the head of the last, would depend mainly on the arrows for the more central paths[8].

Feynman suggests how we might 'fool the light' so that going along a lot of the paths would take the same time and so fewer of them would

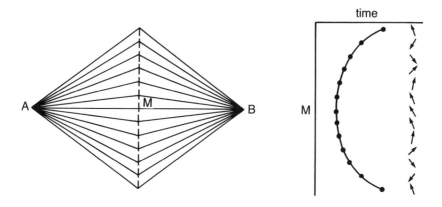

Figure 8.2. Analysis of all possible paths from A to B is simplified to include only double straight lines (in a single plane). The effect is the same as in the more complicated real case: there is a time curve with a minimum (M), where most of the contributions to a final (upward) arrow are made.
From Feynman, Richard. *Q.E.D.* Copyright © 1985 by Princeton University Press. Reproduced by permission of the publishers.

cancel out. Well, light goes slower in glass than in air so the trick would be to put a lot of glass in the way of the shorter paths and then carefully choose smaller amounts of glass for the longer off-centre paths to give them a chance to catch up. Figure 8.3 shows the idea. You know what it is, of course: a *lens*. (You knew all along that light does not always travel in straight lines.)

An even more ingenious way of producing a similar effect is with a device known as a zone plate (figure 8.4). It too can act as a focusing lens. You may like to figure out how it works (note 9 explains).

Feynman gives several other examples which lets us see how mirrors reflect, how colours are produced by oil films or by CD discs . . . 'everything you know about light'. Feynman hardly mentions the wave nature of light: he does it all with his little arrow, providing us with a wonderful example of how with a model which has no pretence to be realistic (light has no arrows) we can 'obtain more extended views of the connections of the subject' as Maxwell had put it.

In getting to the arrows interpretation I chose to start with waves, in the conventional way, to develop the ideas of amplitude and phase. Having done that we could then drop the wave idea if we wanted to. Light is no

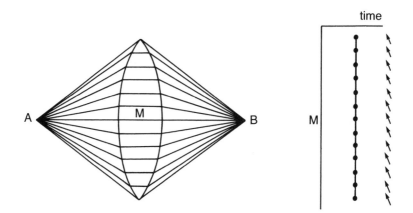

Figure 8.3. As in figure 8.2, except that different thicknesses of glass have
been put in the way to slow down especially light taking the shorter paths,
and so that each of the paths takes exactly the same time. This causes all
the arrows to point in the same direction, adding together to make a giant
arrow. The light is thus highly concentrated at the destination point, B. Such
a piece of shaped glass is called a convex (or focusing) lens.
From Feynman, Richard. *Q.E.D.* Copyright © 1985 by Princeton University
Press. Reproduced by permission of the publishers.

more *really* waves than *really* a whole lot of little arrows. (Nor, for those
of you who know about them, is it really the complex numbers which are
used in place of arrows in computing phases and amplitudes . . .)

The title of Feynman's book is 'QED', which stands for 'quantum
electrodynamics': the quantum update of the theory of electromagnetism
started by Faraday. QED extends to electrons and gives us an insight as
to how the electromagnetic force works – why like charges repel and
unlike charges attract, for example. (We will come to this.)

If you want to know how an electron gets from A to B then again you
have to consider all the possible ways in which an electron might be
imagined to be able to make the journey. Again it can be done by 'adding
arrows' for all the possible ways and coming up with a net arrow with a
net amplitude: 'the amplitude to get from A to B'.

Indeed the term 'amplitude', although derived from ideas of waves, has
an extended meaning in quantum theory. It can be applied generally to
quantum events which are said to have such and such an amplitude to
happen. This sounds like assigning odds, saying that the event has such
and such a probability of happening, but it is more subtle than this. The

Figure 8.4. Magnified view of a zone plate, which can act as a focusing lens (see note 9).
From Jenkins, F. & White, H., *Fundamentals of Optics*, 2nd ed. © McGraw-Hill 1951. Reproduced by permission of the publishers.

probability of the event is the *square* of the net amplitude (as found by combining arrows or however it is done). An amplitude is less definite than a probability: it is a sort of tendency, but as we saw it is a tendency that can help or hinder, it may be positive or negative. If you had several cooks in the kitchen each with a certain *probability* of making broth then the more cooks there were the more broth you would expect to get. But as everybody knows cooks are not like this. Cooks should rather be said 'to have an amplitude to make broth'. Even two cooks may interfere.

What complicates the situation for an electron going from A to B is that electrons have this tendency – amplitude – to emit and absorb photons. In trying to figure out the net amplitude for the event of getting to B you have to take into account all sorts of 'paths', including some quite odd ones in which the electron suddenly decides to emit a photon, or perhaps several along the way, and re-absorb them again (see figure 8.5b,c). Such

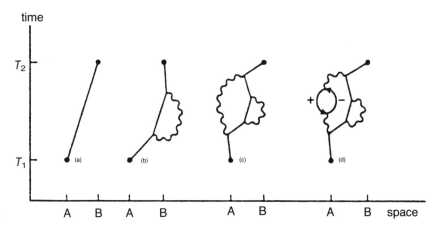

Figure 8.5. Some ways in which an electron may go from A to B (see text).
From Feynman, Richard. *Q.E.D.* Copyright © 1985 by Princeton University
Press. Reproduced by permission of the publishers.

are often called 'virtual photons' because they are not present at either
the start or the finish of a process: nobody can even pretend to be able
to observe them directly.

Now with two or more electrons you can imagine what may happen.
A photon from one may be picked up by another. Well *that* is happening
all the time, according to QED. Any electrically charged particle is continually emitting and absorbing (virtual) photons. That is what charge *is*:
an amplitude to emit and absorb photons. It is through such exchanges
that electromagnetic forces are said to operate 'across space'.

Figure 8.5d illustrates another piece of quantum licence. One of these
virtual photons suddenly turns into an electron and a positron. A positron
is an electron-like particle but with a positive charge. You do not find
many of them about because electrons and positrons annihilate each other
when they meet, and as you might expect these suddenly produced electrons and positrons last for only very short times. They too are 'virtual'.
In fact there is a worse scandal even than this. You do not even need a
photon for an electron plus positron to jump into existence: it can happen
from *nothing*.

These are some of the secret things I referred to in the last chapter
when talking about the principle of indeterminacy. Where does the energy
come from to produce these virtual particles? The answer is from
Nowhere. It turns out that the law of the conservation of energy can be
violated on a very small (*h*-sized) scale.

Can be? I should have said *must be*. One cannot say that there is *no* energy in such and such a region of space over some small interval of time, because like momentum and position, energy and duration cannot simultaneously have an exact measure – and *no* energy is an exact measure. So over short time intervals energy indeterminately flickers in and out of existence in the form of, for example, virtual photons or virtual electron positron pairs: space or 'the vacuum' as it is called in this context, is seething with such activities, called 'quantum fluctuations'. (You thought *Maxwell* was being extravagant?)

So The Bank of Nowhere provides a limited overdraft facility to its quantum customers. An amount of energy, E, can be borrowed from Nowhere for a period t, provided that E multiplied by t does not exceed $h/4\pi$ . . .

The picture which QED gives us is of a world in which very few *kinds* of things happen. Only three kinds, according to Feynman: photons go from place to place; electrons go from place to place; electrons emit and absorb photons. The basic acts are simple, as in a board game such as draughts. There are simple rules but vast numbers of possible forms of play.

What is this QED world in more ordinary language? Well, it is *our* world more or less. It is the electromagnetic domain of science, where gravity and nuclear forces can be pretty well ignored. It is the domain of chemistry, molecular biology, cell biology, and all the intricate things about the brain that we were talking about in chapters 4 and 5[10].

What should a theory of consciousness be like?

So what about that effect which switches on every morning? A theory of consciousness is bound to sound crazy if current theories of matter are anything to go by, but this is not to say that any old nonsense will do. Let us see if we can place some limits, insisting on some features which a *useful* theory should have in the light of our discussions so far.

Connecting with physics and chemistry

It is pretty clear that phenomena of consciousness are caused by activities of brain matter (chapter 5). And the central theory of biology, evolution through natural selection, tells us that states of consciousness must be

goodness' sake? If a purely 'neuronal computer' explanation of behaviour can say it all; if an account in terms of action potentials, etc. can always be a complete account without bringing feelings into the discussion, then it would never make a jot of difference what feelings (if indeed any) ever accompanied the computing needed, say, to find a meal or plan a courtship or seek an avenue of revenge. Inappropriate feelings would be just as likely as appropriate ones. If feelings are biologically redundant the evolution of the means to generate feelings, especially appropriate ones, would be inexplicable.

But in that case why has the forget-about-consciousness programme been so successful? In trying to understand how the brain works most molecular and cell neuroscientists do not really think about consciousness at all. But, as we saw, in terms of complexity of operation very little goes on 'in consciousness' compared with what is going on at the levels of ions going through membranes, allosteric proteins flipping about, membrane potentials building up, neurons firing and puffing little pulses of neuro-transmitters at each other . . . Then, as we discussed in chapter 5, even at higher levels of behaviour almost all that we do we do unconsciously. So we should not be surprised that consciousness need not be considered in relation to most of the detailed goings-on in the brain.

The conscious mind may be a more limited part of our intelligence than we might wish to believe, but it is crucial all the same, and anyway *different* in its talents and its uses. In simple-minded engineering terms we should expect to be able to correlate this difference with different brain components or with different ways in which the same components are working – when on the one hand we *compute* and on the other hand *feel* as well[12].

Then again from chapter 5 it seemed that consciousness, although surely localised in space to the extent that it is a one-brain product, is almost certainly not a highly localised effect within the brain. What makes consciousness, it seems, is not a centre but some 'big place' in the brain, and a number of people have suggested that consciousness is a large scale (macroscopic) effect arising from small scale (microscopic) brain processes[13].

That idea I would go along with too, but not the analogy which is then often made with the way in which the microscopic activities of molecules underlie such macroscopic properties as pressure or temperature. We can easily understand the connection between, say, collisions of the molecules of a gas with the walls of a container and the pressure of the gas; or the ways in which such collisions may give rise to chemical reactions; but there is no such transparent connection between neuronal activity and feelings[14].

In particular, from James's evolutionary argument discussed in chapter 6, I would not expect the microscopic processes underlying conscious experience to be simply and directly identified with the myriads of microscopic processes which we know are concerned with 'the neuronal computing' (a term which you will have seen I am using to mean molecular and cellular processes, which can be understood without bringing consciousness into the discussion). It would not make engineering sense for much the same reason as it does not make evolutionary sense. Let me try to untie this a little further.

Imagine that you have designed and built yourself a beautiful washing machine. Then, to celebrate your achievement, you throw a party which gets a little out of hand when someone discovers that your machine can be used as a sort of roulette wheel. You would not expect it, unmodified, to be a particularly good roulette wheel and you would be amazed if as you later went on to improve your machine (with of course *only* sober clothes washing in mind) it simultaneously got better and better as a roulette wheel (to become perhaps the preferred design for casinos and laundrettes the world over).

There are some morals here. The first is that unintended uses may be found for objects – even for quite complicated machines. In evolutionary theory the term 'preadaptation' is used to describe the 'discovery' of alternative functions for parts of organisms. A structure evolved under one set of selection pressures, for one purpose as we might say, sometimes turns out to have other fortuitous uses; but to begin with these are either rather simple functions or carried out in a rudimentary way. So a second moral is that radically new inventions do not spring fully formed into existence.

A favourite example of this kind of thing was in the evolution of our lungs. Fish discovered that gulping air was an alternative way of taking in oxygen in stagnant waters (you can see goldfish doing it). The mouth and oesophagus just happened to be 'preadapted' as primitive lungs. In some lines of descent this air-breathing system was improved gradually through the evolution of a simple pouch off the oesophagus and then eventually, so the story goes, to highly adapted lungs in the ancestors of present-day lungfish and land vertebrates[15]. So a third moral is that evolution *from* a preadaptation is likely to create features concerned specifically with the new function. Lungs would not have evolved as a sort of automatic concomitant of the evolution of an oesophagus; there had to be continuing selection pressures to establish and perfect the new invention.

At the level of protein molecules, too, preadaptation is the standard way in which new functions are 'discovered'. A protein, say an enzyme catalysing one chemical reaction, turns out to have a weak activity for a rather different but useful reaction, or perhaps for some other purpose altogether. By having a double copy of the DNA specifying this protein the organisms may now evolve two proteins along separate lines: one remains more or less unmodified for the original function while the other is likely to be more highly modified in adapting to the new function. (From similarities in amino acid sequences it is clear that in many cases protein molecules with very different functions have descended from a single type[16].)

I understand that in Las Vegas people need to gamble from the moment they wake up in the morning till they go to bed, putting terrible strains on them when they have to do such mundane things as washing their clothes in the launderette. Well, one day someone discovered that a coin left in a pocket would sometimes get thrown out during the spin cycles. So of course people started to gamble on whether this happened or not ... Then the manufacturers began to modify their washing machines for Las Vegas. A ball put in among the clothing would sooner or later find a special slot and be thrown out on one side or the other side (you could bet on that too), and then in later models to emerge in one of 36 numbered channels ... Of course these machines still had to be good at washing clothes (a clean shirt might be needed as a stake) so it was not a miracle that washing and rouletting both evolved to a high level of efficiency ...

Now consider the evolution of consciousness. We are supposing that feelings are physical effects dependent on brain activity, on physical mechanisms. Now preadaptation is the only way in which quite new functions can appear in evolution. There is a remarkable implication. Conscious effects (of a sort) cannot be that hard to come by if they appeared by accident in an early nervous system which presumably had in no sense been designed to produce them.

We might say that the first appearance of conscious effects would have been like discovering that a washing machine could be an accidental roulette wheel (of a sort) rather than, say, discovering that it was accidentally a television set – which even 'of a sort' would be rather too much to expect. It is not a reasonable conjecture that consciousness was an altogether new effect which could only have emerged at some specific high level of organisation. The forces of evolution, having no eyes, could not have got to such a place.

So there is a second feature for an acceptable theory of consciousness, what we might call the not-hard-to-come-by requirement (that consciousness is not hard to come by in a rudimentary form): or if you prefer **the requirement of evolutionary accessibility**. But there is a further expectation.

Suppose that the critical preadaptation has been made: some aspect of the activity of a System-2 axon–synapse computer happens to generate faint effects, the forerunners of our sensations and urges, which provide a new integrating technique, a rudimentary System-3. What would we expect to happen next? Well, we would *not* expect to find that as ComputerPlus evolved further both System-2 and System-3 would always automatically improve in step: that any improvement in System-2 would automatically represent an improvement to System-3. That would not be at all like the evolution of the lung (or of the Las Vegas washing machine) where from the moment a preadaptation caught on the new function and the old function, being different in kind, created selection pressures for the elaboration of distinct physical apparatus. We would expect new structures or new modifications identifiable in principle with the new function ('lungs' not just a bigger and better 'oesophagus').

So, yes, I think the phenomena of consciousness will turn out to be identifiable with brain processes: but, please, not with exactly the *same* brain processes as underly a computing system for which consciousness need not be invoked. We might call this **the specialisation postulate**. It is my third feature for an acceptable theory of consciousness.

Dependent independence   As an illustration of what I mean by the status of dependent independence, think of that institution so valued by decent democracies 'the independence of the judiciary'. Nobody says that judges do not depend on society to be comfortably maintained, but they are not supposed to have their decisions determined by their paymasters. So if I say that my fourth principle of acceptability is **the independence of consciousness** I do not mean that it is wholly independent, that it inhabits a separate world, only that there is a measure of independence in the control it exerts.

Consider a favourite analogy for things spiritual: a flame. Suppose that consciousness is maintained by brain activity in a way somewhat analogous to the maintenance of the flame of a bunsen burner. Each has a wholly dependent existence. Cut off the gas from the bunsen or cut off the blood supply to the brain and the flame or the consciousness disappears. But to be wholly dependent on some external situation for your existence is not necessarily to be dependent in every detail for your *state* of existence. Indeed states too may be affected by external circumstances. No doubt the flame may be modulated moment by moment by small changes in gas pressure as well as draughts and so on; but that is not to say that you would be able to predict every nuance of the flame's flickerings even if you had perfect knowledge of such external influences. Freeman & Skarda's 'chaotic' theory of consciousness embodies such an idea, and I used a similar weather analogy in discussing it (on page 175); but I want to keep clear for the moment of the question of whether conscious events should properly be regarded as only owing such independence as they have to an element of chaos. The principle of the independence of consciousness says that, however it happens, there should be some events in the flame of consciousness which are not wholly determined by the instrument which daily creates and maintains it.

Summarising, then, consciousness should be seen

    I as a physical effect which
   II is not difficult to produce in a rudimentary form but which
  III is now created by somewhat specialised brain structures, and
  IV is not simply a channel of communication.

Thinking in 'hardware' terms, there are then more precise expectations.

The specialisation postulate (III) is that there is a distinction between brain processes mediating the conscious control system and those concerned with the 'purely neuronal computing' as I have been calling it. There will almost certainly be overlap, but if consciousness is part of such a control system we should nevertheless expect to be able to identify mechanisms in the brain which relate to consciousness. More precisely:

  1 to make and maintain it
  2 to modulate it
  3 to react to modulations

Expectation 3 follows from the arguments in chapter 6 – that 'feelings are causes', as James put it.

Now recall the part of our discussion in chapter 6 which was to do with the appropriateness of subjective sensations (page 206). It seemed that there had to be a conscious part of the self which really makes decisions from moment to moment based upon what we know subjectively are subtle mental values: states of niceness or nastiness to put it more crudely. The gist of the argument was that if consciousness was merely a channel of communication ('global broadcasting' or otherwise) the subjective nature of different states of consciousness would still be irrelevant. 'Going through consciousness' cannot be like going through a wire (or hanks of wire) but more like going through a processor. This led us to a fourth requirement (within IV) – and which is not exactly of the brain – that:

4 some modulations of consciousness are self-generated[17]

Expectation 4 is based largely on subjective experience. We seem to have two selves, do we not? There is our short-term conscious self, the self that comes into being every morning, the self that feels. And then there is the more permanent self embodied in that great unconscious part of our inner model, with its inherited modes and its acquired memory store of things, events, skills . . . the Greater Self. But Evanescent Self, it seems, has one endearing property. It does not act determinately nor does it act at random. It does what it feels like. In doing that it alters and updates the Greater Self, so that in the lifelong accumulation of its effects Evanescent Self affects the way it is today and is remade tomorrow . . .

That at least is how it seems to my two selves. Yet we also have an outside view of it, in watching how *others* behave. If consciousness is a physical effect, another's consciousness is as objective as anything else about them; and if it is a causal agent we should at least be able to see what its effects are as distinct from the effects of System-1 and System-2. Looking forward to a time when we know pretty well everything there is to know about System-1 and System-2, we should expect to find that the intelligent behaviour of others is still not fully comprehensible only in terms of those systems. But by that time I think we *will* understand system-3 much better.

Notes

[1] Niven (1890), volume 1, p. 489; quoted in Torrance (1982), p. 13.

[2] Einstein (*ca.* 1931). 'Maxwell's Influence on the Development of the Conception of Physical Reality.' English translation in Torrance (1982), pp, 29–32.

3 Niven (1890), volume 1, p. 486: quoted in Torrance (1982), p. 13.

4 From a book review by Maxwell (Niven, ed, 1890, volume 2, p, 328): 'We can only express our sympathy with the efforts of men, thoroughly conversant with all that mathematicians have achieved, to divest scientific truths of that symbolic language in which the mathematicians have left them, and to clothe them in words, developed by legitimate methods from our mother tongue, but rendered precise by clear definitions, and familiar by well rounded statements.'

5 Niven (1890), volume 1, p. 155: quoted in Torrance (1982), p. 9.

6 Berkson (1974) comments on this in relation to Maxwell: 'The liberating feature of the 'method of analogies' is the fact that it encouraged the development of what one believes to be *false* analogies for the light they may shed on the truth – a procedure which had been recommended by Faraday. The method also encourages an individual to construct theories other than his pet ones, and in general encourages the invention of theories which *nobody* would believe for their possible fruitfulness.'

7 Feynman (1985/1990), pp. 55–6.

8 We have been talking here about the procedure for adding arrows. Feynman also describes a slightly more complicated procedure for multiplying them – required for estimating amplitudes for events which happen in a sequence of stages rather than in alternative ways.

9 You can see how a zone plate works by looking at figure 8.2 again and thinking about how you might block off half the rays and let through half, in such a way that those rays which got through would have their arrows all in the same general direction.

10 Feynman's favourite example to persuade us of the validity of QED was a calculation analysing dozens of kinds of 'paths' which an electron absorbing a photon from a magnetic field may take – calculating how much effect in general magnetic fields have on electrons. This is a quantity called the magnetic moment of the electron and in 1983 it had been worked out from QED that it should be 1.001 159 652 46. The observed value then was 1.001 159 652 21. As Feynman put it, the accuracy of this estimate was equivalent to knowing the distance between New York and Los Angeles to within the width of a human hair.

11 James (1904).

12 The two 'operating modes' which Baars suggests may have evolved in vertebrates (1988), p. 350; see quotation on page 180.

13 Searle (1984), chapter 1.

14 Gray (1987).

15 Described for example in Rensch (1959); Schmalhausen (1968).

16 Doolittle (1985).

17 Some might say that this contradicts my requirement for a scientific theory that consciousness should be a physical effect. It depends what you mean by 'physical'. I do not of course mean 'a Newtonian physical effect'. I mean an effect which connects 'at both ends', as it were, with physics and chemistry: can be affected by and can affect molecules. But already we know that physics leaves some things open which a Newtonian view would have said should be accounted for – what a photon is up to between A and B, for example, or the simultaneous momentum and position of any very small particle. Consciousness may be produced by brain matter and affect brain matter, but that is not to say that physical rules can be used to keep tabs on everything going on in between.

9

Quantum theories of consciousness

Quantum phenomena underly molecules. Molecules make up neurons. Neurons make up brain circuitry. Brain circuitry becomes active when we think and feel. So perhaps we can express the mind–matter relationship through a hierarchy of levels:

quantum → molecule → cell → circuitry → consciousness ??

Such is a popular notion – and wonderfully unilluminating. But then it is not true. You cannot always forget about quantum theory at the level of molecules; or about molecules at the level of cells; or neuron structure at the level of circuitry – even if for convenience chemists, cell biologists or neural network enthusiasts may reasonably make such simplifying assumptions in trying to understand some aspects of what is going on, blanking out lower levels of structure and activity by using appropriate toy models. But to understand in detail how the circuitry works you have to think about molecules. And understanding in detail how such molecules interact will mean direct reference to the quantum level; balls and springs cannot represent everything about how molecules vibrate, for example, or how energy passes between them.

If there is no simple hierarchy of levels *below* consciousness, why should we assume that to understand consciousness itself we need only consider the immediately lower level of circuitry and software?

Now what defines true quantum theories of consciousness is that they do *not* take a simple hierarchical view of the emergence of consciousness. They seek to make some connections directly between the conscious and the quantum level.

To put a toe in the water, I will start with a theory which was proposed in 1977 by two neurophysiologists, although it was not actually presented as a quantum theory.

Thatcher and John: *the hyperneuron*

Robert Thatcher and Roy John sought to understand consciousness through a 'non-obvious attribute' of organised energy states 'an integrative process which is a function of the state of energy in any form of matter'. They go on:

> This conjecture, fanciful though it may at first appear, has at least the virtue of no special pleading for humankind. It is parsimonious. It suggests that all organised energy possesses a non-obvious attribute, an integrative process reflecting the overall state. The difference between a human being and an elementary particle becomes an enormous quantitative difference in the number of energy states which can be entered. But a qualitative *continuum* can be postulated. What is unique about the brain of human beings, from this viewpoint, is that they are exceptionally well suited to construct an almost infinite variety of energy states[1].

They then come to a more specific identification of the physical substrate for consciousness:

> As these temporal patterns of neuron discharge occur, the membranes of participating cells are depolarised and ionic shifts occur with extrusion of potassium ions and ionic binding on extracellular mucopolysaccharide filaments. If we focus our attention not on the membranes of single neurons, but upon charge density distributions in the tissue matrix of neurons, glial cells, and mucopolysaccharide processes, we can envisage a complex, three dimensional volume of isopotential contours, topologically comprised of portions of cellular membranes and extracellular binding sites and constantly changing over time. Let us call this volume of isopotential contours or convoluted surfaces a *hyperneuron*[2].

'Hyperneuron' is neurophysiologist's language, but in the 'non-obvious' property suggested as being responsible for conscious integration, there is a close enough parallel to a number of quantum theories proposed by physicists and others over the past 25 years. It is time to jump in at the deep end.

Stapp: the feel of events

Henry Stapp's theory of consciousness was inspired by the physics of Heisenberg and the philosophy of James[3].

James had seen clearly that the root problem about the mind–matter connection, as it presented itself at the end of the nineteenth century, was that *matter* was not sufficiently understood (see pages 202–3). In particular the Newtonian and atomic theories of the time could give no good account of the unity of conscious experience – not if, say, a complex object is just a collection of atoms. By contrast the *thought* of a complex object is not made up of tiny parts but is 'one undivided state of consciousness': of a piece, not just because its components are joined up like carpentry, but unified by its very nature. Stapp quotes a passage where James, having concluded that the only reasonable correlate for a state of consciousness would be an entire brain process, goes on to say:

> The 'entire brain-process' is not a physical fact at all. It is the appearance to an onlooking mind of a multitude of physical facts. 'Entire brain' is nothing but our name for the way in which a million of molecules arranged in certain positions may affect our sense. On the principles of the corpuscular or mechanical philosophy, the only realities are the separate molecules, or at most the cells. Their aggregation into a 'brain' is a fiction of popular speech. Such a fiction cannot serve as the objectively real counterpart to any psychic state whatever. Only a genuinely physical fact can so serve. But the molecular fact is the only genuinely physical fact[4].

James's argument here is hardly conclusive. When he says that the realities are molecules and then adds 'or at most cells', one can't help wondering why he should not have said 'and aggregations of cells into higher-order structures and ultimately complete brains', or something of the sort. But I do not think this spoils his general argument. The kind of unity of brain which is achieved by assembling molecules together to make successively higher-order machines gives us no adequate insight into how conscious experience is so much of a piece. Indeed in some ways the intervening years have added to this puzzle. The brain is an even more complex object than James could have known for sure. How can fantastically complicated molecular processes, billions of little pieces at work, underlie our conscious experience, which, even if we may want to argue about how unified this is, does not seem at all to be made up of billions of little pieces. . . ? As it is sometimes expressed, the *grain* seems so hopelessly different for brain and for conscious mind[5].

Stapp rather sees the intervening century as having provided the key which James was looking for in an appropriate depth in our understanding of matter: in Heisenberg's interpretation of quantum theory. Let me explain.

In the last chapter we were discussing 'amplitudes', those strange plus-or-minus 'tendencies- to happen' which when combined appropriately (with 'arrows' or otherwise) let you calculate the probabilities for events to happen in alternative ways. The examples given were to do with photons going from A to B, through pairs of slits, lenses, zone plates and so on; but you can in principle calculate the probability of any quantum event – and indeed (with provisos we will come to) 'events' generally. In this sense 'quantum mechanics', as it is called, is as definite and deterministic as Newton's account of how matter behaves ('classical mechanics').

The difference is that although in principle quantum mechanics allows you to compute the odds for things happening, and to do this as accurately as you like, there is no way, no way even in principle, in which you can calculate just where, for example, any one photon is going to hit a screen. (There is a difference between knowing the odds for sure and knowing which horse will actually win.) When it comes to the crunch point, to 'actual events', you cannot predict further than to say how likely they are: how likely it is, say, that the photon will end up *here*.

Heisenberg's interpretation of quantum mechanics is one of several attempts to provide 'a picture of what is really going on' – *à la* Faraday/ Maxwell. Stapp explains and expands on it along these lines.

We are asked to imagine the entire Universe abruptly changing its state of being from instant to instant as 'actual events' happen in series. The whole Universe is of a piece, and no two quantum events in it ever happen at exactly the same time; they are strung out in a linear time sequence[6]. This Universe can be seen as something like a single fantastically complex mega-wave, which changes ('evolves') according to strict laws. The mega-wave is a representation of tendencies to do with an impending 'actual event'. The mega-wave is indeed a kind of superposition of tendencies: amplitudes for each of the possible forms that this impending event might take. Then the event happens. One possibility becomes actual so that the Universe has now changed to a new evolving state, a somewhat different superposition of tendencies, from which the probabilities of different forms of the *next* event could be calculated in principle. The next event then duly happens – and so on and on in a succession of (determinate) evolutions punctuated by the (indeterminate) jumps of 'actual events'.

Well, the whole Universe is rather unwieldy and you would not have much time to make those calculations between 'Heisenberg events', particularly as you would have to know everything there was to know about the entire Universe to do it properly. But the idea that at least a moderately sized region of space has to be taken into account, to be able to calculate (at least reasonably well) the odds for more modest quantum events to happen, follows from the kind of examples we were discussing earlier.

Recall from the last chapter that where a photon going through a lens is most likely to end up depends on the integration of zillions of possible paths. To make a good estimate of these odds we would have to take into account the 'arrows' (or make some equivalent calculation) relating to a good representative number of such paths extending at least over a lens-sized region of space. Indeed that archetype, the two-slit experiment, makes the point on its own. Closing one slit can affect a pattern of probabilities of photon arrivals spread over several centimetres. (Similar examples have been given for thought experiments on the scale of light years[7].)

That the way in which a quantum event like this is likely to happen should depend upon a situation spread out in space (ultimately on the state of the entire Universe) means that the occurrence of such an event at a particular locality had nevertheless 'to take into account' that spread-out situation. It is as if a man with a clipboard had to go rushing round collecting information – 'yes, I see, there is a double slit over there and a screen here which can catch photons: wait a moment while I measure it up . . .' – and had had to use all this information to make the calculation of where photons should have a better chance, and where they should have a smaller chance of turning up, and estimating quite accurately what these chances should be.

Well, there is no harassed man with a clipboard, but as we saw there is something almost as extraordinary. It seems to be the case that the probability of quantum events like this arises from an integration of factors which are *obviously* to do with a large-scale 'global' situation.

It works the other way too. According to the Stapp–Heisenberg picture, the Universe is a single entity. It is not only that the likelihood of a quantum event can be influenced by an earlier global situation. Once such an event has happened this will also have a global *effect*. Every event changes the Universe, changes the situation for the next event.

It is this integrative character in both the causation and effects of Heisenberg events which lies at the heart of Stapp's theory of consciousness. In his development of the Heisenberg 'ontology' (meaning 'picture of how things are') Stapp suggests that:

> This useful ontology has two defects. The first is its a run away ontology: the supposedly actual things to which the tendencies refer consist only of shifts of tendencies for future actual things, which consist, in turn, only of shifts in tendencies for still more distantly future things, and so an *ad infinitum*: each actuality is defined only in terms of possible future ones, in a sequence that never ends.
>
> The second defect is the omission from the description of nature of the one thing really known to exist: human thought.
>
> These two difficulties fit hand-in-glove: the first is that some authentic actual things are needed to break the infinite regress; the second is that some authentic actual things have been left out[8].

Stapp then proceeds to connect conscious effects with matter:

> . . . to attach to each Heisenberg event an experiental aspect. The latter is called the *feel* of this event, and it can be considered to be the aspect of the actual event that gives it its status as an intrinsic actuality.'

More particularly, Stapp considers brain matter. James had already understood the brain to be in a highly metastable state[9], on a 'hair trigger' between often radically different incipient forms of action, and he saw the role of consciousness as the critical selecting agent[10]. A hundred years later, and based particularly on Edelman's recent accounts of brain action[11] and Pribram's ideas about memory[12], Stapp can make more specific suggestions. For example, he discusses the way in which incipient patterns of activity can be defined by alternative diffuse interweaving patterns of synaptic connections of the sort presumed to be the basis of memory. But for Stapp, unlike Edelman, it is a 'Heisenberg event' that determines the issue.

We cannot put off any longer the dread question of what makes a Heisenberg event – 'an actual event' – happen. The official answer among purists is clear and precise: 'don't know'. (And 'don't care' – because a 'picture' is not necessary to get the sums to work out right.) But we have to do better than this if we are trying to invent models that might allow us to understand such undoubtedly real but rather unmathematical things as feelings. Not only Stapp's but other quantum theories of consciousness that I will be touching on attempt such a picture.

The central problem is to see when and how an event can precipitate from an evolving superposition of tendencies. This mysterious process is called (in wave language or arrow language, respectively) 'the collapse of the wave function' or 'state vector reduction.' Less formally we might ask: 'When does Nature make up her mind?'

It might seem clear enough in some cases: when the photon hits the screen *here* and permanently alters a grain of silver bromide in a photographic plate, or more generally when there is some such large-scale effect. The audible click of a Geiger counter caused by a single quantum particle is a favourite example. Like a Westinghouse brake (p. 107), or a neuron, or a whole brain, a Geiger counter is in a highly metastable state when it is set for action. It is a 'hair trigger' device.

These might seem like special cases, but really all phenomena are quantum phenomena at root and should be subject to the same sorts of 'evolutions of tendencies' as photons or atoms or molecules, and similarly calculable in principle from Schrödinger's famous wave equation, only with even more complex superpositions of tendencies to be included in the calculations.

In analysing this problem, John von Neumann considered a train of processes setting each other off to produce eventually some change in the brain of an observer[13]. Only then, he said, could you be sure that an event had actually happened at some point along the line. But von Neumann concluded that there is no way of deciding exactly where, because it would make no difference to the calculated outcome. (Hence the purist's advice – 'forget it' – but needless to say this is not advice which Stapp takes.)

Here is Stapp going into details:

> The probability for an action-potential pulse to release a vesicle at a cortical synapse appears to be about 50%. If, in some small time window (say a fraction of a millisecond), N synapses receive action-potential pulses then there will be 2^N *alternative* possible configurations of vesicle releases, each with a roughly equal probability. *Each alternative possibility is represented in the evolving quantum-mechanical wave function*[14].

Later in the paper he comes to the question of what determines which of such alternative possibilities is actualised, and expresses the view that 'pure chance' cannot be the whole answer, that if such choices appear to come from nowhere that is because we are taking too local a view. He ends with an enigma:

> ... the fundamental process that is expressing itself through these local events is intrinsically global in character: it cannot be understood as being localized in the brain, or in the body. Rather it must act in a coordinated way over much of space. Neither contemporary science nor the present work addresses the issue of how that global process works. Our ignorance concerning this intrinsically global process is represented in these theories by the introduction of 'pure choice'[15].

Enigma variations

Others have made similar attempts to put the mind-body connection at 'the collapse of the wave function'. I will try now to give some indication of the spread of ideas.

Schrödinger's equation is the basis for calculating the determinate 'evolution of tendencies' part of quantum mechanics; but it deals only in amplitudes and lets you go no further than to say what the probabilities are for any of the superimposed possibilities to 'actualise'. It cannot tell you when or why. Yet we know (or think we know) that the 'collapse' must happen at some point between the very small and the scale of ordinary-sized objects which certainly do not seem to be a superposition of alternative arrangements – they seem to be firmly one thing or another.

Schrödinger himself gave a spoof example (endlessly seriously discussed since) of a chain of events *à la* von Neumann. He asked us to imagine a cat isolated from all external influences. It is left for one hour in a large box with plenty of air (and no doubt a bowl of milk and a cat tray). In the box is 'an infernal device' consisting of a small amount of radioactive material, just enough for there to be a 50% chance of one atom disintegrating and emitting a single particle. This would be detected by a Geiger counter which if it fired would set in train a series of events leading to a flask of cyanide being cracked open and so killing the cat. This chain starts with a quantum event for which the reality should be a superposition of the two possibilities: with an atom disintegrating *and* an atom not disintegrating. The question is: Will the final outcome still be superposition of possibilities – a live cat *and* a dead cat?

For Schrödinger this was a *reductio ad absurdum* casting doubt on the whole quantum mechanical picture: obviously the cat would be either alive or dead. But not everyone agrees. Eugene Wigner, for example, suggested that perhaps the resolution only happens when the box is finally opened and the outcome is observed by somebody. The observer would also be part of the Universe, as liable to remain as a superposition of states as any other part ... Wigner's resolution of *this* was to say that states of consciousness (or perhaps living things generally) are unique in never being a superposition so that, after all, only one thing or another thing is actually observed by anyone[16].

But then there are more problems. What if there are several observers – what makes them all agree? (And did anyone ask the cat?) It would be nice to have something more objective.

Another line is to say that there are classes of *fairly* small-scale events which usually cause the collapse long before the level of large-scale objects; that the Schrödinger equation only applies sometimes. (Schrödinger himself had thought that the answer must be something like this.)[17]

Roger Penrose is highly sympathetic to the idea that in some sense consciousness is a quantum phenomenon, suspecting for example that the 'globality' of consciousness is related to the well-known non-local effects of the quantum world[18]. In his challenge to the adequacy of 'wires and switches' to account for human intelligence[19], Penrose is nevertheless skeptical about the adequacy of current quantum theory: so long as *gravity* is left out of the picture, as it still is, matter theory cannot be complete.

Penrose makes a proposal similar to Stapp's, although with less neurophysiological detail. Summing up he says:

> I am speculating that the action of conscious thinking is very much tied up with the resolving out of alternatives [of brain microstructure] that were previously in linear superposition.

But he adds:

> ... and [an unknown physics] which, I am claiming, depends on a yet-to-be-discovered theory of quantum gravity[20].

Indeed Penrose has a more specific idea here, which had been suggested independently by Paul Davies[21], that in going from the very small to the scale of ordinary objects the wave function collapses when the gravitational field of the participating components exceeds some critical value. Penrose reckons that about 10^{-5} grams might do the trick[22], but the issue is complicated by interactions with the surroundings, which might reduce the critical mass in practice. On the other hand, as Penrose points out[23], what characterises the quantum world is not so much small size as small energy differences. So perhaps we could imagine alternative patterns of neuron firing (like alternative paths of photons) remaining superposed provided their energy *differences* were very small . . .

Everett's suggestion   You will have noticed a tendency for quantum physicists, when in a philosophical vein, to think big. The Heisenberg picture, for example, was framed in terms of the entire Universe. (The main reason, incidentally, was to avoid questions about how the environment might interfere with what goes on in a local region: the whole Universe has no environment.) But for the ontological glutton there is nothing to touch Hugh Everett III's so-called 'many worlds' idea[24]. It starts with a highly satisfactory resolution of the questions of when and how the wave function of the Universe collapses, how it 'decides' from moment to moment which way to 'actualise'. Everett's suggestion was that it *never does*. All the impending outcomes 'actualise' (if we want to put it like that).

   There are various interpretations of Everett's idea. For example, here is Davies on what happens to Schrödinger's cat:

> According to Everett the transition occurs because the universe splits into two copies, one containing a live cat and the other a dead cat. Both universes contain one copy of the experimenter too, each of whom thinks he is unique. In general, if a quantum system is in a superposition of, say, n quantum states, then, on measurement [meaning observation or 'actualisation'] the universe will split into n copies. In most cases n is infinite. Hence we must accept that there are actually an infinity of 'parallel worlds' co-existing along side the one we see at any instant. Moreover, there are an infinity of individuals, more or less identical with each of us, inhabiting these worlds. It is a bizarre thought[25].

Indeed. And not everyone is happy with the idea. Creating and splitting Universes seems rather an upheaval – but this must be a way of speaking.

David Deutsch, a notable advocate of Everett's general idea, prefers to think of an infinity of parallel Universes which start identical but progressively subdivide into groups and subgroups evolving differently[26]. (At least no crow-bars would be needed in this case to prise newly formed Universes apart.)

Michael Lockwood has another way of looking at it which he describes in detail in his deep but highly readable *Mind, Brain and the Quantum*[27]. He agrees that there is no objective collapse of the wave function and that what is 'out there' is immeasurably bigger and more complicated than we can grasp in our imagination. Yes, there are 'many worlds' in a sense, but this is an unhappy term which Lockwood avoids: they should be regarded rather as many self-consistent perspectives of a single entity. It is because consciousness can only deal with one such perspective that there only seems to be one. There is only one which at any moment we can be aware of. In fact there are zillions of such perspectives each equally making physical and chemical sense. In some of these (and there are still zillions) you and your brain exist, each one in some state or other with a corresponding state of consciousness. Spread out in time there are then zillions of *sequences* of states of consciousness, 'biographies', coexisting in different perspectives of the real Universe. Lockwood comes to his crux point:

> Reduction of the state vector or collapse of the wave function, *tout court*, is, I am claiming, a myth. But collapse relative to a *biography* is a fact[28].

Then later:

> It is, incidently, senseless to ask – as do some commentators on Everett – 'Why do I find myself in *this* state?' For it isn't as though I find myself to be in one of the eligible states *as opposed to* any of the others. On the contrary, for each of the parallel states, I have an experience of finding myself in it – though these experiences are not of course co-conscious[29].

I must admit to a liking for Everett's idea and particularly Lockwood's version of it. It goes with the neo-Kantian attitude of chapter 7: that, well, things are not as they seem. And to say that the Universe is a few zillion times bigger than we had been thinking seems neither here nor there, being quite in line with a general expansive trend since Greek times.

On the other hand we *had* rather been hoping to arrive at something more brain-friendly to be going on with, more brain-sized for that matter . . .

Marshall: *Bose condensation*

It seems natural enough that a practising psychiatrist should have something interesting to say about the mechanism of consciousness. Ian Marshall is just that and his short, lucid paper of 1989 *Consciousness and Bose–Einstein Condensates* is an exercise in sharp Holmesian deduction[30].

Part of Holmes's method, if you remember, was to go straight for the most 'singular' aspect of a problem. For Marshall, here, this is the unity of consciousness. It is the first of three considerations leading to the interim conclusion that, anyway, classical physics is not going to provide a physical correlate for consciousness. (This part of the paper is somewhat Jamesian, taking a similar line to Stapp and our earlier discussions.)

The second consideration has to do with the complexity of conscious states. For all that we would say that it is less complex than the underlying neuronal computing, an average state of consciousness is still too complex to have any very small structure underlying it. A state of consciousness, say while reading a sentence or listening to a piece of music, would require *at least* 100 bits of information to specify it. Marshall then uses neurophysiological data of the kind we discussed in chapter 5 further to support the contention that 'the physical correlate of consciousness is extended in space, a pattern composed of many states of many entities'.

A third consideration, to do with locality, now makes the point. Clearly a billiard-ball view of matter will not allow identity with a state of consciousness thus spread out, but nor will other classical concepts such as fields. A field as classically conceived consists of points in space with particular values (e.g. of a gravitational force acting in a certain direction) and this is a kind of atomism too: Marshall sees it as the general assumption of classical mechanics that all systems can be 'analysed into smaller parts having separate identities and only local interactions'. So classical physics will not do.

But nor (fortunately) does quantum mechanics give a blanket reassurance that there is nothing to worry about because non-local effects are so common. Marshall is much sharper than this. The physical components providing the substrate of consciousness must at least lose their identity: in technical terms, their wave functions must overlap. This happens

10

Conversation and coda

When they met in the park Advo and Krit had started talking about a book they had both been reading. Krit as usual was full of Questions and Difficulties – to which, as was his wont, Advo provided Answers and Resolutions. It was a book about the mind. The conversation had started with some rather arcane discussion about whether the author favoured Interactionist Dualism or Central-State Materialism, or what. Not a single 'ism' had appeared in the text so the matter was unclear, until Advo, who had read the book the more carefully of the two, pointed to a note in chapter 7 where an 'ism' was discovered: 'neutral monism' seemed to be what the author was more or less following – that mind and matter are each rooted in the same underlying 'stuff'.

When we join them Krit has got on to one of his Questions.

KRIT You say there are three systems of the mind: briefly these are chemical, neural-computing and conscious – that all three would have to be there before we would start calling a control system a mind, and that the hardware underlying each evolved one from the other. We have so far failed to find the special equipment for making and reacting to consciousness, but you say that if we look a bit harder something will turn up, some sort of global quantum mechanical effect.

Now my concern is this. If a classical account of brain action in terms of atoms and molecules is not going to give us an insight as to what the pain of a toothache is, I don't see that funny quantum effects, in Bose–Einstein condensates or whatever, are going to do any better. I don't see what going from one kind of physics to another kind of physics buys you. All you are ever going to be able to say is: 'When this happens (in the brain) that happens (to our feelings) and I don't know why'.

ADVO I agree with you that at *some* stage we will have to say 'I don't know why', but this is standard practice. Newton had much the same attitude to gravity. Ultimately he didn't know why either. Gravity was just a fact of Nature. But that is not to say that the good Sir Isaac did not have some illuminating things to say on the subject. The whole idea is that when you don't understand something you eventually draw a line under it and call it a fundamental law.

KRIT   Yes, but the progress of science has been precisely a continuing reduction in the number of fundamental mysteries . . .

ADVO   Who says? Some modern cosmologists perhaps, but they are not speaking the truth. In the good old days of Democritus there were only atoms and void . . . But then it turned out that a picture of the world consisting only of atoms in motion was quite simply inadequate to account for the full richness of phenomena. When fields were introduced there were people who felt it was somehow cheating. Yet now fields are on centre stage. There are people like Stapp who would put feelings on centre stage – or anyway in there on an equal footing as one of the great fundamentals – and I think that is the sort of direction to be going. Current physics is too neat, too Democritean still, too simple and too simpleminded: *it* does not account for the full richness of phenomena. Science advances sometimes by making things simpler, sometimes by making them more complicated – or rather by seeing them as being more complicated than had previously been thought. The existence of feelings is such an added complication to be faced.

KRIT   Well, I might be prepared to go along with that as a long-term view, but it is too vague to be useful right now. Let us try and sharpen the immediate argument. If consciousness really is a third system this means that even if we understood everything about systems 1 and 2 we would not be able to explain everything about animal behaviour, including of course human behaviour. Is that correct?

ADVO   Yes indeed: the third system of the mind is *not* just a global way of describing the first and second systems . . .

KRIT   OK. So let me tell you a story of a friend of mine, a computer manufacturer, who once examined a competitor's product to see how it worked. He could see all the electrical circuitry and it was clear that the computer did much better than it should have been able to on the basis of its circuitry. It was some time ago and my friend had not noticed that what he had taken to be insulation were optical fibres carrying information in the form of light signals . . . There were two collaborating systems in the computer. My friend admitted that it had crossed his mind that maybe he was dealing with a conscious product (its efficiency really was baffling), but of course abandoned such whimsy when he knew what was going on.

Is this not perhaps like the brain – that there is some hardware in there which we have not yet understood?

ADVO   Absolutely – except that the hardware that we have not noticed is more subtle than glass fibres, and is not the kind of thing molecular biologists have so far thought much about . . .

KRIT   My point is that it need not be mysterious at all. I understand that your reason for having this third system is that there has to be some overall control – through consciousness behaving something like a low-capacity serial computer strapped on to the high-capacity parallel design of the neural computer. But why do you insist that the system-2 hardware is not enough for this sort of thing and will never be enough to explain consciousness? Why introduce another kind of physics, for goodness' sake?

For example, one could imagine a kind of diffuse supervisory network of long fibres which keeps every region in the brain in close contact – much as Baars suggests in his extended reticular plus thalamic activating system – and that it is the activity of this network, made of ordinary neurons perhaps, which constitutes consciousness.

The 'global' and 'limited capacity' aspects of consciousness and its way of working through switching attention from one thing to another, comes about because the grand network is of a piece, there is only one such network, there can only be one principal use for it at a time. (For example the network gets connected particularly tightly to bits of the brain concerned with speech when we are trying to think of the next word . . .)

ADVO   It is an interesting idea. How are the appropriate connections made: how is it, for example, that different aspects of visual information about objects are analysed in different places in the brain and yet somehow we perceive them together?

KRIT   Of course this is a big problem – it's called the binding problem. There is good evidence now for what is called temporal coding as a 'classical' way of solving it. It is early days yet, but what seems to be happening is that sets of, perhaps distant, neurons in the brain which are analysing aspects of the same object oscillate in phase (at frequencies around

40 Hz) and in little bursts the patterns of which also correspond. So this is perhaps how they keep together. They sing together. Furthermore, artificial neural networks can simulate such effects: they are understandable simply in terms of oscillating circuitry[1].

ADVO   Well, I have always felt there must be system-2 (unconscious) mechanisms for such things. When I look at a stereo pair of pictures and it takes a few seconds for it to develop into a 3-D image I am curiously aware that there are unconscious integrating mechanisms at work over which I have little control. The 'tip of the tongue' effect, when you can't quite remember something but it comes back to you after a few moments thinking about something else, is again evidence that unconscious processors are able to act in concert with consciousness and produce similar effects to conscious thought.

Clearly there is functional overlap. But just as clearly there is some non-overlap – particularly when pains and pleasures come into the logic. Indeed I do not deny that an entirely unconscious mechanism might be imagined that would account for everything that a brain can do. What I deny is that this is actually the way the brain works.

KRIT   Did you really mean *logic*?

ADVO   Of course. Is it not so, that the qualities of our sensations are relevant to our actions? Sensations are evidently part of the control mechanism. It actually matters that suffocation is a horrible feeling, that eating is enjoyable and so on. Such points would seem hardly worth making, if it were not for people like you, Krit, who tell me that such conscious phenomena simply arise from patterns of action potentials, etc. – the *same* such patterns of activity that would bring about the appropriate actions anyway.

Now if pleasures and pains are *not* just passive experiences which might as well not have been there, if they are indeed effective parts of our central control machinery, that means that an explanation of behaviour without them is incomplete. Even if the brain processes accompanying feeding happened to produce sensations there would be no reason for these sensations to be pleasurable unless *their being pleasurable* had effects on future behaviour – as common sense tells us they do.

Then again, various kinds of feelings and sensations are part of the working model we make to understand the world and to deal with it. It uses sensations of colour, of time, of form and so on. Let me give you an example of your use of this feeling-based model. Remember the final hole in the golf match last Saturday?

KRIT   I certainly do. What a putt that was!

ADVO   Well, apart from trying not to notice the little boy on the edge of the green making faces at his sister, what were you doing consciously as you stood there quite still, intent on sinking that vital long putt over a bumpy green with patches of damp moss on it? Were you calculating? No doubt your cerebral processors were working flat out to balance up the factors which they had become informed of as you had strolled over to see where the ball was and how it lay. But consciously as you stood there you were not calculating. You were going by the feel of it. The third system of your mind was in control.

KRIT   But these are subjective matters.

ADVO   Yes, but not purely subjective. You sank the putt. That is an objective, much-talked-about fact. Anyway feelings are not a purely subjective matter if you accept the central theory of biology – evolution through natural selection. Experience tells us that feelings exist, but the argument from then on, the argument for their efficacy, is objective. Without there being *effects* of feelings, natural selection would have been as impotent in connecting them up appropriately as it is in determining any characteristic which is of no biological consequence.

Consider for a moment an example of what happens in such a case – in protein evolution. Sometimes it seems that several related amino acid sequences for, say, an enzyme are just as good as each other – that there is no discernible difference in function between them. What happens in such cases is what is called drift: which of the sequences comes to be established eventually is a matter of pure chance. Now if feelings and sensations could have no effects then connections between sensations and activities such as feeding would similarly have *drifted*, leading to the oddest situation of beings which had all sorts of quite inappropriate sensations associated with nevertheless normal effective biological functions.

We know that this was not the outcome. We know it from our own experiences. So we know that feelings are not just epiphenomena like shadows, but that they are part of the mechanism of the central control system of ourselves and so presumably of other animals too. And so we know that our formulation of science is wrong if it cannot possibly provide a place for causally effective feelings as part of the machinery of the brain.

Now I agree that none of this is going to tell us exactly what formulation of physics and chemistry we should use, but it does allow us to exclude some. It will exclude any which could always in principle provide complete explanations for the movements of atoms and molecules. A hundred years ago that is what physics and chemistry looked like, and it is still more or less the molecular biologist's view of it.

The main thing going for quantum theory was realised decades ago. It is that quantum mechanics is a formulation of physics which is suitably incomplete. Within the framework of quantum mechanics there are certain kinds of question which it is senseless to ask. It is not that the logic of the quantum mechanical frame is loose or rickety. Far from it. It is that the frame is just that – a frame. It leaves room for other things in the Universe than atoms in motion . . .

KRIT What about the theory of chaos? That is not a quantum theory, yet it is also in a sense incomplete. It also says that you cannot predict everything in absolute detail.

ADVO Well, yes, Freeman and Skarda go for that idea, so we should take it seriously. Really I have not thought this through properly – but if you want an opinion all the same it is a bit too understandable for my taste, too mathematical rather than physical . . .

KRIT You prefer 'the surrogate spooks of physics' as Edelman rather rudely put it[2].

ADVO Oh, much. I mean, the real world *is* just incredibly spooky, is it not? Don't get me wrong: I too like models framed in terms of our our inherited forms of thought, but the bad news is that such models never go all the way. Spooks have been coming in all the time: immutable atoms, force at a distance, potential energy . . . Physics has always been full of this. It cannot be framed exactly according to our inherited 'common sense', so we invent compromise models – and they do remarkably well. All too soon we forget their origins and begin to believe them, as if they *were* reality, which of course they are not. Like everything else in science they are provisional, even if it is true that we cannot *always* be doubting ideas which have served us well in the past and have become fundamental to our thinking.

So it is natural and proper to try to explain as much as we can in terms of the models we have; to try to explain brain action, for example, in similar terms to those we use for the fundamental processes of life – i.e. in terms of current models of molecular biology. But this approach, however successful to begin with, and however successful still in uncovering unconscious mechanisms of perception, thought, memory, etc., fails at consciousness. If I were to choose a single sentence from the book to make this point it would be from near the end of chapter five, the chapter on neural correlates of consciousness (you know, what goes on in the the brain to correspond to particular feelings, that sort of stuff). Let me read it to you:

> Yet the elusive Ultimate Correlate cannot really be anything we understand in terms of current models of molecular biology and computing: the more we understand the functions of consciousness in these terms the less comprehensible the phenomenon of consciousness becomes, because the less reason there is for ever feeling anything.

Similar points have been made often enough, but it is time to stop ignoring them as some of the most prominent thinkers on this subject still do.

KRIT   It sounds to me like throwing in the sponge.

ADVO   No, no. We have to extend our understanding of the nature of matter. Those masses of organised molecules in the box behind your eyes are definitely doing something spooky. They are making pains and pleasures – and making *use* of them for the central control mechanism. Long ago natural selection discovered some properties of matter for which we have still no agreed models.

KRIT   Well, maybe, but let's come down to earth again. The brain as a physical object does not seem that spooky. For example, I can ask you firmly enough: 'Where is the specialised equipment for system-3?'

ADVO   An absolutely fair question, and Marshall and Zohar have an answer anyway: oscillating molecules in the membranes of neurons which get pushed into something like a Bose condensation through being continually supplied with energy. Walker and then Domash had come up with rather similar ideas. I have all sorts of doubts about the details, but I think consciousness should be seen as something *like* that, something which, for all its dependence on brain action for its existence, has a certain integrity, an integrity based on a different physical principle than 'the long wires' of system-2, and which accounts for system-3's distinctive features. Our conscious selves *seem* to be quasi-independent agents which operate through feelings. And I think they are that.

I take it that like every other inheritable aspect of our being our forms of consciousness evolved. Now any invention of natural selection has to be specified by DNA molecules. So there is no question: if consciousness evolved then it is part of the material world. It depends nevertheless on properties of organised matter which simply do not come in anywhere else in physics and chemistry as far as we know. Of what other kind of matter except brain matter would you seriously say 'it behaved this way so as to feel better'? Or of what other kind of mechanism except an awake brain do we feel any need to suppose that there is a whole vivid perceptual world inside it?

KRIT   How do you know that feelings are not everywhere – that ions, say, don't 'feel better' when they move in an electric field? The difference might be that an ion has no way of telling us about the subtle psychological pressures that made it behave as it did . . .

ADVO   We don't know, of course. All I am saying is that we don't need to assume any psychology for atoms or ions in describing how they behave. Brains are different in this respect. To speak very cautiously, the difference seems to be something to do with scale and organisation – a kind of organisation accessible to evolution. Let me try to explain what I mean using again the boson speculation.

We have been speculating, in effect, that consciousness is a form of energy, or perhaps we should say a convoluted energy flow, a kind of complex eddy. A state of consciousness, a feeling, is (say) one of an immense number of different dynamic patternings of short-lived bosons – maybe phonons or virtual photons – set up by the brain through mechanisms influenced by but not identical to the mechanisms responsible for unconscious processing. (*like* a laser perhaps, as Marshall suggested, but a laser would be a crass photon organiser by comparison.)

Now *why* such a dynamically maintained eddy should also be a state of consciousness would have to be seen in the meantime at least as just one of those fundamental mysteries as, say, the gravitational force was for Newton (still is as far as I am concerned). It is just one of those things, and incidentally, like gravity, it is something whose effects may be imperceptible on a very small scale. I may say the gravitational force between two protons is only about one part in 10^{39} of the electrostatic force between them: a fat chance that gravitation would ever have been discovered just by watching protons. So I imagine consciousness to be a higher-order large-scale effect: somewhat like gravity in this sense, but with properties which are much more complex than the gravitational force – the outcome of a much more structured set of circumstances 'engineered' by natural selection. I have a preference for protein molecules as being central players, in spite of difficulties discussed in chapter nine of the book, because these are the most minutely 'engineerable' structures in biology; they can be complex machines and sets of billions of closely similar ones[3] can be easily manufactured by cells. I mean, just think of motor proteins, muscle molecules, those actin polymers within cells, or microtubules which Stuart Hameroff sees as tied to consciousness – all those seemingly magical things which can happen when ATP energy is in abundant supply[4]. Well, perhaps feelings are other such magical things 'discovered' by evolution, the most surprising of all because based on physical effects which we have yet to come to grips with . . .

KRIT A bit of a coincidence, wasn't it? I mean, natural selection beavering away at making computer control machinery when, hey presto!, the machinery begins to feel things, to have urges . . .

ADVO It's a serious point. There could have been no sudden 'hey presto', of course, any more than, say, lungs or hands burst upon the world all of a sudden. New inventions in evolution start off as accidental side effects, alternative uses being made of pre-existing structures – which are said to be preadapted to the new functions. To begin with such functions will be useful rather than essential – 'optional extras' – and are likely to be rather inefficiently carried out.

Now your question should have been: What was it about evolving nervous systems which preadapted them to become conscious? It is of course not enough just to answer 'because even a primitive consciousness would have been useful for such systems', true though that might be. We want some ideas about *how*. I made an attempt a moment ago. The essential preadaptation came from the ability of organisms to make sets of billions of similar yet complex machines – protein molecules, cells – as well as to maintain a reliable head of energy in the form of ATP. As far as we know there is nothing like this in Nature outside organisms.

As usual for preadaptations, feelings would have been 'optional extras' when the first forms of them appeared, weak effects perhaps, biasing the odds slightly between one thing happening or another. Later, as more specialised machinery evolved, the effects would become more integrated, and more powerful and sophisticated . . .

In discussing Marshall's ideas, and the question of where the specialised equipment for consciousness might be, Lockwood remarked that it might not only be neurons, but other sorts of cell as well, whose cell membranes help to sustain the collective oscillatory states that, on this view, constitute consciousness[5].

Following from the evolutionary considerations just touched on, we might actually *expect* cells other than neurons to be the primary makers of consciousness. We might suppose that neurons have quite enough to do making and being sensitive to action potentials, etc. They seem to be highly evolved for this. Making consciousness – a concert of a zillion bosons or whatever it is – looks like a different job. We might expect that the instruments most active here would be in cells (or of cells) that were in touch with but not at the heart of the system-2 computer. Glial cells look to be well placed . . .

KRIT   Mmm. We might come back to that, but first let me set you a trap. Are you saying that our consciousness actually has a location in space?

ADVO   Well, yes, as much as anything can ever be said to have a location. Feelings are made in the head.

KRIT   I would agree, but how does this square with quantum theories of consciousness, which make much of the non-local aspects of quantum causes and quantum effects? I am thinking particularly of the more grandiose theories which bring in the whole Universe. It seems clear that our consciousness is indeed well located in our heads, or telepathy would be more evident than it is.

Indeed the question of the location of consciousness is greatly sharpened by those 'split-brain' phenomena. Crudely and approximately, if you cut the connecting wires between the two hemispheres of a brain with a

that system-3 has no power beyond the motor cortex and presumably intervenes before it.

Another clue is provided by people suffering from Parkinson's disease, who may be unable to carry out their intentions. A typical remark here: 'My fingers won't do what I tell them'[10]. The situation is less clear here, since Parkinsonism is a complex disease resulting from insufficient supplies of dopamine to various places in the brain, but the main blockage seems to be at the striatum. So it seems that such Parkinson patients are telling us that general conscious intentions to act must be arrived at before the striatum.

Well, it is the whole cortex, more or less, which feeds information into the striatum: very many separated processors working away frantically at detailed calculations of the sort that never 'reach consciousness'. It would fit the facts as far as they go to say that it is on the way across between the cortex and the striatum that it all comes together: because the machinery for consciousness – for making feelings – is located in the intervening white matter . . . It is an amusing thought.

KRIT   They 'reach consciousness' in the process of transmission between the two sets of grey matter processors, those in the cortex and those in the striatum (and other basal ganglia)? Certainly consciousness *is* associated with signals being transmitted over long distances through the central white matter in the brain. It would be nice to have something more definite about how it works, this spooky stuff slurping about inside the brain. How is it affected by System-2? How does it act on System-2?

ADVO   That I can answer easily. Don't know.

KRIT   Ignorance doesn't usually stop you, Advo.

ADVO   True. And come to think of it there are some more things to be said, indications of where the answers may lie. In the first place the organisation of bosons, if that is the kind of theory we are following, must be able to exist in different states: very many such states which correspond to – sorry, *are* – states of consciousness as seen from the outside as it were. These would be excited states somewhat analogous to excited states in an atom only with very many more possible ones. Marshall and Zohar have suggested an analogy with complex patterns of waves on the surface of a pond or indeed complex sound waves.

An interesting thing about a wave form, however complicated, is that it can be said to be made up of a superimposition of simpler wave forms[11]. It can be mathematically analysed into simpler forms – and can be synthesised from them too. So a waveform has that odd feature about consciousness, which William James emphasised: although consciousness can be said to have 'contents', it is at the same time a single indivisible whole.

Now to make some attempt at your questions, think about a piano (just an ordinary piano). You can play a chord on it and generate quite a complex wave form. But you can do the opposite too. You can *give* the piano a sound. With the loud pedal down to free the strings, sing a simple note and you will set one or a few strings going. Give them a more complex sound, bashing a biscuit tin or shouting, and you will set most of the strings going more or less.

Indeed, our ears work somewhat like this. In the cochlea of the inner ear there are innumerable bundles of actin-filled 'stereocilia' of graded sizes and positions, each bundle tuned to a slightly different sound frequency. But like a set of open piano strings, sets of these respond according to the detailed waveform that is coming through to them. You can hear a whole orchestra this way. A sound generated in the first place by separate orchestral instruments comes to activate another set of separate instruments, the microscopic bundles of your inner ear. But in between, for all its multiple causes and effects, there is a single wave form.

KRIT   At the last concert I was at the second trumpet dropped his spectacles during the slow movement – I could hear the clatter. It was definitely not of a piece with the music . . .

ADVO   So you say, but all such judgments are in the ear of the hearer. Actually there is only one fantastically complicated wave form: your ear-brain decides how to analyse it into trumpets and oboes and clattering spectacles. Such a wave form can be written down as one immensely squiggly line. It *is* written down like that on an LP disc, and is in effect transmitted like that in a radio broadcast.

KRIT   So are you suggesting that the condensate 'sings different tunes' as it were in different parts of the brain which are somehow 'received' by protein molecules or whatever in appropriate brain cells?

ADVO   I imagine the state of the condensate reacting back on the brain in some way very broadly analogous to the way we hear sounds. But as to your idea of the different parts of the condensate singing different tunes, no, I think that's wrong.

I don't think it can be generally so that modulations are made in different ways in different places, so that over there in the right frontal lobe there is one complex wave pattern, while on the other side or away over there in an occipital lobe another pattern holds sway. Such things may happen, presumably in split-brain patients, perhaps in schizophrenics[12] – perhaps in all of us to the extent that our consciousness is never entirely of a piece. But this is a side issue. It would be like saying that in a different part of the concert hall you get a different acoustic, or hear too much of the double basses. But really you hear all the music everywhere. That is the whole idea of a concert hall.

Now the price you pay for this way of doing it – using space to broadcast in – is that you do not then have it so easily available for modulation, for making spatial structures. We have to say that the main structuring of the flame of consciousness must be in time not space (a form *à la* Mozart rather than Michaelangelo) – that generally speaking there is only one waveform, however complicated it is, however much it changes, however many molecules in however many places are used to create it: or however many molecules in however many places may come to be affected by it. What happens in one place within the flame is happening everywhere. That again is the whole idea. That is the nature of the 'global broadcasting' which for Baars provides the *raison d'être* of consciousness. It is not in System-3 but in System-2 that a spatial diversity of structure and activity is standard practice.

We might suppose that a memory is recalled, in so far as consciousness plays a part in its recall, not by locating it in space – the condensate shifting around, say, to find and light up some particular location – but by tuning for it in some way rather as a radio receiver can be tuned for a particular carrier wave. Here, though, it would be signals which were being tuned for. (It would be like having a radio that could be tuned, say, to pick up Mozart whatever station was transmitting it . . .) Notice that with such a procedure there would be no need for the instruments which are to be activated to be close to each other: what is to be 'lit up' could as well be distributed as a million sparks all over the brain even if more concentrated in some regions than others. Memories then of the kind which can be brought to consciousness could be (as they probably are) so distributed throughout the cortex.

KRIT   What about PET scans where different small areas of cortex can be seen to be active when a subject is thinking in different ways?

ADVO   By revealing changing patterns of blood supply, PET mainly monitors differences in energy requirements. I would guess that PET scans monitor system-2 processors. System-3 would also have energy requirements, but I would guess not nearly so patchy.

KRIT   EEG then: what about the findings that very often the same quite complex EEG signals may be recorded from distant electrodes attached to the head[12]? Might this be some sort of indicator of the kind of concerted activity you are talking about? EEG signals are known to correlate with states of consciousness to some extent. On the other hand they seem to be straightforward global potentials caused by concerted activities of neurons. They certainly don't seem to *be* consciousness – I mean I don't feel, see, hear or in any way become conscious of a regular tenth-second pulse when I close my eyes, although I am told that electrodes attached to my head would register this 'α-rhythm'. Ditto for more complex patterns which would be produced when I am alert.

ADVO   I agree with most of that. In so far as we are imagining the phenomena of consciousness as arising from the activities of large numbers of brain cells, there might be some connection. For example, EEG signals might reflect brain mechanisms for generating the contents of consciousness. Alternatively it might be a response to conscious states acting on the brain. (Or of course sometimes one, sometimes the other.)

Thinking more generally, in so far as we are imagining that system-3 is activated 'by the whole brain' (more or less), then system-2 of the whole brain has to get its act together so that the required neural activities are concerted. On the other hand, in so far as system-3 acts 'on the whole brain' (more or less) this should *result* in concerted activities in separated parts of the system-2 circuitry. One might be able to decide between these two possibilities. The activation *of* system-3 should be through concerted system-2 neuronal processes which are explicable in the sense that you would be able to see what prior brain processes had brought them about – but you would not be able to see what the point was in system-2 (and/or system-1) terms. On the other hand the activation of system-2 *by* system-3 would produce some neuronal activity out of the blue, as it were. Here, though, they would be understandable in the sense of contributing to neuronal processes which ultimately produced appropriate behaviour.

KRIT   I see that you mean by 'system-3' not only consciousness but specific apparatus which you imagine is producing it and responding to it. You are saying now that there should thus be some things about the brain about which one could understand *how* but not *why*, and others *why* but not *how*? This might be a useful guide. But I suspect this sort of thing is a general property of gaps in understanding control machinery of any sort. Like my friend's mysteriously effective computer, this could simply be because there were aspects of system-2 which were not yet understood. Merely to find apparent gaps in brain circuitry would not be to establish that such gaps must be filled by consciousness or have anything to do with it.

ADVO   Indeed. But there must be such gaps somewhere if feelings are to be part of our central control mechanism and not inconsequential epiphenomena.

KRIT   If this is so one really ought to be able to say *where* more precisely. For example, would you not expect the 'how but not why' puzzles to appear in the input perceptual circuitry, while the 'why but not how' ones should turn up in brain processes leading to motor outputs?

ADVO   Things might be a bit more complicated than this. There is a continual to and fro between conscious and unconscious. For example you may need to be be consciously aware of the results of your actions . . . But I get the idea. We might be able to make some sensible guesses about circuitry by concentrating on what we think consciousness does, and forget for the moment such questions as what it is in physical terms or how in detail it works.

Well, we are supposing that consciousness as whole simulates a piece of computing hardware. But it has quite a low capacity – nothing like as complex as system-2. And it *is* somewhat ephemeral, coming and going. But it makes up for this by being in touch with (and highly switchable between) different activities, adding assistance, as it were, where need be. Above all it seems to be a decider between divergent possible outcomes set up by system-2. It might seem to be like a coin tosser in this respect: one can easily think of neuronal mechanisms which could be 'deciders' of this sort (one neuron would do, come to think of it). But that, it seems, is not how consciousness works. 'It does not act determinately nor does it act at random. It does what it feels like' as it says rather cryptically in the book [p. 251] – but now we are trying to do a little bit better than this. We are still not asking the deep question – how *could* it do what it feels like? – but how in circuit terms would it have to, to make biological sense.

You imagine this little box of changing feelings. How are pains curtailed and pleasures enhanced? Let me put up some Aunt Sally ideas for you to shoot at.

First idea: It is in the very nature of feelings that once they have been produced by the brain they are self-manipulating.

KRIT   Of course this is no good. If our consciousness had developed that sort of power it would have been *eliminated* by natural selection. We would all be psychological junkies dreaming ourselves into beautiful states, never getting on with the hard tasks of finding food, stuffing it inside ourselves, reproducing and so on and on. Consciousness cannot be so directly self-manipulating.

ADVO   Second idea: Feelings cannot change themselves directly, but they can act on their immediate means of production in the brain and change themselves that way.

KRIT   This is still too direct – the same objections apply.

ADVO   Third idea: Feelings cannot act on their immediate means of production but can act on certain other brain mechanisms – 'receivers' – which are in turn wired up to the feeling generators.

KRIT   Now we're just going round in ever-increasing circles . . .

ADVO   Increasing circles, yes, but there is some point in this. Now there would be opportunities for connections with behaviour. The 'receivers' might now both set in train unconscious processes – act on system-2 – and alter states of consciousness by acting back on the state generators. And then of course things would have been so arranged that system-2 is influenced so that (on the whole) biologically effective behaviour results.

KRIT   And it was natural selection which set up the critical connections. How, I wonder? It is far more than just a system-3 'wheel' meshing (sometimes) with system-2 machinery. It is more than just reacting to an itch . . . Think of all the to-ing and fro-ing that must go on in conscious *thought*! Myriads of wheels, myriads of contrived connections . . .

ADVO   Well, conscious thinking would have been a late invention. By all accounts the 'downtown' area of the brain, the limbic system, with its 'centres' of pleasure and anguish, has a longer history than the model-making, thinking, cortex, which seems to have developed later.

I would imagine that it was through a rudimentary pleasure–pain system that conscious effects first caught on. But then we might speculate that feelings of different sorts appeared through mutations in genes controlling their means of production, with new kinds of pleasures and pains appearing. More neutral feelings with little or no pleasure–pain aspect to them could have had a use, however, in evolving perceptual models which were now no longer wholly unconscious. So, perhaps, there arose such sensations as colours, sounds, and so on[13]. And then there are sensations associated with what we call forms, forces, movement . . . the stuff on which our perceptual dreams are largely made.

To get to conscious thinking we would have to imagine still further derivatives of the original pains and pleasures: feelings of doubt and certainty, of puzzlement and recognition . . .

In all this I have in mind the idea that the underlying instruments that produce feelings of different sorts and react to conscious states are very plural indeed, that they are microscopic structures distributed widely in brain matter. As you know, I rather fancy the notion that it is in or around the wiring of the brain, the white matter, that the 'generators' and 'receivers' will be mainly found. This may be quite wrong of course. But what does seem clear from the most general evolutionary considerations – and indeed from your golf – is that our feelings are part of our control circuitry; that they are brain-made physical effects which are physical causes also.

I think Lucretius was on the right lines when he described mind as an exceptional kind of matter ('particles exceptionally small and smooth and round'), although nineteenth- and twentieth-century science may have let us improve on this a bit. No doubt twenty-first-century neurobiology and matter theory will produce some weird and wiser insights into the substrate of our inner being, into what it is, this consciousness, that Nature discovered in evolving the mind.

KRIT   Let's agree on that, and go and have some coffee.
We leave the friends on this note. Their discussions over coffee drifted to more political matters. They got on to a polemical piece which Krit, I think it was, had found in a newspaper. The writer was saying that with so many urgent

problems in the world it was a waste of time and money to be concerned with research on 'the mystery of human consciousness'. They both of them wondered if the writer had ever known anyone suffering from a disease of consciousness – severe depression, Alzheimer's, schizophrenia . . .

Notes

[1] For accounts of temporal coding etc see Engel *et al.* (1992); Llinás (1990); Gray & Singer (1989); Stryker (1989), Singer (1994), Sillito *et al.* (1994); Tank *et al.* (1994); Laurent & Davidowitz (1994).

[2] Edelman (1992), p. 217.

[3] Similar, not identical. Any two protein molecules are almost bound to be different because of differences in isotopic composition: for example, of the carbon atoms in the molecule about one in a hundred, distributed in a random way, will be slightly heavier – i.e. ^{13}C instead of ^{12}C.

[4] The anaesthesiologist Stuart Hameroff was perhaps the first to suggest that an abundant cellular protein (tubulin in microtubules) was directly associated with consciousness (Hameroff & Watt 1982; Hameroff, 1987).

[5] Lockwood (1989), p. 258.

[6] Sperry (1966), pp. 302–3.

[7] Barres (1991); Dani, Chernjavsky & Smith (1992). See comment on consciousness in Kimelberg & Norenberg (1989), p. 52. Also Nedergaard (1994) on signalling from astrocytes to neurons via gap junctions.

[8] Jasper (1966), pp. 259–60.

[9] Penfield (1958); Penfield & Roberts (1959); Baars (1988), p. 256.

[10] Flowers (1987).

[11] This is true anyway for a waveform at a particular instant, or for cases where the mechanisms producing the component forms are simple (linear) and not, for example, affected indirectly by their own activities. In such more complex cases the systems may evolve in ways which are more or less unpredictable and anyway not a superposition of separately evolved elements. As discussed in chapter 6 ('an orchestral metaphor', p. 204, such situations might provide more realistic models for consciousness, which, although it may have features such as moods which may change only slowly, has other characteristics that are far more evanescent. See also Freeman (1991) on chaos in perception, and Gleick (1988), which contains descriptions of how chaotic effects in general are produced.

[12] See Thatcher and John (1977), ch. 13, and Freeman (1991) on correlations between EEG signals.

[13] Smells in particular can register very directly as pleasant or unpleasant –
but then smells are largely dealt with by more ancient parts of the cortex
(see chapter 5, page 160).

Reference list

Abercrombie, M. (1980). The crawling movement of metazoan cells. *Proceedings of the Royal Society*, B **207**, 129–47.

Aghajanian, G. K. & Rasmussen, K. (1987). Physiology of the mid brain. Serotonin systems. In *Psychopharmacology: The Third Generation of Progress*, ed. H. Meltzer, pp. 141–9. New York: Raven Press.

Albert, D. Z. (1994). Bohm's alternative to quantum mechanics. *Scientific American* **270**, no. 5, 32–9.

Alberts, B., Bray, D., Lewis, J., Raff, M., Roberts, K. & Watson, J. D. (1989). *Molecular Biology of the Cell*, 2nd ed. New York: Garland Publishing.

Alkon, D. L. (1989). Memory storage and neural systems. *Scientific American* **261**, no. 1, 26–34.

Allen, R. D. (1987). The microtubule as an intracellular engine. *Scientific American* **256**, no. 2, 26–33.

Amato, I. (1993). Theory meets experiment in high-T superconductivity. *Science* **261**, 294.

Amos, L. A. (1985). Structure of muscle filaments studied by electron microscopy. *Annual Review of Biophysics and Biophysical Chemistry* **14**, 291–313.

Animalu, A. O. E. (1977). *Intermediate Quantum Theory of Crystalline Solids*, p. 68. Englewood Cliffs, New Jersey: Prentice-Hall.

Aoki, C. & Siekevitz, P. (1988). Plasticity and brain development. *Scientific American* **259**, no. 6, 34–42.

Artola, A., Bröcher, S. & Singer, W. (1990). Different voltage-dependent thresholds for inducing long-term depression and long-term potentiation in slices of rat visual cortex. *Nature* **347**, 69–72.

Atkinson, E. R. (1940). *Journal of Chemical Education* **17**, 3–11.

Baars, B. J. (1988). *A Cognitive Theory of Consciousness*. Cambridge University Press.

Baldwin, R. L. (1990). Protein chemistry: Pieces of the folding puzzle. *Nature* **346**, 409–410.

Barres, B. A. (1991). New roles for glia. *Journal of Neuroscience* **11**, 3685–94.

Barrow, J. D. (1990). *The World within the World*. Oxford University Press.

Bechgaard, K. & Jérome, D. (1982). Organic superconductors. *Scientific American* **247**, no. 1, 50–9.

Bement, W. M. & Mooseker, M. S. (1993). Molecular motors: keeping out the rain. *Nature* **365**, 785–6.

Bendall, D. S. (ed.) (1983). *Evolution from Molecules to Men*. Cambridge University Press.

Bennett, C. H. (1987). Demons, engines and the second law. *Scientific American* **257**, no. 5, 88–96.

Bennett, W. S. Steitz, T. A. (1980). Structure of a complex between yeast hexokinase A and glucose. *Journal of Molecular Biology* **140**, 211–30.

Berkeley, G. (1710/1713/1988). *Principles of Human Knowledge* and *Three Dialogues between Hylas and Philonius*, ed. R. Woolhouse. Harmondsworth: Penguin.

Berkson, W. (1974). *Fields of Force: the Development of a World View from Faraday to Einstein*, p. 142. London: Routledge.

Bohm, D. (1980). *Wholeness and the Implicate Order*. London: Routledge.

Bourne, H. R., Sanders, D. A. & McCormick, F. (1991). The GTPase superfamily: conserved structure and molecular mechanism. *Nature* **349**, 117–27.

Bradford, H. F. (1987). Neurotransmitters and neuromodulators. In *The Oxford Companion to the Mind*, ed. R. L. Gregory, pp. 550–60. Oxford University Press.

Brodal, A. (1981). *Neurological Anatomy*, 3rd ed. New York: Oxford University Press.

Brodmann, K. (1914). Physiologie des Gehirns. *Neue Deutsche Chirurgie* **11**(1), 88–398.

Brokaw, C. J. (1986). Future directions for studies of mechanisms for generating flagellar bending waves. *Journal of Cell Science*, Supplement, 4, 103–13.

Brown, R. (1828). Microscopical observations. *Philosophical Magazine* 4, 161–73.

Bunge, M. B. (1986). The axonal cytoskeleton. *Trends in Neurosciences* 9, 477–82.

Bycroft, M., Matouschek, A., Kellis, J. T. Jr, Serrano, L. & Fersht, A. R. (1990). Detection and charactrisation of folding intermediate in barnase by NMR. *Nature* 346, 488–90.

Cadée, G. C. (1991). Brownian Emotion. *Nature* 354, 180.

Cairns-Smith, A. G. (1971). *The Life Puzzle*. Edinburgh: Oliver & Boyd.

Cairns-Smith, A. G. (1982). *Genetic Takeover*. Cambridge University Press.

Cairns-Smith, A. G. (1985). *Seven Clues to the Origin of Life*. Cambridge University Press.

Calford, M. (1991). Curious cortical change. *Nature* 352, 759–80.

Churchland, P. S. (1981). On the alleged backwards referral of experiences and its relevance to the mind-body problem. *Philosophy of Science* 48, 165–81.

Clerk Maxwell, J. (1864/1983). *A Dynamical Theory of the Electromagnetic Field*, ed. T. F. Torrance. Edinburgh: Scottish Academic Press.

Coleridge, S. T. (*ca.* 1820). *Theory of Life*, p. 42. Quoted in Snyder, A. D. (1929). *Coleridge in Logic and Learning*. (1816 and 1823 are alternative suggestions for the publication date of *Theory of Life*; see Snyder, A. D. (1928). *Review of English Studies* 4, 32–4.)

Collingridge, G. L. & Bliss, T. V. P. (1987). NMDA receptors – their role in long-term potentiation. *Trends in Neurosciences* 10, 288–93.

Constantine-Paton, M. & Law, M. I. (1982). The development of maps and stripes in the brain. *Scientific American*, 247, no. 6, 54–62.

Cooper, J. R., Bloom, F. E. & Roth, R. H. (1986). *The Biochemical Basis of Neuropharmacology*, 5th ed. New York: Oxford University Press.

Craik, K. J. W. (1943). *The Nature of Explanation*. Cambridge University Press.

Creighton, T. E. (1993). *Proteins – Structures and molecular properties*, 2nd ed. New York: W. H. Freeman.

Crick, F. (1979). Thinking about the brain. *Scientific American* **241**, no. 3, 181–8.

Crick, F. (1994). *The Astonishing Hypothesis*. New York: Scribner.

Crick, F. & Koch, C. (1992). The problem of consciousness. *Scientific American* **267**, no. 3, 152–9.

Crossland, M. P. (1971). *The Science of Matter*. Harmondsworth: Penguin Books.

Dani, J. W., Chernjavsky, A. & Smith, S. J. (1992). Neuronal activity triggers calcium waves in hippocampal astrocyte networks. *Neuron* **8**, 429–40.

Darwin, C. R. (1859). *On the Origin of Species by means of Natural Selection*. London: John Murray.

Davies, P. C. W. (1981). Is thermodynamic gravity a route to quantum gravity? In *Quantum Gravity 2*, ed. C. J. Isham, R. Penrose & D. W. Sciama, pp. 183–209. Oxford: Clarendon Press.

Davies, P. C. W. & Brown, J. R. (eds) (1986). *The Ghost in the Atom*. Cambridge University Press.

Dawkins, R. (1986). *The Blind Watchmaker*. Essex: Longman.

Deeke, L., Grötzinger, B. & Kornhuber, H. H. (1976). Voluntary finger movements in man: cerebral potentials and theory. *Biological Cybernetics*, **23**, 99.

Deutsch, D. & Lockwood, M. (1994). The quantum physics of time travel. *Scientific American* **270**, no. 3, 50–6.

DeYoe, E. A. and Van Essen, D. C. (1988). Concurrent processing streams in monkey visual cortex. *Trends in Neurosciences* **11**, 219–26.

Dixon, N. F. (1987). Subliminal perception. In *The Oxford Companion to the Mind*, ed. R. L. Gregory, pp. 752–5. Oxford University Press.

Dobzhansky, T. (1973). Nothing in biology makes sense except in the light of evolution. *American Biology Teacher* **35**, 125–9.

Dobzhansky, T., Ayala, F. J., Stebbins, G. L. & Valentine, J. W. (1977). *Evolution*. San Francisco: Freeman.

Domash, L. H. (1977). The transcendental meditation technique and quantum physics: is pure consciousness a macroscopic quantum state in the brain? In *Scientific Research on the Transcendental Meditation Program*, ed. D. W. Orme-Johnson & J. T. Farrow, pp. 652–70. Weggis, Switzerland: Maharishi European Research University Press.

Donnelly, R. J. (1988). Superfluid turbulence. *Scientific American* **259**, no. 5, 66–74.

Doolittle, R. F. (1985). The genealogy of some recently evolved vertebrate proteins. *Trends in Biochemical Sciences* **10**, 233–7.

Eccles, J. C. (1953). *The Neurophysiological Basis of Mind*, pp. 265–6. Oxford: Clarendon Press.

Eccles, J. C. (1987). Brain and mind, Two or one? In *Mindwaves*, ed. C. Blakemore & S. Greenfield, pp. 293–304. Oxford: Blackwell.

Eccles, J. C. (1989). *Evolution of the Brain: Creation of the Self*. London: Routledge.

Edelman, G. M. (1989). *The Remembered Present: A biological theory of consciousness*. New York: Basic Books.

Edelman, G. M. (1992). *Bright Air, Brilliant Fire*. London: Allen Lane, The Penguin Press.

Ehrenberg, W. (1967). Maxwell's Demon. *Scientific American* **217**, no. 5, 103–10.

Einstein, A. (1979). *Autobiographical Notes*. Chicago: Open Court.

Engel, A. K., König, P., Kreiter, A. K., Schillen, T. B. & Singer, W. (1992). Temporal coding in the visual cortex: new vistas on integration in the nervous system. *Trends in Neurosciences* **15**, 218–26.

Everett, H. (1957). 'Relative state' formulation of quantum mechanics. *Reviews of Modern Physics* **29**, 454–62.

Faraday, M. (1844). *Matter*. London: Library of the Institution of Electrical Engineers. (See Crossland, 1971.)

Fersht, A. (1985). *Enzyme Structure and Mechanism*, 2nd ed. New York: Freeman.

Feynman, R. P. (1985/1990). *QED: the strange theory of light and matter*. Princeton: Princeton University Press/Harmondsworth: Penguin.

Feynman, R. P., Leighton, R. B. & Sands, M. (1965). *The Feynman Lectures on Physics*, vol. III. Reading, Massachusetts: Addison–Wesley.

Fisher, R. A. (1930). *The Genetical Theory of Natural Selection*. Oxford University Press.

Flowers, K. A. (1987). Parkinsonism. In *The Oxford Companion to the Mind*, ed. R. L. Gregory, pp. 587–91. Oxford University Press.

Foot, C. (1992). Atoms brought to a new focus. *Nature* **355**, 303–4.

Freeman, W. J. (1975). *Mass Action in the Nervous System*. New York: Academic Press.

Freeman, W. J. (1991). The physiology of perception. *Scientific American*, **264**, no. 2, 78–85.

Freeman, W. J. & Skarda, C. A. (1991). Mind/brain science: Neuroscience on philosophy of mind. In *John Searle and his Critics*, ed. E. Lepore & R. van Gulick, chapter 7. Oxford: Blackwell.

Fröhlich, H. (ed.) (1988). *Biological Coherence and Response to External Stimuli*. Berlin: Springer-Verlag.

Frydman, J., Nimmesgern, E., Ohtsuka, K. & Hartl, F. U. (1994). Folding of nascent polypeptide chains in a high molecular mass assembly with molecular chaperones. *Nature* **370**, 111–17.

Gazzaniga, M. S. (1967). The split brain in man. *Scientific American* **217**, no. 2, 24–9.

Geschwind, N. (1979). Specialisations of the human brain. *Scientific American* **241**, no. 3, 158–68.

Ghirardi, G. C., Rimini, A. & Weber, T. (1986). Unified dynamics for microscopic and macroscopic systems. *Physical Review* **D34**, 470–91.

Gleick, J. (1988). *Chaos*. London: Heinemann.

Glynn, I. M. (1990). Consciousness and time. *Nature* **348**, 477–9.

Glynn, I. M. (1991). Conscious vs. neural time. *Nature* **352**, 27–8.

Glynn, I. M. (1993). The evolution of consciousness: William James's unresolved problem. *Biological Reviews of the Cambridge Philosophical Society* **68**, 599–616.

Goldman–Rakic, P. S. (1992). Working memory and the mind. *Scientific American* **267**, no. 3, 111–17.

Gould, S. J. (1989). *Wonderful Life: The Burgess Shale and the Nature of History*. New York: W. W. Norton.

Gray, C. M. & Singer, W. (1989). Stimulus specific neuronal oscillations in orientation columns of cat visual cortex. *Proceedings of the National Academy of Sciences, USA* **86**, 1698–702.

Gray, J. (1987). The mind-brain identity theory as a scientific hypothesis: a second look. In *Mindwaves*, ed. C. Blakemore & S. Greenfield, pp. 460–83. Oxford: Blackwell.

Graybiel, A. M., Aosaki, T., Flaherty, A. W. & Kimura, M. (1994). The basal ganglia and adaptive motor control. *Science* **265**, 1826–31.

Green, N. P. O., Stout, G. W. & Taylor, D. J. (1990). *Biological Science*, 2nd ed., ed. R. Soper. Cambridge University Press.

Greengard, P., Valtorta, F., Czernik, A. J. & Benfenati, F. (1993). Synaptic vesicle phosphoproteins and regulation of synaptic function. *Science* **259**, 780–5.

Gregory, R. L. (1984). *Mind in Science*. Harmondsworth: Penguin.

Gregory, R. L. (1987). Split-brain and the mind. In *The Oxford Companion to the Mind*, ed. R. L. Gregory, pp. 740–7. Oxford University Press.

Grivell, L. A. (1983). Mitochondrial DNA. *Scientific American* **248**, no. 3, 60–72.

Gustafsson, B. & Wigström, H. (1988). Physiological mechanisms underlying long-term potentiation. *Trends in Neurosciences* **11**, 156–62.

Haldane, J. B. S. (1927). A mathematical theory of natural and artificial selection. Part V. Selection and mutation. *Proceedings of the Cambridge Philosophical Society* **23**, 838–44.

Hameroff, S. R. (1987). *Ultimate Computing: biomolecular consciousness and nanotechnology*. Amsterdam: North-Holland.

Hameroff, S. R. & Watt, R. C. (1982). Information processing in microtubules. *Journal of Theoretical Biology* **98**, 549–61.

Heath, R. G. (1963). Electrical self-stimulation of the brain in man. *American Journal of Psychiatry* **120**, 571–7.

Hebb, D. O. (1949). *The Organization of Behaviour*. New York: John Wiley.

Herapath, J. (1821). A mathematical inquiry into the causes, laws and principal phenomena of heat, gases, gravitation, etc. *Annals of Philosophy*, new series, vol. 1, 278–9.

Herbert, N. (1985). *Quantum Reality*. London: Rider.

Hertz, H. (1893). *Electric Waves* (English translation by D. E. Jones), p. 21. London: MacMillan.

Hesse, M. B. (1961). *Forces and Fields: the concept of action at a distance in the history of physics*. London: Nelson.

Hirokawa, N. & Heuser, J. E. (1981) *Journal of Cell Biology* **91**, 404.

Hodgson, D. (1991). *The Mind Matters: consciousness and choice in a quantum world*. Oxford: Clarendon Press.

Hökfelt, T., Johansson, O. & Goldstein, M. (1984). Chemical anatomy of the brain. *Science* **225**, 1326–334.

Hollenbeck, P. J. (1990). Cell biology: Cytoskeleton on the move. *Nature* **343**, 408–9.

Hoover, J. E. & Strick, P. L. (1993). Multiple output channels in the basal ganglia. *Science* **259**, 819–21.

Horgan, J. (1992). Quantum philosophy. *Scientific American* **267**, no. 1, 72–80

Horgan, J. (1994). Can science explain consciousness? *Scientific American* **271**, no. 1, 72–8.

Horne, M., Shimony, A. & Zeilinger, A. (1990). Two particle interferometry. *Nature*, **347**, 429–430.

Hubel, D. (1988). Quoted in a conference report: Who knows how the brain works? *Nature* **335**, 489–91 (on p. 490).

Humphrey, N. (1983). *Consciousness Regained*. Oxford University Press.

Humphrey, N. (1987). The inner eye of consciousness. In *Mindwaves*, ed. C. Blakemore & S. Greenfield, pp. 377–81. Oxford: Blackwell.

Humphrey, N. (1992). *A History of the Mind*. New York: Simon and Schuster.

Huxley, J. (1962). Higher and lower organisation in evolution. *Journal of the Royal College of Surgeons of Edinburgh* **7**, 163–79.

Iversen, L. (1979). The chemistry of the brain. *Scientific American* **241**, no. 3, 118–29.

Iversen, L. (1992). Dopamine receptors: Which D4 do *you* have? *Nature* **358**, 109.

James, W. (1890/1983). *The Principles of Psychology*. New York: Holt (1890). Reprinted Cambridge, Massachusetts: Harvard University Press (1983).

James, W. (1904/1977). Does consciousness exist? Reprinted in J. J. McDermott (ed.), *The Writings of William James*, pp. 169–83. Chicago: University of Chicago Press.

Jasper, H. H. (1966). Brain Mechanisms and states of consciousness. In *Brain and Conscious Experience*, ed. J. C. Eccles, pp. 256–82. Berlin: Springer–Verlag.

Jenkins, F. A. & White, H. E. (1951). *Fundamentals of Optics*, 2nd ed. New York: McGraw–Hill.

Johnson, K. A. (1985). Pathway of the microtubule-dynein ATPase and structure of dynein: a comparison with actomyosin. *Annual Reviews of Biophysics and Biophysical Chemistry* **14**, 161–88.

Johnson-Laird, P. N. (1983). *Mental Models*. Cambridge University Press.

Johnstone Stoney (1891). *Scientific Transactions of the Royal Dublin Society* **4**, 583.

Kalaska, J. F. & Crammond, D. J. (1992). Cerebral cortical mechanisms of reaching movements. *Science*, **255**, 1517–23.

Kalil, R. E. (1989). Synapse formation in the developing brain. *Scientific American* **261**, no. 6, 38–45 (esp. pp. 44–5).

Kandel, E. R. Hawkins, R. D. (1992). The biological basis of learning and individuality. *Scientific American* **267**, no. 3, 79–86.

Kent, A. (1950). *An Eighteenth Century Lectureship in Chemistry*. Glasgow: Jackson and Sons.

Kimelberg, H. K. Norenberg, M. D. (1989). Astrocytes. *Scientific American* **260**, no. 4, 44–52.

Kimura, M. (1983). *The Neutral Theory of Molecular Evolution*. Cambridge University Press.

Kolbe, H. (1877). Zeichen der Zeit. *Journal für Praktische Chemie* **15**, 473–7.

Körner, S. (1955). *Kant*. Harmondsworth: Penguin.

Land, E. H. (1977). The retinex theory of colour vision. *Scientific American* **237**, no. 6, 108–28.

Latham, R. E. (1951). *Lucretius: On the Nature of the Universe.* Harmondsworth: Penguin Books.

Laurent, G. & Davidowitz, H. (1994). Encoding of olfactory information with oscillating neural assemblages. *Science* **265**, 1872–5.

Leicester, H. M. (1956/1971). *The Historical Background of Chemistry.* New York: Dover.

Libet, B. (1991). Conscious vs neural time. *Nature* **352**, 27.

Libet, B., Wright, E. W., Feinstein, B. & Pearl, D. K. (1979). Subjective referral of the timing for a conscious sensory experience. *Brain* **102**, 193–224.

Livingston, R. B. (1967). Brain circuitry relating to complex behavior. In *The Neurosciences, a Study Program*, ed. G. C. Quarton, T. Melnechuk & F. O. Schmitt, pp. 499–515. New York: Rockefeller University Press.

Livingstone, M. S. (1988). Art, illusion and the visual system. *Scientific American* **258**, no. 1, 68–75.

Livingstone, M. & Hubel, D. (1988). Segregation of form, color, movement and depth: Anatomy, physiology and perception. *Science* **240**, 740–9.

Llinás, R. R. (1982). Calcium in synaptic transmission. *Scientific American* **247**, no. 4, 38–47.

Llinás, R. (1990). Intrinsic electrical properties of nerve cells and their role in network oscillation. *Cold Spring Harbor Symposia on Quantitative Biology* **55**, 933–8.

Lockwood, M. (1989). *Mind, Brain and the Quantum.* Oxford: Blackwell.

London, F. (1950). *Superfluids*, vol. 1, p. 8. New York: John Wiley & Sons.

McCrone, J. (1990). *The Ape that Spoke.* London: Picador.

McGeer, P. L., Eccles, J. C. & McGeer, E. G. (1978). *Molecular Neurobiology of the Mammalian Brain.* New York: Plenum Press.

MacKay, D. (1987). Divided brains – divided minds? In *Mindwaves*, ed. C. Blakemore & S. Greenfield, pp. 5–16. Oxford: Blackwell.

MacLean, P. D. (1954). Studies on the limbic system ('visceral brain'). and their bearing on psychosomatic problems.

In *Recent Developments in Psychosomatic Medicine*, ed. E. Wittkower & R. Cleghorn. London: Pitman, pp 101–125.

Maddox, J. (1990). Maxwell's Demon flourishes. *Nature* 345, 109.

Maddox, J. (1993). Calculating the energy of fullerenes. *Nature* 363, 395.

Madison, D. V. (1992). Knocking out memory's door. *Nature* 358, 626–27.

Marshall, I. N. (1989). Consciousness and Bose-Einstein condensates. *New Ideas in Psychology* 7, 73–83.

Masland, R. H. (1986). The functional architecture of the retina. *Scientific American* 255, no. 6, 90–9.

Mason, S. F. (1956/1962). *A History of the Sciences.* New York: Collier Books.

Maynard Smith, J. (1975). *The Theory of Evolution*, 3rd edn. Harmondsworth: Penguin Books.

Milner, P. M. (1993). The mind and Donald O. Hebb. *Scientific American* 268 no. 1, 104–9.

Minsky, M. (1988). *The Society of Mind*, p. 287, London: Pan Books.

Mishkin, M. & Appenzeller, T. (1987). The anatomy of memory. *Scientific American* 256, no. 6, 62–71.

Mollon, J. D. (1989). 'Tho' she kneeled in that place where they grew . . .' the uses and origins of primate colour vision. *Journal of Experimental Biology* 146, 21–38.

Mollon, J. (1992). Worlds of difference. *Nature* 356, 378–9.

Montemurro, D. G. & Bruni, J. E. (1988). *The Human Brain in Dissection*, 2nd ed. New York: Oxford University Press.

Morell, P. & Norton, W. T. (1980). Myelin. *Scientific American* 242, no. 5, 74–89.

Morris, R. G. M., Kandel, E. R. & Squire, L. R. (1988). Learning and memory. *Trends in Neurosciences* 11, 125–81.

Nagel, T. (1979). *Mortal Questions.* Cambridge University Press.

Nathan, P. W. (1987). Nervous system. In *The Oxford Companion to the Mind*, ed. R. Gregory, pp. 514–34. Oxford University Press.

Nauta, W. J. H. & Feirtag, M. (1979). The Organisation of the Brain. *Scientific American* 241, no. 3, 78–105.

Nedergaard, M. (1994). Direct signalling from astrocytes to neurons in cultures of mammalian brain cells. *Science* **263**, 1768–71.

Nieuwenhuys, R., Voogd, J. & van Huijzen, C. (1988). *The Human Central Nervous System: A Synopsis and Atlas*, 3rd ed. Berlin: Springer-Verlag.

Niven, W. D., ed. (1890). *James Clerk Maxwell, Scientific Papers.* Cambridge University Press.

Noback, C. R., Strominger, N. L. & Demarest, R. J. (1991). *The Human Nervous System*, 4th ed. Malvern, Pennsylvania: Lea & Febiger.

Okabe, S. & Hirokawa, N. (1990). Turnover of fluorescently labelled tubulin and actin in the axon. *Nature* **343**, 479–82.

Ostwald, W. (1904). Faraday lecture. *Journal of the Chemical Society, Transactions* **85**, part 1, 508–9.

Partington, J. R. (1960). *A Short History of Chemistry*, 3rd ed. London: Macmillan.

Pashler, H. (1993). Doing two things at the same time. *American Scientist* **81**, 48–55.

Pauling, L. (1960) *The Nature of the Chemical Bond*, 3rd ed. Ithaca, New York: Cornell University Press.

Pauling, L. (1970). *General Chemistry*, 3rd ed. San Francisco: W. H. Freeman.

Pauling, L. & Pauling, P. (1975). *Chemistry*. San Francisco: W. H. Freeman and Co.

Penfield, W. (1958). *The Excitable Cortex in Conscious Man*. Liverpool University Press.

Penfield, W. (1959). The interpretive cortex. *Science* **129**, 1719–25.

Penfield, W. (1966). Speech, perception and the uncommitted cortex. In *Brain and Conscious Experience*, ed. J. C. Eccles, pp. 217–37. Berlin: Springer-Verlag.

Penfield, W. & Roberts, L. (1959). *Speech and Brain Mechanisms*. Princeton, New Jersey: Princeton University Press.

Penrose, R. (1987). Minds, machines and mathematics. In *Mindwaves*, ed. C. Blakemore & S. Greenfield, pp. 259–76. Oxford: Blackwell.

Penrose, R. (1989). *The Emperor's New Mind*. Oxford University Press.

Perutz, M. F. (1964). The haemoglobin molecule. *Scientific American* **211**, no. 5, 64–76.

Perutz, M. F. (1990). *Mechanisms of Cooperativity and Allosteric Regulation in Proteins*. Cambridge University Press.

Pons, T. M., Garraghty, P. E., Ommaya, A. K., Kaas, J. H., Taub, E. & Mishkin, M. (1991). Massive cortical reorganisation after sensory deafferentation in adult macaques. *Science* **252**, 1857–60.

Popper, K. R. & Eccles, J. C. (1977). *The Self and its Brain*. Berlin, New York: Springer International.

Pribram, K. (1990). *Brain and Perception*. East Sussex, Hove: Erlbaum (Lawrence) Associates.

Priest, S. (1991). *Theories of Mind*. Harmondsworth: Penguin Books.

Proust, J. L. (1799). Recherches sur le cuivre. *Annales de Chimie* **32**, 26–54.

Psaltis, D., Brady, D. Xiang–Guang, G. & Lin, S. (1990). Holography in artificial neural networks. *Nature* **343**, 325–30.

Raichle, M. E. (1994). Visualising the mind. *Scientific American* **270**, no. 4, 36–42.

Ramón y Cajal, S. (1909–11/1972). *Histologie du Système Nerveux de l'Homme et des Vertébrés*. Paris: Maloine, 1909–11; reprinted Madrid: C.S.I.C., 1972.

Ravin, A. W. (1977). The gene as catalyst; the gene as organism. *Studies in the History of Biology* **1**, 1.

Rensch, B. (1959). *Evolution above the Species Level*. London: Methuen.

Richards, R. J. (1987). *Darwin and the Emergence of Evolutionary Theories of Mind and Behaviour*, p. 433. Chicago: University of Chicago Press.

Ridley, M. (1993). *Evolution*. Cambridge, Massachusetts: Blackwell.

Roder, H., Elöve, G. A. & Englander, S. W. (1988). Structural characterization of folding intermediates in cytochrome *c* by H-exchange labelling and proton NMR. *Nature* **335**, 700–4.

Rolls, E. T. (1989). Information processing in the taste system of primates. *Journal of Experimental Biology* **146**, 141–64.

Rothman, J. E. (1994). Mechanisms of intracellular protein transport. *Nature* **372**, 55–63.

Ruskin, J. (1860). *Modern Painters*, vol. 5, pt. 8, ch. 1 'The law of help'. London: Smith Elder and Co. (Page 174 of 1897 edition, Orpington: George Allen.)

Russell, B. (1927). *An Outline of Philosophy*. London: Allen and Unwin.

Russell, B. (1946). *A History of Western Philosophy*, p. 565. London: Allen & Unwin.

Ryle, G. (1949). *The Concept of Mind*. London: Hutchinson.

Sarnat, H. B. & Netsky, M. G. (1981). *Evolution of the Nervous System*, 2nd ed. New York: Oxford University Press.

Schirmer, T. & Evans, P. R. (1990). Structural basis of the allosteric behaviour of phosphofructokinase. *Nature* **343**, 140–5.

Schlichting, I *et al.* (1990). Time resolved X-ray crystallographic study of the conformational change in Ha-Ras p21 protein on GTP hydrolysis. *Nature* **345**, 309–15.

Schmalhausen, I. I. (1968). *The Origin of Terrestrial Vertebrates*. New York: Academic Press.

Scholey, J. M. (1990). Multiple microtubule motors. *Nature* **343**, 118–20.

Searle, J. (1984). *Minds, brains and science* (Reith Lectures). London: BBC Publications.

Serebriakoff, V. (1987). *The Future of Intelligence*. Carnforth: Parthenon Publishing.

Sewell, G. L. (1986). *Quantum Theory of Collective Phenomena*. Oxford: Clarendon Press.

Sharon, N. & Lis, H. (1993). Carbohydrates in cell recognition. *Scientific American* **268**, no. 1, 74–81.

Shepherd, G. M. (1988). *Neurobiology*, 2nd ed. New York: Oxford University Press.

Sherrington, C. (1940). *Man on his Nature*. Cambridge University Press.

Shimony, A. (1988). The reality of the quantum world. *Scientific American* **258**, no. 1, 36–43.

Sillito, A. M., Jones, H. E., Gerstein, G. L. & West, D. C. (1994). Feature-linked synchronization of thalamic relay cell firing induced by feedback from the visual cortex. *Nature* **369**, 479–82.

Silva, A. J., Stevens, C. F., Tonegawa, S. & Wang, Y. (1992a). Deficient hippocampal long-term potentiation in α-calcium-calmodulin kinase II mutant mice. *Science* **257**, 201–6.

Silva, A. J., Paylor, R., Wehner, J. M. & Tonegawa, S. (1992b). Impaired spatial learning in α-calcium-calmodulin kinase II mutant mice. *Science* **257**, 206–11.

Singer, C. (1959). *A Short History of Scientific Ideas to 1900.* Oxford University Press.

Singer, W. (1994). A new job for the thalamus. *Nature* **369**, 444–5.

Snyder, S. H. (1984). Drug and neurotransmitter receptors in the brain. *Science* **224**, 22–31.

Spencer, H. (1855). *The Principles of Psychology*, pp. 578–9. London: Longman, Brown, Green and Longmans.

Sperry, R. W. (1966). Brain bisection and mechanisms of consciousness. In *Brain and Conscious Experience*, ed. J. C. Eccles, pp. 298–313. Berlin: Springer-Verlag.

Sperry, R. W. (1975). In search of psyche. In *The Neurosciences: Paths of Discovery*, ed. F. G. Worden, J. P. Swazey & G. Adelman, pp. 425–34. Cambridge, Massachusetts: MIT Press.

Sperry, R. W. (1976). Changing concepts of consciousness and free will. *Perspectives in Biology and Medicine* **20**, 9–19.

Sperry, R. W. (1983). *Science and Moral Priority.* New York: Columbia University Press.

Sperry, R. W. (1987). Consciousness and causality. In *The Oxford Companion to the Mind*, ed. R. L. Gregory, pp. 164–6. Oxford University Press.

Stapp, H. P. (1993). *Mind, Matter, and Quantun Mechanics.* Berlin: Springer-Verlag.

Stevens, C. F. (1979). The Neuron. *Scientific American* **241**(3), 48–59.

Stevens, C. F. (1990). A depression long awaited. *Nature* **347**, 16.

Stones, G. B. (1928). The atomic view of matter in the 15th, 16th and 17th centuries. *Isis* **10**, 444–65.

Stryker, M. P. (1989). Is grandmother an oscillation? *Nature* **338**, 297–8.

Tank, D. W., Gelperin, A. and Kleinfeld, D. (1994). Odors,

oscillations, and waves: Does it all compute? *Science* **265**, 1819–20.

Tank, D. W. & Hopfield, J. J. (1987). Collective computation in neuronlike circuits. *Scientific American* **257**, no. 6, 62–70.

Thatcher, R. W. & John, E. R. (1977). *Foundations of Cognitive Processes*. New York: John Wiley & Sons.

Thayer, H. S. (1953). *Newton's Philosophy of Nature*. New York: Haffner.

Tilley, D. R. & Tilley, J. (1986). *Superfluidity and Superconductivity*. New York: Van Nostrand Reinhold.

Torrance, T. F. (1982). Introduction to Clerk Maxwell's *A Dynamical Theory of the Electromagnetic Field*. Edinburgh: Scottish Academic Press.

Toulmin, S. & Goodfield, J. (1962). *The Architecture of Matter*. London: Hutchison.

Travis, J. (1993). Fullerene superconductors heat up. *Science* **261**, 1392.

Udgaonkar, J. B. & Baldwin, R. L. (1988). NMR evidence for an early framework intermediate on the folding pathway of ribonuclease A. *Nature* **335**, 694–9.

Vos, M. H., Rappaport, F., Lambry, J.-C., Breton, J. & Martin, J.-L. (1993). Visualisation of coherent nuclear motion in a membrane protein by femtosecond spectroscopy. *Nature* **363**, 320–5.

Waddington, C. H. (1968). The basic ideas of biology. In *Towards a Theoretical Biology*, vol. 1, *Prolegomena*, ed. C. H. Waddington, p. 3. Edinburgh University Press.

Walker, E. H. (1970). The nature of consciousness. *Mathematical Biosciences* **7**, 131–78.

Wallace, A. R. (1870). *Contributions to the Theory of Natural Selection*. London: Macmillan.

Wallich, P. (1991). Silicon babies. *Scientific American* **265**, no. 6, 83–91.

Warren, G. (1990). Vesicular consumption. *Nature* **345**, 382–3.

Watson, J. D., Hopkins, N. H., Roberts, J. W., Steitz, J. A. & Weiner, A. M. (1987). *Molecular Biology of the Gene*, 4th ed., vol. 1. Menlo Park, California: Benjamin/Cummings Publishing Co.

Webster, B. (1990). *Chemical Bonding Theory*, figure 3.1a on p. 44. Oxford: Blackwell Scientific Publications.

Whitlock, F. A. (1987). Capgras' syndrome. In *The Oxford Companion to the Mind*, ed. R. L. Gregory, p. 125. Oxford University Press.

Wigner, E. (1960). The unreasonable effectiveness of mathematics in the natural sciences. *Communications in Pure and Applied Mathematics* **13**, 1–14.

Wigner, E. P. (1962). Remarks on the mind-body problem. In *The Scientist Speculates. An anthology of partly-baked ideas*, ed. I. J. Good, pp. 284–302. London: Heinemann.

Wright, S. (1931). Evolution in Mendelian populations. *Genetics* **16**, 97–159.

Wurtman, R. J. (1982). Nutrients that modify brain function. *Scientific American* **246**, no. 4, 42–51.

Young, T. (1802). On the theory of light and colour; and An account of some cases of the production of colours not hitherto described. *Philosophical Transactions of the Royal Society* **92**, 12–48; 387–97.

Zangwill, O. L. (1987). Isolation experiments. In *The Oxford Companion to the Mind*, ed. R. L. Gregory, pp. 393–4. Oxford University Press.

Zohar, D. (1990). *The Quantum Self.* New York: William Morrow.

Zohar, D. & Marshal, I. (1993). *The Quantum Society*. London: Bloomsbury Publishing.

Index

The suffix F refers to a figure or figures.

135596